A Cognitive Grammar Approach to the Fuzziness in the English Voice Category

从认知语法视角看英语语态范畴的模糊性

by
LI JINGYING

李静莹 著

西北工业大学出版社

西 安

【内容简介】 本书主要从认知语法的角度分析了英语语法范畴中语态的模糊性特征,共分为八章,内容包括绪论、文献回顾、理论框架、语法语态的一般属性和语言中的语态分类、主动结构范畴化的模糊特征及其认知模式、被动结构范畴化的模糊特征及其认知模式、七种中间语态结构范畴化的模糊特征及其认知模式以及结论。本书内容丰富,全面而又深入地呈现了英语语态体系的模糊性,丰富了该研究领域的成果。

本书既可以作为英语专业本科生及研究生英语语态学习的参考书,也可供语言学、心理学及社会文化学方向的研究员及高校教师使用。

图书在版编目(CIP)数据

从认知语法视角看英语语态范畴的模糊性 ＝A Cognitive Grammar Approach to the Fuzziness in the English Voice Category 李静莹著. —西安:西北工业大学出版社,2022.12

ISBN 978 - 7 - 5612 - 8563 - 3

Ⅰ.①从… Ⅱ.①李… Ⅲ.①英语-态(语法)-研究 Ⅳ.①H314

中国版本图书馆 CIP 数据核字(2022)第 224463 号

CONG RENZHI YUFA SHIJIAO KAN YINGYU YUTAI FANCHOU DE MOHUXING

从 认 知 语 法 视 角 看 英 语 语 态 范 畴 的 模 糊 性
李静莹 著

责任编辑:杨 军 张 炜	策划编辑:张 晖	
责任校对:胡莉巾	装帧设计:蒲 一	

出版发行:西北工业大学出版社

通信地址:西安市友谊西路 127 号 邮编:710072

电 话:(029)88491757,88493844

网 址:www.nwpup.com

印 刷 者:西安五星印刷有限公司

开 本:787 mm×1 092 mm 1/16

印 张:16

字 数:370 千字

版 次:2022 年 12 月第 1 版 2022 年 12 月第 1 次印刷

书 号:ISBN 978 - 7 - 5612 - 8563 - 3

定 价:75.00 元

如有印装问题请与出版社联系调换

前　言

本书探讨了语言学研究中备受关注的一个语法问题：英语语态的范畴。尽管先贤们在此方面做出了卓越的贡献，但英语学习者仍然有很多困惑之处。事实上，很多语法学家致力于这样的问题并给出了相应的答复，究竟是什么构成了英语语态？语态分类的标准虽各不相同，但不可否认的是，语态的模糊性既存在于语态的定义上，也存在于语法语态各子类的边界上。这种模糊性与认知语法中的离散性和连续性的概念相呼应。

本书主要从认知语法的角度分析了英语语法范畴中语态的模糊性特征。其研究的主要目的有三个：其一，将离散性与连续性两个概念应用到英语语态范畴的范畴化分析过程中。其二，运用识解理论、力动态理论和图式理论，详细、具体地描述英语语态分类中各子类中的原型和非原型。其三，勾画多个图式并建立多个语态类型的认知模式从而形成认知网络，将语法语态的每个子类别的所有可能属性联系起来，从认知层面切实帮助英语学习者深入理解英语语态的本质，夯实语法基础。

关于目的一，本书认为，考虑到语言离散性和连续性的特征，英语语法语态范畴包括主动语态、被动语态和中间语态三个主要子类。具体来说，主动语态是语态类别中的缺省代表，没有标记。中间语态和被动语态在不同程度上与主动语态有所不同。另外，中间语态并不是一个独立的语态类型，它可以分为中动语态（middle voice）、使役语态（causative voice）、逆使役语态（anticausative voice）、逆被动语态（antipassive voice）、互惠语态（reciprocal voice）、反身语态（reflexive voice）和应动语态（applicative voice）七个子类。

关于目的二，本书认为英语语法语态的每个子类都有原型和非原型。每种语态类型中的论元（arguments）或参与者（participants）的数量以及参与者之间的互动是不同的，这是因为观察者倾向于从不同的角色原型视角来观察事件，例如，施事（agent）、受事（patient）、感知者（experiencer）、工具（Instrument）等。识解模式将决定哪个参与者会被置于突显位置，并传递能量或对其他参与者施加影响。本书还指出，不仅仅是及物动词，所有的动词都应该包括在英语语态的讨论中，因为动词及物性的概念不是一个二元实体，而是一个连续体。

关于目的三，本书提出可以使用代表语义和语音结构复杂性的符号单位（Σ）来描绘每种语态类型的图式。每个语态子类的认知模型可以基于原型的离散特征和非原型的连续特征生成，并在子类别的边界上与其他语态类型重叠。

本书共分为八章。

第一章为绪论，介绍了本书的研究动机、背景、目的、意义以及本书的大体结构。

第二章批判性地回顾了四个主要语言学派（传统语法、生成语法、功能语法和认知语法）对英语语态进行的基本研究，通过对不同语言学派的不同解释进行比较和对比，指出本研究基于认知语法的理由。

第三章介绍了模糊性、离散性、连续性三个基本概念，以及四种基本的认知理论——原型理论、图式理论、力动态理论和识解理论。此外，本章还介绍了研究方法和步骤，为构建离散－连续图式和认知模型提供了理论框架。

第四章讨论了语法语态的一般属性和语言中的语态分类。此外，本章还对语态的概念进行了重新定义，并对英语语态的子类进行了分类。

第五章分析了英语主动结构的模糊特征及其认知模式。首先，从论元的角色原型与复合动词互动的角度讨论了主动结构原型的选择，然后总结了形成主动原型的离散性特征。其次，以原型的离散性特征为标准，对这些非原型进行衡量，探析它们偏离原型的离散性特征并与原型共享的连续性特征，以及识解在理解扩展过程中所起的作用。最后，在原型及其扩展的基础上，勾勒出英语主动语态范畴的图式和认知模型。

第六章研究了被动结构的分类及其认知模式中所表现出的模糊特征。本章主要从三个方面展开论述：首先，着重讨论被动语态范畴中的原型问题。通过考察 Be+V-en 被动句结构的梯度特征，从形式特征、角色原型和复合动词三个方面选取能动真被动（Agentful True Passive）句作为原型。然后通过对被动语态范畴中的非原型性的讨论，论述了被动语态范畴内的连续性。由于被动语态结构的多样性，在讨论这些结构时，笔者勾勒出了六个独立的图式，分别对应于被动语态的六个子类型：Be+V-en 被动结构、Get +V-en 被动结构、介词被动结构（Prepositional Passive）、非宾格进行体被动结构（Unaccusative in Progressive）、Be+V-able 被动结构及 [V1+V2-ing] 被动结构。最后，根据上述离散和连续特征，笔者构建了被动语态的总体认知模型。

第七章讨论了中间语态的模糊特征及其认知模式。在这一章中，笔者详细分析了中动语态、使役语态、逆使役语态、逆被动语态、互惠语态、反身语态和应动语态七个子类是如何在小句层面表现出来的。此外，笔者还关注其连续性特征，以解析它们与其他语态类型的关系，本章中讨论的每一种语态类型都有七个独立的图式和认知模型。

第八章为结论部分，主要介绍本研究的重要发现及研究的局限性，并提出了进一步研究的方向。

在撰写本书过程中，参阅了相关文献资料，在此对其作者表达感谢。本书为陕西省教育科学"十四五"规划课题（SGH21Y0203）成果，咸阳师范学院博士科研启动计划成果。

由于水平有限，书中的内容难免存在疏漏，敬请读者批评指正！

著者

2022 年 9 月

CONTENTS

Introduction

1　The Motivation of the Study

The present book addresses a topic that has been receiving great attention in past and present-day linguistic study: the category of grammatical voice in English. Despite the impressive contributions of the previous research, there is still so much bewilderment concerning voice.

It might look like a trivial issue if voice is only attributed to the correlation between the active and passive as in (1), where all the components of the clauses seem to cater completely to the definitions of the voice everyone observes in a great number of traditional grammar books.[①]

(1) a. Jeanne made a cake.

b. A cake was made by Jeanne.

However, in the discourse, the sentences vary greatly. Viewing the sentences in (2) from the traditional dichotomy of active and passive, the ESL and EFL learners seem to always have trouble in identifying the grammatical voice of the sentences.[②]

(2) a. The key opened the door. (Active, Non-prototype)

b. His suggestion was proven useful. (Passive, Non-prototype)

c. He had his secretary deliver the letter. (Causative Active)

d. She got her dress altered. (Causative Passive)

e. Mary and John saw each other. (Reciprocal)

---

① See Eckersley's (1958: 68) definition of voice and Greenbaum's (1996: 57). The former states that "voice is the form of the verb which shows whether the subject of the sentences is the doer of the action or the receiver of the action expressed by the verb." and the latter says that "an active sentence contains an object as one of its constituents. Active sentences can generally be made passive."

② The definitions of active and passive voice are fuzzy in many grammar books.

     f. His suggestion proved itself useful. (Reflexive)

     g. The door opens easily. (Middle)

     h. Mary ate (in a hurry). (Antipassive)

     i. The window broke. (Anticausative)

     j. Jack outran his pursuer. (Applicative)

In fact, what exactly constitutes the grammatical voice has been an ongoing discussion involving the unremitting efforts of many grammarians. The classifications of voice may vary in their strictness, but there is no denying that the fuzziness resides in both the definition of grammatical voice and the boundaries of the subcategories of grammatical voice. Taking an eclectic view, the fuzziness fits comfortably within the concept of relativity, and it echoes the concepts of discreteness and continuity in cognitive grammar. [①] If we take a closer look at the discrete features of each sentence in (2), we can ascribe them as examples of nine independent voice types.

If there are some difficulties in determining the voice types in (2) for ESL and EFL learners, we assume it is understandable in that most of them may not have had much input about fine-grained classifications of voice. However, the problem may not only lie in defining the boundaries of voice types but also exist within the subcategories of the voice itself. A question is thrown out for a few intermediate EFL learners to test their grasp of the passive voice. They were given four sample sentences, as illustrated in (3) and (4), and ask to choose the ungrammatical sentences and explain the reason for the ungrammaticality.

    (3) a. They told John to be fired.

       b. They told John to get fired.

    (4) a. She was found wandering on the beach.

       b. She got found wandering on the beach.

It is evident that the sentences in (3) and (4) deal with the differences between Be-passive and Get-passive. Both passives have their discrete features, but they are related in one way or another. There is fuzziness within the passive category for sure. Most of these EFL learners feel baffled in that they cannot figure out the answer, let alone give an exact explanation of the ungrammaticality of (3)a and (4)b. It is unforgivable for them since they believe that they understand the passive well. A natural question which arises here is that the problem they have is a personal one or a common

---

①   For a more detailed interpretation, see Langacker (2006).

one for ESL and EFL instructors and learners in general. This confusion motivates us to explore what is going wrong here and inspires us to dig out the root cause.

Hence, a survey about using of passive voice in English is conducted. First, 60 subjects are chosen and divided equally into three groups, namely a group of native speakers, a group of EFL instructors, and a group of advanced learners of English. Then we use the question illustrated in (3) and (4) to test them. After checking the answer and consulting 20 subjects for each group, we find that 95% of native speakers get the right answer based on their intuition but it is not easy for 40% of them to give an exact explanation. They confide to us that they have chunks of internalized knowledge of English that help them to discern the grammatical sentences with certainty. About 50% of the EFL instructors we interviewed can offer the right answer, but the rest of them get lost. The teachers who can give an exact explanation of the selection are 20% of the total. All the 20 advanced learners we chose have got their master degree in English, but only 40% of them get the right answer; the subjects who can give the exact reason are 10% of the total. The overwhelming majority of instructors and learners affirm that they have a good command of the grammatical rules of using passive in English, but things become complicated in practice.

This result seems to prove that being incapable of giving an exact account of the ungrammaticality of (3)a and (4)b is not only a personal problem for the intermediate English learners involved in the test, but a general problem for native speakers, EFL instructors, and advanced learners of English as well.

On reflection, it seems that some academic support for the commonality of the problem is also needed. To confirm our suspicions, we investigate all the relevant academic research on teaching the English passive voice. In addition to the subjects' puzzle, we gain some support from academic research as well. For example, according to Hinkel (2002, 2004), teaching the English passive voice represents one of the thorniest problems in L2 grammar instruction. Speakers of many L1s appear to have difficulty with passive constructions. Although they were studying at the intermediate level, they were considered to be beginners in using the passive voice correctly in writing (Rivandi et al. 2012: 284).

Moreover, both the subjects' bewilderment and academic support validate the complexity of using the passive in English and motivate us to look into the reasons why EFL instructors and advanced learners fail to solve the above problem since they are regarded as veteran language users. It is assumed that there are language external factors as well as language internal factors.

The first question which occurs to us while we analyze the language external factors is whether there are any gaps among the teaching (or learning) materials, teaching (or learning) practices and the actual use of the passive in English. In terms of teaching (or learning) material, 50 popular English grammar books from 1969–2019 are consulted and the contents about the voice are assessed and reviewed. One of the discoveries we can make from this analysis is that content arrangement of voice is disproportioned and comparatively simple, even though almost every book regards voice as an integral part of the English language teaching grammar syllabus. The evidence shows that although most English grammar books we consulted cover English voice, most of them confine their discussion only to the most basic passive construction rather than active construction, middle construction, etc.

Furthermore, a significant caveat that should be noted in relation to teaching (or learning) material is teaching practice. According to many EFL and ESL teachers' experience, grammar instruction in real practice still mainly focuses the derivation of passive structures from active structures and demonstration and identification of passive verb forms in various tenses and aspects.[①]

In addition, there are some problems with formal definitions of the passive voice. For example, Sweet (1892: 112) claims that "the passive is formed by combining the finite forms of the auxiliary verb to be with the preterite participle of the verb in English." Visser (1973: 1788) holds that "a passive construction must necessarily consist of a form of *to be + past participle*." Applying the label of *passive* only to the clauses or sentences whose main verb is a passive past participle fails to account for other passive constructions in English.

Moreover, additional support for that assumption is that language internal factors are responsible, at least in part, for the above failures of comprehension evidenced by the practical observation that the English voice per se is actually quite complicated. In order to have a clear view of the intricacies of English passive, it is necessary to take a close look at some backup examples.

The central assumption about English voice underpinning traditional grammar and pedagogical grammar is that voice usually falls into two types: active voice and passive voice, representing two different ways of viewing an event denoted by a transitive verb. However, the boundary between transitive verb and intransitive verb is not clear cut. The verb *suffer* that serves as an intransitive verb in (5)a does not have corresponding passive form. By contrast, the verb *suffer* functions as a transitive verb in (5)b which can be converted into a passive form. The verb sleep is an intransitive verb which cannot have a corresponding passive form. However, when it combines with the preposition in, the passive form is widely accepted as being grammatical, as in (6).

    (5) a. I suffered from a cold and feel terrible.

       (*I am suffered from a cold and feel terrible.)

---

①   See Hinkel (2002, 2004) for reference.

b. He suffered a head injury.

(A head injury is suffered by him.)

(6) a. Queen Elizabeth the First slept in this bed.

b. This bed was slept in by Queen Elizabeth the First.

Furthermore, some verbs may have dynamic meaning as well as stative meaning. Just as the sentences in (7) and (8) show, *weigh* behaves differently in different situations.

(7) a. The nurses carefully weigh the children every day.

b. The children are always weighed by the nurses before they are bathed.

(8) a. The baby weighed 8 pounds.

b. *8 Pounds was/were weighed by the baby.

In addition, the intricate features of passive are also reflected in their verb constraints: some verbs can only be used in the active voice and some in the passive voice. As examples in (9) illustrate, *have* and *lack* can only be used in the active form while in (10), *say* can only be used in the passive form.

(9) a. They have a nice house.

b. He lacks confidence.

(10) a. John was said to be a good teacher.

b. *They said him to be a good teacher.

So far, we have examined several causes of the confusion of English passive. The characterization of the external factors shows that both the teaching (or learning) material and teaching (or learning) practices fail to give the instructors and advanced learners enough knowledge resources to improve their understanding of English voice. The analysis of the internal factors suggests that the complexity of English passive itself may pose a barrier to correct use in real context. In addition, the mechanism of passivization and process of categorization may differ across-languages, and thus English passive may not be easily understood by ESL and EFL learners.

The overall generalization to be drawn from above analysis is that there is a gap between teaching (or learning) actuality and complexity of this grammatical issue. As a result, we arrive at a conclusion that this topic is worthy of discussion and dedicated research.

2   The Background of the Study

Thus far, we have argued that there is a gap between teaching (or learning) actuality and complexity of a grammatical issue. Undoubtedly, a natural question to ask at this point is how we can bridge (or at least minimize) the gap between teaching (or learning) actuality and complexity of English passive. Based on the above analysis, we are certain about the loophole that needs to be fixed here.

Initially, this dissertation aims to make an attempt to answer ESL/EFL instructors' and learners' questions about meanings, uses and functions of passive constructions. However, one of the questions posed by this assumption is how the instructors and learners can have a thorough understanding of passive construction without knowing other types of voice in English. In order to establish a comprehensive and panoramic cognitive model of English passive, it is better to take all members of the English voice category into consideration rather than choose one subcategory. Given this, the need for holistic grammatical voice knowledge in English leads us to expand the scope of research from the passive voice to the whole voice category in English.

Against this background, a tentative hypothesis that can be formulated here is as follows: Are there any possible ways to establish a cognitive model or a cognitive network to connect all the possible knowledge points of grammatical voice in English together and present them in a mind-mapping graph?

In order to confirm this hypothesis, the first thing we need to do is to sort out the category of passive voice. There are several reasons for trying to ascribe passive to a certain category. First and foremost, it has been generally claimed that understanding the world starts from categorizing things. Every time we see something as a kind of thing, we are categorizing. To put our discussion on a concrete footing, we retrieve the related literature in the past and present to find what constitutes the English grammatical voice. Altogether, nine types of voice are presented in the English voice category, which are represented respectively by active voice, passive voice, middle voice, antipassive voice, causative voice, anticausative voice, reciprocal voice, reflexive voice and applicative voice.

A close look at the literature provides evidence that English voice has been one of the perennially popular topics of grammar studies. For one thing, it is an essential part of almost every grammar teaching syllabus. For another, it is complicated in nature and function and constrained by many subtle rules. On the other hand, a review of literature on the scholarship of English voice reveals that grammarians, linguists and scholars (Sweet 1892; Jespersen

1924; Chomsky 1957; Svartvik 1966; Siewierska 1984; Shibatani 1985; Quirk et al. 1985; Palmer 1987, 1994; Croft 1994; Dik 1997; Biber et al. 2000; Dixon 2005; Kulikov 2011; Authier and Haude 2012; Malchukov and Comrie 2015, to name just a few) from different schools of grammar study—traditional grammar, structural grammar, transformational generative grammar, functional grammar, cognitive grammar, etc.—have involved themselves in discussing its definitions, classifications, distributions, functions and cross-language comparisons, etc.[①]A considerable amount of research has sprung up in the past many years. It is gratifying to note that a considerable number of publications reveal the contentions among different schools of grammar study and consistently provide new perspectives and a large number of useful and valid references for better understanding the nature of English voice.

However, a survey of current literature also reveals the undeniable fact that not only grammar books but also academic studies lay emphasis on passive construction. The uses, functions, constraints and contrastive studies across languages of passive constructions are discussed and probed in various ways, as shown in Alsina (1996), Collins (1996), Meints (1999), Blevins (2003), Hirtle (2007), Keenan and Dryer (2007), Toyota (2007, 2008, 2009), Rubin (2009), Wanner (2009), Sleeman (2011), Alexiadou and Doron (2012), etc.

One point that needs to be pointed out here is the concept of passive gradient, which was first developed in Svartvik (1966). Quirk et al. (1985) present the most typical categorization of the passive gradient, but their discussion is based purely on a formal definition of the passive. They claim that the clause containing the construction 'be (or get)+ed participle' is very broad and would include the true passives,[②] semi-passives and pseudo-passives, all of which form a passive gradient. Toyota (2009) reinforces the continuum concept in his study, but taking a diachronic perspective on English passive voice makes it impossible to show gradience between different members of English voice category in his diagram. Croft (2012) also reiterates his support for voice continuum, but his study puts emphasis on typological analysis and cross-language comparison with little concern for an English-specific account.

Having discussed the current research status of passive, it is necessary to turn to look at the research on the active voice. Indeed, the above literature does mention active construction while discussing the passive construction in English, but only as an entry point for introducing passive construction and with no more detailed discussion. There are a few studies concerning the uses, distributions and features of active voice, as represented by Hopper and Thompson (1980), Rice (1987a, 1987b), and Næss (2007). Despite these contributions, it is worth noting that active voice research is always put in a subordinate position in contrast to passive voice or

---

① The more detailed discussion will be offered in Chapter II to generate the contribution and the defects of each school of grammar study concerning grammatical voice.

② It can also be called central passive, see Quirk et al. (1985: 167)

middle voice.

Comparatively speaking, the systematic study of middle voice in English began from Keyser and Roeper in 1984 later than that of active and passive voice. However, because of its peculiarity in form and usage, middle construction has attracted the attention of many linguists and scholars. They spare no effort to clarify its generation process, characteristics, and cognitive motivation as well as its cross-language difference, which are represented by Hale and Keyser (1987), Roberts (1987), Fagan (1988, 1992), Massam (1992), Kemmer (1993), Zribi-Hertz (1993), Hoekstra and Roberts (1993), Ackema and Schoorlemmer (1994, 1995), Kitazume (1996), Stroik (1992, 1995, 1999), Sung (1994), Langacker (1987a, 1991a), Condoravdi (1989), (Levin 1993), Goldberg and Ackerman (2001) and Lekakou (2005, 2006). In contrast to the attention given to the three above major voice types, when the remaining voice types are mentioned in the literature in most cases, it is concerning a typological study or special constructions.

When we put all the facts together and conduct a comprehensive analysis of relevant studies, we see that the research contributes substantially to understanding the nature of the English voice system. However, there are still some research gaps worth mentioning here.

Firstly, in the category of English voice, the members are supposed to possess the discrete features as well as continuous features. However, some asymmetrical and disproportionate properties can be found while reviewing the literature. Taking the individual member of the English voice category as research object is conducive to revealing the discreteness of language but still fails to give due attention to its continuous features. Though there are some publications that have discussed the gradient features that passive voice exhibits, a corresponding discussion of active voice, middle voice and other voice types is rarely seen.

Another gap worth noting is that all the possible members of the English voice category are assumed to be included in the scope of study even though there are some peripheral cases that are rarely seen in English. It is better to include them in the research in order to have a comprehensive understanding of the voice system in English. However, except the passive, active and middle voice, these atypical voice types may only have some sporadic research from the perspective of voice as a comprehensive categorization. Few systematic studies on a complete voice system in English can be found.

In addition, the literature shows that various schools of grammar give rise to different assumptions concerning English voice and make significant contributions to it. However, there are always theoretical defects or practical drawback for every school. Schools of formalism such as structural linguistics and transformational generative linguistics claim that language is composed of different types of discrete components—syntax, semantics, lexicon, and phonology—with the semantic feature of the grammatical structure often neglected. The formalists' preference for discreteness is further proved by regarding language as a distinct mental *organ or faculty*. They describe English voice in an accurate way based on form and individuality but neglect the connections between form, meaning and other voice categories. On the contrary, functionalists see many things as *matters of degree* and tend to posit gradient rather than discrete boundaries.

It has been generally claimed by cognitive linguists that grammar does not exist independently of semantics. The language is human-oriented and the structure and use of language are largely influenced by the cognitive system and mental ability. It is a pseudo-issue to draw a line between linguistic meaning and general knowledge. In order to describe and explain language completely and accurately, it is necessary to connect discreteness with continuity while analyzing language (Langacker 2006: 108).

3   The Purpose of the Study

In the light of the discussion given above, the two key assumptions embodied in the analysis can be generated. For one, a panoramic study of English voice is supposed to take both the discreteness and continuity features of language into account. For another, every approach to voice study has its strengths and weaknesses. In contrast to other schools of linguistic study, cognitive linguistics is usage-based (Langacker 1988, 2000), though it has also some theoretical limitations, such as subjectivity and illogicality. As the analysis goes on, we still prefer to choose a cognitive approach as our main research perspective in this dissertation for it may necessarily account for the complexities of language as a social phenomenon. In addition, we may resort to other grammar for extra explanations.

Based on the above two assumptions, the overall objective of this dissertation can be characterized as follows: in an attempt to answer ESL/EFL instructors' and advanced learners' questions about meanings, uses and functions of complex voice constructions in English and bridge or minimize some gaps in the English voice continuum now partially under construction in the existing literature, the primary purpose of this study is three-fold: (1) to address two significant concepts—discreteness and continuity—in studies of the categorization of the English voice category; (2) to give a detailed and concrete account of English voice category from the perspective of cognitive grammar; (3) to establish a cognitive model or a cognitive network to connect all the possible knowledge points of grammatical voice.

To put our discussion on a concrete footing, let us provide a more detailed elaboration. As illustrated above, in the English voice category, there are nine voices available, but in most cases only three of them (active voice, passive voice, middle voice) are even partially understood by most ESL/EFL instructors and advanced learners. In addition, there is no prototype in the superordinate category of voice in English but only a schema—a grammatical category that describes the relationship between the action (or state) that the verb expresses and the participants identified by its arguments (subject, object, etc.). However, there are two poles in this category—active voice and passive voice—which serve as two typical members in the category. The rest of voice types serve as members that are more or less similar to active voice or passive voice.

It is also worth noticing that the passive subcategory still has many subcategory members such as Be+V-en construction, Get+V-en construction, prepositional passive construction, unaccusative progressive construction, [V1+V2-ing] construction, Be+V-able construction, etc.

It appears that a hierarchy exists in the English voice category where schematization serves the purposes of discreteness as well as continuity. An established schema implicitly defines a category by making evident what its members have in common. But, by the same token, it heightens the contrast with elements that do not conform.

By resorting to the theory of prototype, schema, force dynamic and construal, this research aims to construct a linguistic discreteness-continuity schematic representation model which is clearly shown in the category of English voice. In order to get a holistic as well as fine-graded view of English voice, we will not only deal with the common or partial attributes shared by all members and some members but also the precise defining idiosyncrasies of each member. In addition, we attempt to connect all the attributes of the members together and try to establish a schematic network by a using mind-mapping graph.

To be more specific, it is argued that a fuzzy feature that instantiates itself as being both discrete and continuous is essential for grammatical voice category. Given this, this study examines the discrete and continuous features of English voice category from the cognitive perspective and endeavors to answer the following research questions:

(1) What are the possible members of English voice category according to the discrete feature?

(2) How are the prototype effects shown in English voice category?

(3) What is the prototype in the subcategory of active voice and passive voice respectively? How is it extended? What is the schema of active voice and passive voice respectively?

(4) What are the discrete features for each medial voice and how are they related to the active and passive? What are their respective schemas?

(5) How is the fuzzy feature shown within each subcategory of grammatical voice and at the boundary of all subcategories?

(6) What are the possible cognitive models of each voice based on the ICM[①], prototype and

---

① It refers to the Idealized cognitive model. For a more detailed introduction, see Chapter Ⅲ.

their deviations, extensions and overlaps?

(7) What are the implication of this study on grammar instruction and grammar learning?

4   The Significance of the Study

The strong motivation for solving the practical problems at the very beginning of the research and filling the research gap in current literature scholarship are two decisive factors to make this study meaningful. Specifically, the significance of this study is shown in three aspects:

Above all, we will propose a discrete/continuous cognitive model of the English voice category which may have never been discussed until now. Thus, this study would be a significant endeavor in remedying the deficiencies of the current linguistic theory and teaching practice. Following the basic assumptions of cognitive grammar: human experience–conceptualization–prototype–deviation–schema–cognitive model for English voice, this research aims to construct a discreteness/continuity linguistic schematic cognitive model which is operable in understanding English category system. On the one hand, this model will provide a sound reference for language teaching and learning. ESL and EFL learners can take this continuum as a reference point to understand and analyze different types of voice. It will bridge the gap between concentration on theory and the neglect of practice.

Secondly, it has been claimed by structuralists and formalists that the voice of the English verb has only two subcategories, the active voice and the passive voice, while functionalists propose three subcategories: the active voice, the passive voice and the middle voice. Contrary to other beliefs or opinions, this research reveals that there are nine subcategories. They form a continuum of English voice category that takes passive voice and active voice as two prototypes which extend to other peripheral members. This coarse-graded classification and investigation can give EFL and ESL teachers and students a panoramic schematization of the English voice category and show the continuous nature of language.

In addition, we describe the defining idiosyncrasy of each member from its morphosyntactic, semantic, and pragmatic features. By making comparison and contrast, th e fine-graded explanations will give EFL and ESL teachers and students specific information about independent schematization of each member of the English voice and in turn show the discrete nature of language.

5   Layout of the Book

The present study consists of eight chapters. Chapter I is introduction, which presents the motivation, background, purpose, significance of the study and the layout of the dissertation.

Chapter II critically reviews the previous studies on English voice conducted by researchers from four leading linguistic schools: traditional grammar, generative grammar, functional grammar and cognitive grammar. By making comparison and contrast among different explanations from different linguistic schools, it is argued that the present research is conducted from a cognitive perspective by presenting some feasible reasons.

Chapter III introduces three basic concepts—fuzziness, discreteness, continuity —and four cognitive theories—prototype theory, schema theory, force dynamic theory and construal theory. Moreover, the research methodology and procedure of this study are also presented. This chapter serves as the theoretical framework on which the discrete/continuous schema and cognitive model are based.

Chapter IV discusses the general attributes of the grammatical voice and classifications of the voice in language. Moreover, it redefines voice and clarifies the classification of the subcategories of voice in English in this book.

Chapter V characterizes the fuzzy feature embodied in English active constructions and their cognitive model. We begin with discussing the selection of active prototype in terms of interactions between role archetypes and composite verbs, and then generate the discrete features of the prototype. Next, taking the discrete feature of the prototype as the yardstick, we gauge those non-prototypes to see how they deviate and share continuous features with the prototype, and how the construal works in the understanding of the extensions. Finally, the schema and cognitive model of the active voice category are sketched based on the prototype and its extensions.

Chapter VI investigates the fuzzy feature shown in the categorization of passive constructions and their cognitive model. The discussion falls into three major parts: first, the emphasis is laid on the prototype of the passive category. By looking into the gradient feature of the Be+V-en passive construction, the agentful true passive is selected as the prototype in terms of its formal features, role archetypes and composite verb. Then the continuous feature of the passive is addressed by discussing the non-prototypes of the passive. Due to the diversity in the voice construction in the passive category, six independent schemas corresponding to six subtypes of the passive voice are sketched while discussing these constructions. Finally, a cognitive model is generalized according to the discrete and continuous features discussed above.

Chapter VII deals with the fuzzy feature shown in the medial voice and their cognitive models. In this chapter, detailed analyses go to how the middle voice, antipassive voice, causative voice, anticausative voice, reciprocal voice, reflexive voice and applicative voice are shown at the clausal level. Moreover, it devotes attention to the continuous features to see how they are related to other voice types. In addition, seven separate schemas and cognitive models are illustrated for each subtype of voice discussed in this chapter.

Chapter   Ⅷ is the conclusion. It mainly presents the major findings of this study. In addition, it points out the limitations of the dissertation and suggests some areas for further studies.

II

Literature Review

As a point of departure for enhancing understanding of English voice, this chapter makes an attempt to review the influential literature on English voice contributed by different schools of linguistic study and examine how they deal with English voice. In addition, we also point out the limitations and problems with their studies. Such a review will naturally put our study in a larger background and lay a foundation for the discussion in the following chapters.

1　Traditional Approach to English Voice Category

The treatments of English grammatical category today are inseparably intertwined with the grammatical scholarship of the earlier traditional grammar. The notion of "traditional" in traditional grammar comes from its origin in the descriptive and pedagogical treatments of the structures of ancient European languages, chiefly Greek and Latin, but later it gradually eliminates the rigid rules of Latin and Greek and develops its own method of description.

A review of literature on the traditional scholarship of English grammatical voice reveals that voice has received great attention from traditional grammarians such as Sweet (1900), Jespersen (1927), Poutsma (1926), Leech and Coates (1980), Quirk et al. (1985), and Huddleson (1984), to name a few. Their contributions are vital to the study of English voice and can be summarized as follows:

Firstly, for traditional grammarians, grammatical voice is generally said to be a function of the verb that enjoys the comparable status as that of tense, aspect, and mood (Klaiman 1991; Quirk et al.1985; Möhlig-Falke 2012). It mainly manifests at two levels: the verb phrase, and the clause. According to Quirk et al. (1985: 159), two grammatical levels are involved while dealing with active-passive relations. At the level of verb phrase, the two-voice category is always discussed in terms of various tenses and aspects of the main verb or whether the main verb is changed in a form of the auxiliary *be* followed by the past participle of it. However, the description at verb phrase level is not concrete at all. Thus, most traditional grammarians turn to the clausal level explanation by considering the rearrangement of clause elements and relationship among the verb, its subject and object while discussing the relationship between active and passive voice.

Another crucial contribution made by traditionalists is that the notion of English voice is commonly embodied in binary oppositions of active voice and passive voice (Sweet 1900; Jespersen 1924, 1927; Quirk et al. 1985; Haspelmath 1990; Huddleston and Pullum 2002). What they accentuate is that there is an interrelation between active and passive voice in both structure and meaning, and the formation of the passive construction comes from transforming their corresponding active construction at the syntactical level.

Thirdly, though the traditional grammarians attach great importance to the syntactic correlation between active voice and passive voice, they also notice that active and passive sentences are not in systematic correspondence. There are a number of exceptions where felicitous conditions must be satisfied and constraints must be executed. To argue for the inconsistency between the active-passive transformations, Jespersen (1927) puts forward two points. First, he stresses that in most languages there are certain restrictions on the use of the passive turn, which are not always easy to account for. Second, he claims that intransitive verbs in the passive are common in some languages by using non-English examples. Moreover, Quirk et al. (1985: 160-167) make an elaborate analysis on the five types of voice constraints, involving the constraints on the verb, the object, the agent, meaning as well as frequency of use.

Finally, a crucial point related to traditional study worth mentioning here is the *gradience* or, in other words, *continuality* in English Voice Category. According to Aarts et al. (2014), gradience refers to the phenomenon of categorical indeterminacy between linguistic elements on a graduated continuum (or cline).

It is generally said that the term gradience was introduced by Dwight Bolinger (1961). In fact, a similar phenomenon had been discussed by traditional grammarians preceding the coining of term. Jespersen (1924: 165) comes up with two concepts to show this categorical indeterminacy between active and passive voice: syntactic and notional active or passive. Likewise, Curme (1931) argues that transitivity is not always a crucial factor to make voice distinction because there is not always a clear-cut borderline between the passive and intransitive. He also posits out that there are two passive forms of the verb whose borderline is rather obscure. One is the passive with passive form; the other is the passive with intransitive form.

Contrary to the popular belief held by Joos (1950: 702), who argues that "all continuity, all possibilities of infinitesimal gradation are shoved outside of linguistics in one direction or the other." Bolinger (1961) explicates that linguistics cannot rigidly adhere to discrete rules as in mathematics. Rather, the properties of generality and ambiguity are both found in referent ranges of lexical items in general as well as grammatical categories.

Following in Bolinger's footsteps, many traditional grammarians take note of gradient properties of linguistic categories and apply the notion to almost every domain of linguistic studies. Among them, five research works are worth our attention. Svartvik (1966) introduces the concept of *passive scale* which is similar to the concept of *gradience* and has direct bearing on the relations of the two voice terms. Quirk et al. (1985: 167-171) detect that there is a gradient or scale among different passive sentences and divide passive into central passives with expressed agents or without expressed agents, semi-passives and pseudo passives with current copular verbs or with resulting copular verbs. Palmer (1987: 85) points out some combinations of Be+V-en forms that are obviously not true passives. Shibatani (1985) claims that passives are germane to other constructions in two dimensions: one is that passives are correlated with constructions such as the reflexive, reciprocal, etc. The other is that passives form a continuum with active sentences. Aarts (2007) probes into the syntactic gradience and argues that gradience is an undeniable property of grammar.

2   Generative Approach to English Voice Category

Those who are familiar with the history of generative grammar know that its theoretical system has constantly been in flux since its establishment. Though the theoretical paradigm has been constantly revised and improved in the past decades, the correlation between the active and passive construction has always been the main theme of their study. Someone even proposes that the evolution of passivization theory from the perspective of generative grammar is exactly the epitome of the evolution history of generative grammar. Some scholars criticize the instability of Chomsky's theory, but it is its evolving process that makes generative grammar more scientific.

It is generally known that there have been four periods of theoretical development for generative grammar in (more than) 60 years (Manninen 2013; Fowler 2017). The treatment of active-passive correlation is closely related to Chomsky's four most representative and significant books.

The first influential book is *Syntactic Structures* which is regarded as an epoch-making work in linguistic history. In this book, Chomsky (1957) claims that one essential requirement that a grammar must satisfy is that it be finite. To be concrete, grammar need to be simple, and infinite number of sentences can be generated based on a finite number of rules. Three rules—the phrase structural rule, the transformational rule and the morphophonemic rule—are illustrated in this book. We will have a close look at the first two rules because they have a direct bearing on our present study. First, sentences can be analysed into hierarchies of constituents based on phrase structure rules. However, there are some limitations of the phrase structure description. One of the crucial examples used to illustrate the inadequacy of the conceptions of phrase structure rules is the case of the active-passive relation.

Two fatal weaknesses of the phrase structural rule are worth noting here. First, the phrase structural rule can generate well-formed sentences as well as ill-formed ones. For example, according to the three rules in Table 1, we may generate sentences like (1)a and (1)b, but they are semantically unacceptable. Second, it lacks descriptive adequacy because it cannot explain the similarity of sentences with different surface structures. For example, it cannot explain the fact that (2)a has the same meaning as (2)b, but it has a different meaning in contrast to (2)c. Nor can they illustrate the systematic difference between statement and their corresponding interrogative, as in (2)d.

Table 1   Phrase Structure Rules in Syntactic Structures (1957: 26-27)

(i) S → NP + VP
(ii) NP → DET +N
(iii) VP → V + NP

(1) a. *The girl hit honesty.

　　b. *The apple eats Mary.

(2) a. Bob hit Charlie.

　　b. Charlie was hit by Bob.

　　c. Bob was hit by Charlie.

　　d. Was Charlie hit by Bob?

According to Chomsky (1957: 42), passive sentences are formed by selecting the element be+en according to the following rule: Aux→C(M) (Have+en) (be+ing) (be+en).[①] However there are unrefined replications and heavy constraints imposed on the element be+en. Then Chomsky reintroduces transformational rules rather than restates the restrictions arduously. It assumes that the grammar should be as simple as possible and all the generative descriptions of language should be based on kernel sentences. These sentences refer to affirmative, declarative statements in the present tense and active voice. It clearly points out that sentences in passive voice are generated by transforming the kernel active sentences according to the well-defined

---

① Only three basic rules are listed here to illustrate the defects of the phrase structure rule. See more detailed explanation in Chomsky (1957: 26-27).

rules as follows:

$$NP_1—Aux—V—NP_2 \text{ is rewritten } NP_1—Aux+be+en—V—by+NP_2$$

(Chomsky 1957: 78)

In 1965, Chomsky published another influential book named *Aspects of the Theory of Syntax*. In this book, Chomsky discards the notion of kernel sentence and coins the term deep structure as the underlying constituents of sentences. Transformational Grammar assumes that there exists two levels in a sentence: surface structures and deep structures. It is generally said that deep structures are generated by phrase structure rules while surface structures are derived from deep structures by a series of transformations. For example, in terms of active-passive relations, sentences like (3)a and (3)b are argued to be cognitively synonymous. Passive sentence (3)b is claimed to have a deep structure in which the noun phrases are in the same order in the corresponding active sentence (3)a.

(3) a. An expert will examine Tom.

　　b. Tom will be examined by an expert.

However, according to Chomsky, semantics only lies in the deep structure rather than the surface structure. Thus, syntax is put at the core while semantics is purely interpretative.

This active-passive transformational rule does not shed light on those verbs with NPs that cannot be passivized or go through the passive transformation. As can be seen in examples (4)a, (5)a, and (6)a. If we exert transformational rules on these sentences, we will generate the ungrammatical sentences in (4)b and (5)b. For (6)b, though acceptable in sense, the meaning of (6)a is totally different from that of (6)b which means Alice's marriage ceremony was conducted by a preacher named Bob. According to Lees (1960: 8) verbs such as resemble, have, marry, fit, cost, weigh can be collected into a category of middle verbs that cannot take manner adverbials freely.

(4) a. Mary closely resembles her sister.

　　b.*Her sister is closely resembled by Mary.

(5) a. I have a book.

　　b.*A book is had by me.

(6) a. Alice marries Bob.

　　b. Alice was married by Bob.

The third influential book named Lectures on Government and Binding was published in 1981 based on lectures Chomsky given at the GLOW conference and workshop held at the Scuola Normale Superiore in Pisa in April 1979. This book combined with two other importants books—*Some Concepts and Consequences of the Theory of Government and Binding* (1982) and *Barriers* (1986)—are Chomsky's major contributions to the formation of the tenets of the Government and Binding (GB) theory of syntax.

In these books, a variety of movements have been discussed within the framework of generative grammar. It is generally said by generative grammarians that the conversion of sentence from active voice into passive voice involves *Argument Movement* (or *A-movement*) which refers to displacing a phrase into a position where a fixed grammatical function is assigned. As sentences in (7)a and (7)b show, there is a movement of the object to the subject position in passive.

(7) a. John read the poem.(active)

   b. The poem was read___ (by John). (passive A-movement)

According to Black (1998: 29), the movement analysis of passives by transformational grammarians capture the generalizations as follows: (i) Most transitive verbs have passive alternates. (ii) No intransitive verbs have passive alternates. (iii) The subject of a passive verb corresponds to the object of its transitive alternate.

However, GB theory claims that there are basic principles that must be followed while exerting movement. One of the crucial tenets is the principle of no loss of information, which stipulates that nothing can move to a position that is already phonetically occupied. In this respect, the explanation made by GB theory for active-passive conversion does not resemble the account made by previous generative grammarians because the principle of no loss of information will be violated if the object is moved to a previously occupied subject position. Regarding this, GB theory deals with not only the generalization by previous transformational grammarian but also makes an attempt to account for the synonymy between active and passive sentences by expanding the lexical entries to include semantic roles such as agent, patient, theme, instrument, recipient, goal, locative, etc., which indicate the grammatically relevant relations between arguments and predicates. In addition, lexical entries are also constrained by the notion of subcategorization which designates a word's (most often verb's) complement options. There are some felicitous conditions for lexical items under which only certain types of syntactic arguments can coexist. It is generally accepted that intransitive verbs take just one argument while transitive verbs and ditransitive verbs take two and three arguments respectively.

(8) a. The students invited Professor Lee to their party.

b. Professor Lee was invited by the students to their party.

As we can see in (8)a and (8)b, the students gave the invitation. Professor Lee was the one invited and their party is what Professor Lee was invited to. Thus, the lexical entry for invite would be [__NP (PP$_{[to]}$)]. As indicated by GB theory, each syntactic complement must be assigned a semantic role. Here NP serves as a theme and (PP$_{[to]}$) functions as a goal. The underline in front of NP indicates there is one additional role which may be given to the subject: external argument.

Another assumption made by GB theory is the uniformity of theta assignment hypothesis. According to Baker (1988: 46), theme role is always assigned to the direct object when it is present. In the case of a passive, the theme should not be assigned to the object in one case and to the subject in a related entry. Hence, in the light of above constraints, the interpretation of active-passive relation under the guidance of GB theory must be partly done in the lexicon and partly by movement.

It is said that the movement is allowed since it makes no difference in the linking between syntactic arguments and semantic roles except that there is a coindexed trace left after the movement indicating the link between the moved element and the position it occupied at the deep structure. Therefore, at the surface structure level, semantic roles still stay with the original position and subcategorization requirements are also satisfied. Given these, the full lexical entry for the passive form invited, including semantic roles should be as follows.

The deep structure and surface structure for (8)b are shown in the tree diagram as Figure 1 and Figure 2 show:

$$\text{invited} \quad V_{[+pass]} \quad [\ \_\ NP\ (PP_{[to]})\ (PP_{[by]})\ ]$$

invited '　　　<THEME, GOAL, AGENT>

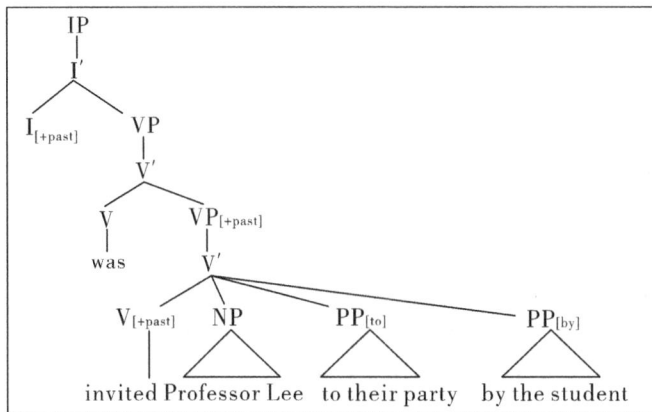

Figure 1 Deep Structure of Passive Sentence in Terms of GB Theory (Baker 1988)

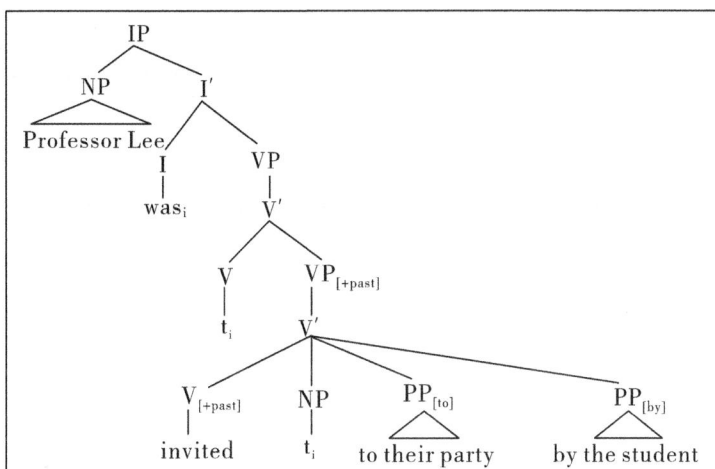

Figure 2   Surface Structure of Passive Sentence in Terms of GB Theory (Baker 1988)

Since 1992, the theoretical framework of generative grammar has shifted gradually from GB theory to Minimalism. With the publication of *The Minimalist Program* in 1995, generative grammar was launched into a new phase. One of the advantages Minimalism have over the previous theoretical models is its clarification of the concept of simplest grammar, because its leading concern is to get rid of complex principles and minimize the theoretical and descriptive apparatus. It is committed to uncovering to what extent minimal conditions are adequate to determine the nature of the correct theory.

In order to cater to the simple and optimal inclinations of generative language research, the modules of grammar under the guidance of the minimalist program have been abstracted, replaced, or even discarded. It is said that within the framework of the minimalist program that phrases and sentences are built up by a series of merge operations. The notion of deep structure and surface structure was abandoned. Radford (2009: 211) claims that one of the crucial properties which differentiate passive sentences from their active counterparts is that the expression which serves as the complement of an active verb surfaces as the subject in the corresponding passive construction. Since Minimalism still lays emphasis on A-movement, so the syntax of the superficial subjects of passive sentences are of great importance. It is claimed that a passive subject originally serves as the thematic complement of a subjectless passive participle, and later is raised into Spec-T via A-movement in order to satisfy the EPP feature of T.

To be concrete, passivization is the first step of computation in passive derivation. First, the base-generated transitive verb merges with the passive morpheme contained in transitivity, which absorbs the Agent θ-role and produces V with a negative transitivity feature. Then the theme object can be proposed to the grammatical subject position to value uninterpretable features of core function categories, or keeps in-situ and values number feature on V_{def} and T via Agree, person feature on T is valued by an expletive via Merge or Move in English (Nan 2012: i).

3 Functional Approach to English Voice Category

Several linguistic theories can be ascribed to functional grammar as against formal grammar. They claim that syntactic, semantic and pragmatic elements are supposed to be unified in explaining linguistic items. Among them, Systemic functional grammar, initiated by Michael Halliday in 1961, and the discourse-pragmatic approach to grammar, which takes Talmy Givón as one of the leading representatives, have been the two most substantial branches whose theories have been applied widely in linguistic analysis and explanations. Moreover, they also pay special attention to the discussion of English voice.

Systemic functional grammarians handle two main aspects of English voice study: (i) voice types were reclassified based on the transitivity analysis. (ii) English voice category is analyzed based on the thematic-rheme structure and information structure from the perspective of textual functional category.

Halliday (2004) holds that transitivity is closely related to the English voice system. Two concepts are introduced to make a distinction between the transitive and intransitive. One is *actor* and the other is *goal*. It is said that in a material clause, there is always one participant — the *actor* that brings about the unfolding of the process through time, leading to an outcome that is different from the initial phase of the unfolding (Halliday 2004: 180).

There are two alternative conditions here:(i) the unfolding of the process only exerts influence on the *actor* which is the only one participant in the process, just as shown in example (9)a, the doing was confined to the lion, we define such a clause as an intransitive one which represents a happening. (ii)The unfolding of the process may transfer to another participant, the *goal*, and exert some impacts on it in some way, just as shown in example (9)b, the outcome of the doing was extended to the tourist. We define such a clause as transitive for it represents a doing.

(9) a. The lion sprang.

   b. The lion caught the tourist.

   c. The tourist was caught by the lion.

(Adapted from Halliday 2004: 180)

Obviously, the operational rules are similar in the English voice system. There are often two participants in a transitive pattern: *actor* is obligatory while *goal* is optional. If there is only *actor* available, the verb is intransitive and the representation is active in voice, as shown in (9)a. Instead, if both the *actor* and *goal* are available, the verb is transitive and the representation may come in either of two forms: either operative (active), as shown in (9)b or receptive (passive), as shown in (9)c.[①]

In line with above assumption, functionalists argue that the English voice system falls into two major types: middle and non-middle. The former refers a clause with no feature of agency, or without the involvement of an external causer or the agent in the clause, just as exemplified in (10)a, the process of *cut* is actualized through the medium without an external causer. The latter, non-middle refers to a clause with agency, or effective in agency. Non-middles can be divided into two subcategories—operative and receptive voice. As the examples below illustrate, (10)b is an operative clause in which the subject is the agent, and the process is realized by an active verbal group. (10)c is a receptive clause in which the subject is the medium, and the process is realized by a passive verbal group.

(10) a. The cake cut easily. (middle)
     b. Mary cut the cake. (operative)
     c. The cake was cut by Mary.(receptive)

In addition to the above generalization, systematic functional grammarians also introduce two concepts to explain voice. One is theme and the other is rheme. The former is the point of departure of the clause as message and sets up an orientation or local context for each clause while the latter represents the non-thematic part of the clause and its role is to present the development of the message of the clause within the local context set up by the *theme*.

It is said that textual clause function operates with the system of *theme* and *rheme*. The syntactic structures formed by using different voices can be analyzed from *theme* and *rheme* of the textual function category and information structure.

In general, the information structure consists of given information and new information and in most occasions new information is preceded by given information. In the same vein, theme and rheme structure often starts with given or old information in *theme* position and extends to new information in *rheme* position. Given this, the symmetrical information units in the syntactic structure of both operative and receptive voice are likely to be the information focus alternatively.

---

① For Systematic Functional grammarians, there are two subsystems of voice: at the clausal level, the binary terms "operative" / "receptive" are adopted, indicating that the contrast between operative and receptive is a textual one and is pertinent to the flow of information within the clause as message (Cf. Matthiessen 2010: 151-174).

(11) a. Nadal defeated Federer in the French Open.

b. Federer was defeated by Nadal in the French Open.

As illustrated in (11)a and (11)b, the information units in the symmetrical syntactic structure of both active and passive construction have the same odds to become the focus of information in a specific communicative context. The preposition by plus agent at the end of the passive sentence like (11)b can be regarded as *theme* because of the change of word order and being marked as a passive. The thematic prominence and end-focus co-occur in the passive construction. Though there are differences, there is no denying that both the agent and patient are put in the salient position if we observe from different perspectives.

In contrast to the systematic functional approach adopted by Halliday, Givón takes a discourse-pragmatic approach to voice. For Givón, two notions are deeply entrenched in his theoretical framework.

Givón's primary concern is the dimensions of transitivity and de-transitivity. In line with the dimension of transitivity, he notes that a syntactic description of the grammar of a language falls into two steps: first, describing the simple clauses and second the complex clauses. The structure of the former may be compared to the theme which refers to a main, declarative, affirmative, active clause while the structure of the latter may be assimilated though variations on the theme. For example, (12)a is the simple-clause theme while the complex clause (12)b corresponds to the theme in that it is a passive rather than an active.

(12) a. Bill ate a sandwich.

b. A sandwich was eaten by Bill.

More generally, Givón's discussion suggests that the active-transitive clause is the reference point, namely, theme, for syntactic description. Thus, the active-transitive voice, the neutral unmarked, and de-transitive voice, the peripheral marked, stand in stark contrast with one another and constitute the core of his approach to the voice category.

In regard to de-transitivity, he refers to the clause that the constructions deviate from the theme in terms of either being less active or less transitive. In accordance with his generalization, not only the traditional canonical voice types (such as, passive voice, middle voice), but also some less canonical voice types (such as, impersonal construction, antipassive construction, reflexive construction, and reciprocal construction), thereby, make up the category of de-transitive voice.

Givón's second main concern is the semantic and pragmatic distinction in his discussion. He argues that semantics and pragmatics, instead of being disparate concepts or categories, are overlapping and interactive on the edge of category. They resemble other prototype-like categories that occupy neighbouring spaces along a continuum (Givón 1993b: 45). Regarding this, he differentiates semantic features and pragmatic features from different types of constructions involving de-transitive voice. His discussion can be divided into two parts: the semantics of de-transitive voice and the pragmatics of de-transitive voice. In terms of the former, it is closely tied with active-transitive voice in three semantic dimensions of the prototypical transitive event, namely, agent, patient, and verb. By and large, semantics of de-transitive voice constructions are those that tamper with transitivity in regard to the following three main semantic parameters: (ⅰ) decreased agentivity of the agent/subject, (ⅱ) decreased affectedness of the patient/object, and (ⅲ) decreased telicity or perfectivity of the verb (Givón 2001b: 93).

In addition, the pragmatics of de-transitive voice suggests that very same semantic transitive event can be rendered by several de-transitive voice constructions. Though the semantics of transitivity is unaffected while viewing the events, these de-transitive constructions differ in pragmatic perspectives which concern chiefly the relative topicality of the agent and patient participants of the event. In other words, the interlocutor's choice of voice hinges on the cognitive salience of the participants in the event.[①] Moreover, three main functional dimensions of de-transitive voice are also given a concrete illustration: (ⅰ) agent demotion, (ⅱ) promotion of a non-agent, and (ⅲ) verb stativization.

Moreover, there are still some publications that share the similar notion with above two influential grammarians. For example, Slobin and Bever (1983) restate the fact that canonical sentences are simple active affirmative declarative sentences, and transitivity and active voice correlate with one another.

In addition, some studies (Rice 1987a, 1987b; Lehmann 1991, Kittilä 2002) explicate the close relationship between transitivity and passive voice. They hold that the degree of transitivity is proportional to the degree of passivization. That is to say, the plausibility of passivization colligates to some extent with transitivity: the more transitive a clause is, the more readily it can be passivized. Kittilä (2002: 31) claims that, passivization is a sufficient criterion for high transitivity in many cases. However, it cannot be a sole factor to influence transitivity due to variation in different languages. Therefore, special caution should be exercised when using it. In the main, those functionalists indeed contribute a lot to the study of English voice category. Broadly speaking, modern linguistics consists of two camps: the formalist and the functionalist. In fact, cognitive linguistics is just one branch of functional study. Though both schools pay special attention to the semantic features of the voice, different

---

① For a more detailed and easy-to-follow introduction, see Cooreman (1982, 1985, 1987, 1988) and Cooreman et al. (1984).

notions are adopted by cognitive linguists and functional linguists. Therefore, let us discuss how cognitive linguists explain the category of English voice in next section.

4   Cognitive Approach to English Voice Category

In this section, our discussion falls into four aspects. First, the basic notion of cognitive linguistics is introduced. Then, the relationship between ICM and voice is discussed. Next, we explain how cognitive grammarians deal with voice. Finally, the concepts of prototype and continuum in English voice category are explained.

4.1   Basic Notions of Cognitive Linguistics

Cognitive linguistics is an approach to the study of natural language that began to arise in the late 1970s in the research of George Lakoff, Ron Langacker, and Gilles Fauconnier has become more and more dynamic since the early 1980s. Nearly four decades later, cognitive linguistics has developed into one of most influential and thriving schools within theoretical and descriptive linguistics. A great amount of research has been conducted by using of the theory of cognitive linguistics. Though certain amount of research discusses syntax, morphology, language acquisition, a majority of studies have addressed semantics.

Cognitive linguistics is delineated by compliance with three central guiding principles. First, it objects to the notion there is an autonomous linguistic faculty in the mind as opposed to generative grammar. Second, it comprehends grammar in terms of conceptualization as opposed to truth conditional semantics. Third, it holds that knowledge of language arises out of language use as opposed to a reductionist tendency in both generative grammar and truth-conditional semantics (Croft and Cruse 2004: 1).

To be concrete, cognitive linguists see language as an instrument for organizing, processing, and conveying information and it is embedded in the overall cognitive capacities of that make up being human. Given this, they attach great importance to the characterization of the conceptual and experiential basis of linguistic categories. The formal structure, rather than being autonomous, serves as the representation of conceptual structure that has experiential and environmental influences. All aspects of conceptual structure are subject to interlocutors' construal of situations, not on objective truth conditions. Linguistic meaning is not a separate modular component that is immune to the influence of semantics and pragmatics, but is preferentially represented in our mind as a conceptualization of the embodied experience.

Categorization does not typically involve necessary and sufficient conditions, but rather prototype and non-prototype senses. Language variation is due to interlocutors' creativity rather than being constrained by a universal grammar.

The major function of language is to meet communicative needs rather than satisfy computational requirements. Grammatical constructions are pairings of form and meaning rather than surface representations of underlying innate computational operations. Therefore, cognitive linguistics often resorts to large amount of data and its research method is empirical in principle.

Thus far, we have dealt primarily with the rudimentary ideas and fundamental approaches of cognitive linguistics. In what follows, we will review briefly how cognitive linguists interpret English grammatical voice within the cognitive theoretical framework. Though a lot of works on voice have been generated, three of them are the most typical and trendsetting approaches worth discussing here. In the next three sections, we will discuss these approaches in turn.

4.2   Event Idealized Cognitive Model (ICM) and Voice

In this section, our discussion is concerned with how ICM is used to shed light on the understanding of English grammatical voice. As it is commonly known, ICM is an analysis model proposed by Lakoff (1987).[①] He argues that we organize our knowledge by means of structures called idealized cognitive models or ICMs, and that category structures and prototype effects are by-products of that organization (Lakoff 1987: 68). However, as suggested by Xiong (2001), there is always a mismatch between ontological entities and epistemological entities since the semiotic relationship may not be totally objective. As put by Lakoff (1987: 70), "an ICM may fit the understanding of the world either perfectly, very well, pretty well, somewhat well, pretty badly, badly, or not at all."

Following the above analysis, Croft (1990b, 1991, 1993) successfully combines the notion of events with the ICM and presents an EICM, that is, an idealized cognitive model of events to conceptualize and categorize verbs in natural language.

According to Croft (1990b), a verb is defined as denoting a segment of a causal chain which represents in some way an ICM of a single event proposed by Lakoff (1987). The lion's share of simple verb types can be put into the three categories as follows: (1) causative, (2) inchoative, and (3) stative. These three categories are three subsets of the idealized event structure, oriented toward the endpoint of the event: the last segment corresponds to stative, the last two segments correspond to inchoative, and the whole event type correlates to causative. This tripartite structure is illustrated in Figure 3 by Croft (1990b). We can see that three examples and their accompanying causal chains are shown in the figure.

The three categories seem to correspond respectively to transitive verb, intransitive verb and adjective to a large extent and serve as the ICM for each of the verbal categories. However, there are always variations and flexibility in the utilization of event views for events. Croft (1990b) suggests that there are always marked cases and unmarked cases among which the latter represents the most natural or typical construal of the event. The notion of event

---

① See Chapter III for more details.

construal appears to be highly compatible with Klaiman's (1988) basic voice category.

Given this, Croft (1993: 102) maintains that the causative, inchoative and stative event views

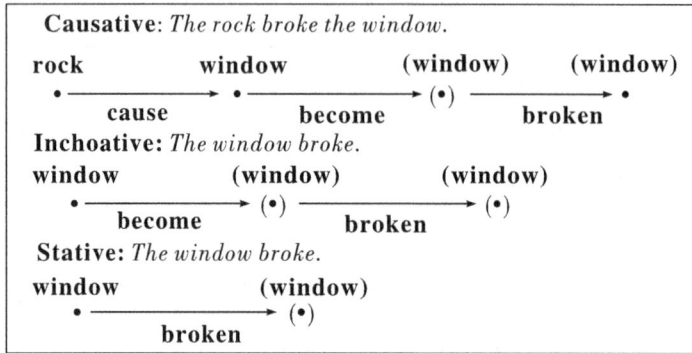

> **Causative**: *The rock broke the window.*
>
> rock   window   (window)   (window)
> • ——————→ • ——————————→ (•) —————————→ •
>   cause   become   broken
> **Inchoative:** *The window broke.*
> window   (window)   (window)
> • —————————→ (•) ——————————→ (•)
>   become   broken
> **Stative:** *The window broke.*
> window   (window)
> • —————————————→ (•)
>   broken

Figure 3   Tripartite Structure of EICM in Croft (1990b: 49-50)

characterise the active, the middle and the passive basic voice type respectively. As Table 2 shows, the same ICM of events falls into three different states: cause–become–state, become–state, and state. It is also shown in four different grammatical constructions, namely, simple verb form, diathesis verb form, basic voice verb form and derived voice verb form. Four different sets of terminologies: (1) transitive–intransitive–adjective; (2) causative–inchoative–stative; (3) active–middle–passive; (4) process passive–antipassive–stative passive are adopted here to represent the same ICM from different perspectives, as shown in Table 2.

Table 2   The Relationship Between Event Views and Voice

Verb Form	Event Views		
	Cause-Become-State	**Become-State**	**State**
simple	transitive	intransitive	adjective (stative)
diathesis	causative	inchoative	stative (resultative)
basic voice	active	middle	(passive)
derived voice	(causative) process process passive	antipassive	stative passive

4.3   Cognitive Grammar and Voice

In this section, our discussion is devoted to how cognitive grammar, as a subbranch of cognitive linguistics, deals with English voice category. As one of the major approaches to structure and meaning of grammar, cognitive grammar was developed by Ron Langacker in the early 1970s as a brand-new theoretical system. It launched a challenge to generative grammar which was the mainstream of linguistics at that time. Its framework was published under the rubric of *space grammar* at very beginning based on the publications of Langacker in 1981 and 1982. Later, space grammar was rechristened as *cognitive grammar* after being given a comprehensively detailed interpretation of their theoretical framework in Langacker's two significant works: *Foundations of Cognitive Grammar Volume One* (1987a) and *Foundations of Cognitive Grammar Volume Two* (1991a).

It has to be pointed out that Langacker is extremely interested in voice study. One piece of evidence is that in his landmark essay "Space Grammar, Analysability, and the English passive", in which many pages are devoted to the discussion of passive construction and the relationship between the passive voice and active voice. In this article, he questions the traditional and generative approach to the roughly synonymous pair of sentences in (13)a and (13)b.

His arguments fall into three points: first, he contends that there is no transformational relationship between active clause and passive clause. Though (13)a and (13)b possess substantially the same composite structure and illuminate approximately synonymous relationships, the two sentences have gone through different compositional paths. Therefore, they are semantically distinct due to their analysability. Second, he maintains that the object *Alice of by* in the passive sentence (13)b should not be treated as a demoted deep-structure clausal subject, but it is simply the object of *by*. Demotion does not occur and under no condition can the object of *by* be the clausal subject. Finally, it is claimed that grammatical morphemes (like *be*, *by*, and the participial inflection) which mark passive constructions, instead of being meaningless entities with purely formal function, are all meaningful. They play an active role in the semantic structure of passive expression and indicate the unique features in contrast to their active counterpart.

(13) a. Alice approached Bill.

   b. Bill was approached by Alice.

Furthermore, Langacker (1991b) employs the concept of the coding of events to expound his view on semantic value with voice. Here, he borrows Talmy's notion of transmission of energy and role archetype in describing the events. He claims that the world is often envisaged as being composed of many discrete objects, each of which occupies a different location. These objects may move and interact with others and in turn the motion is driven by energy. Naturally a certain degree of force will be initiated and energy will be transmitted when there is physical contact with other objects. This is so called billiard-ball model which serves as one of the archetypal conceptions.

The second archetypal conception concerns the stage model, in which the observation of sequences of external events are concretized, each involving the interactions of participants within a setting (Langacker 1991b: 210). Therefore, the typical agent role indicates that a person's volitional action results in contact with some external objects and in turn transmits energy to that object. By contrast, the typical patient absorbs the energy transmitted by external physical contact and consequently goes through some change of state.

In addition, some linguistic coding is unmarked while some are marked. In terms of the voice, Langacker (1991b) points out that transitive sentences in the active voice describing physical interactions among third-person participants are highly unmarked while the passive event coding are marked. Another assumption he made is that interactions between the participants are to be construed as forming action chains which have a head and a tail. The construal falls into different dimensions among which profile/base distinction is the most significant pair. The base for a linguistic predication is its domain while the profile is a substructure of the base that is elevated to a distinctive level of prominence as the entity which the expression designates (Langacker 1991b: 61). Regarding to action chains, profiling enables different portions of a chain to be located into prominent positions as the designated process. Moreover, it is also claimed that there is always an asymmetry exhibited in relational predications in the process of delineation of the relational participants.

Following the above analysis, let's see how voice is interpreted by Langacker (1991b). He proposes that the active and passive voices instantiate alternative philosophies concerning the linguistic coding of events. An active clause is able to align the two asymmetries together by matching the relational figure with the most energetic participant. Each asymmetry assumedly manifests the ranking of participants in terms of their subjective prominence, and directionality in the objectively construed flow of energy coalition.

The two voices thus represent alternative philosophies with respect to the linguistic coding of events. By equating the relational figure with the most energetic participant, an active clause achieves the coalignment of two asymmetries, each of which presumably reflects the order in which conceived entities tend to be accessed at some level of cognitive processing: the ranking of participants in terms of their subjectivity.

Conversely, a passive clause, the most prominent participant locates downstream in the energy flow. Therefore, conflict in alignment occurs and an unnatural construal is executed in the profiled process. The focused participant no longer represents the origin but the terminus relative to its inherent directionality, which naturally make the passive a marked voice.

4.4   Prototype and Continuum in English Voice Category

Prototype approach to linguistic phenomena reveals that every member of a category does not have equal status and the boundaries between categories are fuzzy rather than being clear-cut [①]. This notion gives rise to the grey area that is defined as a continuum by Langacker (1987a). He contends that grammatical structures reveal the structuring and conventional symbolization of conceptual content rather than being inherently symbolic. Within the framework of cognitive grammar, lexicon, morphology, and syntax are all assumed symbolic in nature, forming a continuum of symbolic units.

The prototype theory has enjoyed great popularity and has since been applied to all levels of linguistic analyses. Later, prototype and continuum often went hand in hand in explaining linguistic phenomena. English voice category is also to the point. For better understanding, let's come to some representative works concerning grammatical voice, prototype and continuum.

Admittedly, Van Oosten (1984) is a pioneer who combines the passive study with the prototypical agents and topics. She proposes that a passive should occur when the subject of the passive sentence is unable to have one of the prototypical agent or topic properties.

In the same vein, Shibatani (1985) revisits passives and related constructions under the framework of prototype theory and argues that currently acquirable accounts of passives fail to elucidate the comparatively unfamiliar association of passives to reflexive, reciprocal, spontaneous, potential, honorific, and plural formations and are unable to determine the nature of pseudo-passives, impersonal passives, etc. Therefore, the employment of a prototype approach and the defining of a passive prototype is an alternative way to solve the problem. He also resorts to the concept of continuum and points out that passives form a continuum with active sentences.

Meint (1999) investigates the acquisition sequence of the English passive by dividing passives into prototypes and non-prototypes. He maintains that English passives have gradable structures which have something to do with the canonical action event. It reveals that children acquire prototypical passives earlier than marginal ones.

Croft (2001: 283-319) also involves himself extensively in the study of voice continuum from the perspective of radical construction grammar. His contribution lies in the fact that he makes full use of conceptual space—a structured representation of functional structures and their relationship to each other—to interpret voice continuum. He maintains that though constructions are specifically language-oriented and constructions encoding similar functions across languages are diversified, passives seem to always have something to do with not only the active but also other constructions such as middle voice, inverse voice, anticausative voice, etc.

Another proponent for the notion of voice continuum is Toyota (2008), who gives a clear definition of voice continuum, which refers to a feature of grammatical voice that demonstrates

---

① See Chapter III for more details.

how each voice does not exist independently: they are somehow related to each other, whether the relationship is syntactic, semantic or functional (Toyota 2008: 137). However, he mainly addresses voice continuum in the category of the English passive and lays emphasis on the passive-diathesis. Moreover, Toyota (2011) further elucidates that voice continuum involves numerous structures varying across languages. These structures fall into two categories, one concerning valency increasing operations including the structures such as causative and applicative, and the other valency decreasing operations involving passive, reflexive, middle, and anticausative.

5   Problems and Limitations Concerning Different Linguistic Schools

So far, our discussion of different approaches to English grammatical voice has tacitly assumed that various linguistic schools have come up with different elaborations on voice category from different perspectives. Their research not only enhances our comprehension of English voice but also paves the way for our current study. Despite their contributions, every school seems to have unavoidable theoretical inadequacies and practical deficiencies. An interesting question posed here is what the limitations and problems with each linguistic school concerning English voice are. With this question, let us summarize the drawback of each aforementioned school in turn.

As seen in the preceding section, traditional grammarians give more weight to the grammatical features of both the active and passive voice in English. They lay emphasis primarily on the syntactic features and prescribe some rules for voice conversion, believing that grammar is supposed to be taught clearly in terms of the correct surface of the sentence form discretely by obeying certain rules rather than in context. Though their analyses of English voice offer references for pedagogical grammar, their interpretation for English voice is merely descriptive. They notice the exceptional cases such as active without corresponding passive or passive without passive configurations. The only thing they can do is to list the exceptional cases and take it as a constraint for the verb or some other thing, and no theoretical explanation is offered. In addition, traditional approaches seem to be unable to offer proper principles for choosing the right voice in some special cases, let alone to catch sight of the process of human cognition.

Unequivocally, the relationship between actives and passives has been examined extensively in traditional grammar. However, it is only when a linguistic phenomenon is analyzed with reference to relevant theoretical framework that can make it a theoretical issue. Generative grammar in its various guises including case grammar, relational grammar, etc., has worked out some solutions theoretically. Admittedly, Chomsky and his followers have been endeavoring to offer a good explanation to various linguistic phenomena by revising their theory successively. The intention to minimize theories and maximize the learnability makes the theory more scientific.

However, their argument for autonomy of syntax and less attention to semantics often make them the target of questioning and challenges. As regards the English voice, generative grammarians' interpretation of the relationship between actives and passives is of great significance, but its defects are also obvious. One defect is the purpose for conducting voice research. Just as put by Granger (1983: 48), the complexity and richness of the passive structure are not even hinted at the transformational accounts of the passive. The main reason why generativists offer so less enlightenment underlying this comment is that most of them, particular Chomsky have not investigated the passive for its own sake but as a tool to demonstrate the validity of the different transformational models. Another defect of the generative approach concerns its failure to cast light upon human cognition in dealing with linguistic phenomena. Further evidence comes from Langacker (1987b: 128), where he argues that "simple sentences do much more than simply provide structural templates. They actively interact with the ways in which we apprehend and interpret real world situations." Following Langacker's generalization, the adoption of different voices in expression is done to convey diversified meanings so as to meet communicative needs rather than to generate sentences in accordance with grammaticality confined to certain specific generative rules.

In contradiction to traditional grammar, as suggested by Schleppegrell (2004), functional grammar considers language as a meaning-making resource rather than a set of rules. Contrary to the generativists' belief, as discussed by Dik (1983), grammatical structures are envisaged not essentially as one part of an abstract and autonomous linguistic system by functionalists, but rather as being sensitive to, and co-determined by, the pragmatic determinants of human verbal interaction. The operating principles of functional grammar are conceived in connection with functional notion within which semantic, syntactic and pragmatic factors are all taken into account. After developing for over sixty years, function grammar has already formed a comparatively complete theoretical system. Though they have made great contributions to the study of voice, such as reclassifying voice from their transitivity, putting voice in the text or discourse, etc., defects are unavoidable. One of the weaknesses concerning the functional grammar is that they put too much emphasis on the social factor of the voice while the cognitive process of choosing a proper voice in certain context is hardly discussed. Another drawback concerns the conflict between the wider theoretical system and requirements for a refined interpretation of some special voice cases. Some theoretical analyses need to be considered carefully to avoid cyclic redundancy.

In contrast to the three aforementioned linguistic approaches, cognitive linguistics represents a comparatively new approach to the study of language in its short history, but it has been one of most prosperous schools in recent years. One of the significant differences between cognitive linguistics and other schools of linguistics is the assumption that language is neither self-contained nor describable without essential references to cognitive processing (Langacker 1991b: 1). Due to the neglect of language external factors such as human cognitive devices, the three above approaches may fail to give a complete explanation of English voice. Indeed, some cognitive linguists have already conducted some research on English voice by adopting the prototype theory, ICM theory, etc. However, as reviewed above, their studies are not systematic at all. There are some weaknesses when compared with both generative and functional approaches to voice. Set against the former, cognitive linguistics mainly focuses on the subjective descriptions and interpretation of voice, hence, a more logically theoretical analysis and objective judgment are needed. Compared with the latter, the members of English voice category are not well-defined. In other words, there is no agreement among cognitive linguists on how many types of grammatical voice even exists in English.

6   The Approach of the Current Book

As discussed above, every approach to English voice category has some pros and cons. Despite this, this dissertation mainly takes a cognitive approach to English voice category and takes some functional analysis or other approaches into account if it necessary. The reasons why we combine cognitive approach and functional approach together are as follows:

For one, in broad sense, cognitive linguistics is said to be included in one of the subbranches of functional linguistics—external functionalism, as suggested by Newmeyer (1998) and Croft (1990). The underlying motivation to put cognitive linguistics under the name of functional orientation is that there is great compatibility between the two approaches. First, both schools emerge in opposition to generative linguistics. On the grounds of this, both the functionalists and cognitivists give top priority to the study of meaning, favoring the argumentations that form and meaning are inseparable. Variations in form indicate discrepancy in meanings and there always exists justification between the form and meaning. Second, both approaches back up a dialectical relationship between language and thinking. For functionalists, the selection of language form and meaning inevitably exerts some influence on human thought and outlook but it is rooted in social structure and culture background. For cognitivists, language is said to be the vehicle of thought and cognition on the one hand, as put by Wittgenstein (1953: 329). On the other hand, cognition underpins language. Third, both the functional theories and cognitive theories have strong operability and practicality in contrast with a generative approach.

With regard to English voice category, both the functionalists and cognitivists accept the prototype theory rather than classical theory, holding that there is voice continuum between different types of voice and the boundary between the different constructions is not clear-cut but fuzzy.

For another, it has been claimed that the functional approach and cognitive approach can be complementary in several aspects. First, according to Halliday, the basic assumption of functional linguistics is that there is social meaning interface between the objective world and language symbol. Cognitivists are in favor of the above proposition, but, nevertheless, they assume that, as suggest by Svorou (1994), there is still another interface between the objective world and language symbol, that is, cognition, which plays a significant part in interpreting language. Second, a functional approach to grammatical metaphor and a cognitive approach to conceptual metaphor can be complementary in linguistic analyses. Stratification view and context view of functional linguistics may offer some insights to cognitive linguists while the basic notions such as image schema, ICM, iconicity, grammaticalization, etc. may also offer help to functional linguists to some extent.

Given the above analysis, this book will mainly take cognitive theories as the operation principle in discussion of the English voice category. In addition, we may partially resort to functional approach or other approaches while dealing with the interface between semantic and pragmatic features concerning each individual type of English voice.

III

Theoretical Framework

The organization of this chapter is as follows: section one is devoted to three crucial concepts–fuzziness, discreteness and continuity—that are fundamental to a thorough understanding of the underlying operating principle, and the must-have determinants for formulating the cognitive model in current study. Section two presents the essential tenets of prototype theory by comparing it with the classical view. Section three addresses the schema theory which is drawn on frequently in our present study in that it is one of the cognitive mechanisms that exert great influence that on our categorization. Section four discusses construal theory from many perspectives. Section five deals with force dynamic theory conceived by Talmy and others, which are given top priority in our study due to its great contribution made in interpreting the event model of different voice types. The last section summarizes what has been discussed.

1 Fuzziness, Discreteness, and Continuity

It is an indisputable fact that natural language does not observe explicit and precise rules all the time. The fuzzy features seem to be omnipresent in our language. For example, when somebody tells you that Tom is old, the notion of being old is rather vague. You are supposed to know how old Tom is. Even if you know Tom is 70 years old, the number 70 is still a rough notion in that the precise calculation of Tom's age may involve the month, days, even hours. However, we will not allow such the trivial things to inhibit our communication in daily life because there is always a compromise between fuzziness and preciseness.

The notion of fuzziness is not coined in linguistics, instead, it can be traced to the fuzzy set studied in mathematics where Zadeh (1965) uses it to make comparison and contrast with standard set. In his view, the classes of objects encountered in the real physical world, more often than not, do not have precisely defined criteria of membership but has a graded membership with the values ranging from 0 to 1, written as [0,1], as Figure 4 demonstrates below. His findings shed the light on discrepancy between classical binary logic and the multifarious indistinctness of the real world. It, to some extent, echoes the contradictions between the classical view of categorization and prototypical view of categorization.

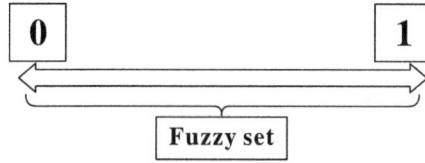

Figure 4   A Graded Membership in a Fuzzy Set

After the notion of fuzziness was introduced in the linguistic field, it was well-adopted and applied to linguistic analysis. Modern descriptive linguistics has always been conscious of the fact that grammatical systems are subject to fuzziness (Aarts et al. 2004).

For example, Wittgenstein (1953) points out that concepts in natural languages tend to possess extendable boundaries, and members in a category vary in their status. Quirk et al. (1985: 403-404) accept the notion of fuzziness. When discussing adjectives, they allow for membership of the adjective category varying from the prototypical to marginal cases. Moreover, Lakoff (1987: 70-74) argues that even non-graded concepts, such as the idealized cognitive model, cannot be totally devoid of the feature of the fuzziness because the ICM of certain concept rarely makes a perfect seamless fit with the world as we know it.

In line with the prototypical and fuzzy feature in the process of categorization, cognitive grammarians have a more liberal view on the gradient feature of language and are more willing to address the non-discreteness in the categorization of word meaning as well as syntactic patterns. As put by Langacker (1987b: 135), to posit a continuum is not to abandon the goal of rigorous description: we must still describe the individual construction in explicit detail, even as we articulate their parameters of gradation. This seems to strengthen the argument that, it is instructive to take an eclectic view in dealing with the fuzzy feature in the category and beyond category. That is, it is feasible to combine the discrete and continuous features in dealing with the categories.

As for the fuzziness and its context, Ma (2011) gives us a comparatively clear explanation. As can be seen, Figure 5 demonstrates the fuzziness in the category and beyond the category. The Rectangle Y indicates the natural context which may consist of several categories. X represents a category in Y. The dots a and e may serve as the prototype of the X category that has discrete features. The dots c, d, f, h, i are members of Y, but not X. However, for the dots of b and g, they are fuzzy in that they locate at the boundary of the X and Y and belong to the both X and Y. But it is no denying that all the dots in the Y, including e and a, have some shared features. They manifest continuous feature in the category of Y for sure.

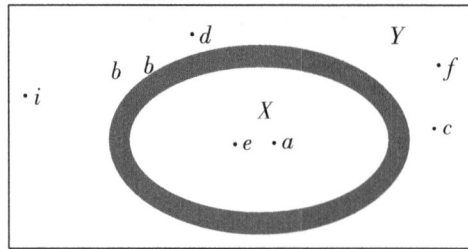

Figure 5   Fuzziness and Its Context (Ma 2011)

Even a quick glance at the linguistic literature makes clear that the term discreteness is on many occasions allied with continuity. In practice, the two terms are so closely interwoven that it is hard to define one without resorting to the other. Originally, as put it by Raper (2000: 63), the duality of continuity and discreteness is probably at the root of the Greek philosophy of space where mathematics, physics and geometry originated and evolved. Therefore, the use of the two terms is hardly a linguistic innovation, but a concept that is applied widely and deep-rooted in the abovementioned natural sciences.

It seems that the term *continuity* is relatively easier to understand than that of discreteness in that we know that it is a word that is omnipresent in everyday conversation, referring to the fact of not stopping or changing. In addition, its conventional meaning is in accordance with its technical meaning in science. Contrastingly, the term *discreteness*, referring to the fact of being individually separate and distinct, is not a colloquial or common word that frequently occurs in daily conversion. To define the technical term, one has to go through some notion of mathematics such as set and one-to-one correspondence between sets, albeit less hard to understand. Two interpretations of discreteness are available, i.e. the use of discrete units (phonemes and morphemes), and the categorization of these units in terms of discrete grammatical categories. The second interpretation is what our dissertation is aiming at.

In the context of human language or semiotic systems, as suggested by Crystal (1985: 96-97), discreteness can be defined as "the elements of a signal which can be analysed as having definable boundaries, with no gradation or continuity between them", whereas a system lacking discreteness is said to be continuous or non-discrete.

The notion of discreteness and continuity has aroused great interest among many linguists from different schools. As maintained by the generativists, the boundaries between phonemes and morphemes, or between words and sentences do not form a continuum but are clear-cut (Chomsky 1970). Following Chomsky's line of thinking, sometimes it is a grueling task to demarcate a clear-cut boundary between various syntactic categories. Functionalists and cognitivists, thereby, hold the opposite position, maintaining that syntactic categories are not discrete but form a continuum (Langacker 1987b; Comrie 1989; Croft 1991). In order to put our discussion on a concrete footing, let us see how the two terms are illustrated by cognitive linguists.

According to cognitive linguists, categorization is one of the essential tenets of conceptual and linguistic organization, which involves putting things into categories based on their shared features. In grammatical scope, this strategy works well in most cases while we define a certain category. But there are always some problems with some grammatical categories. As far as our topic in this dissertation is concerned, a passive is a passive, an active is an active, but this division cannot be maintained one hundred percent of the time. A traditional semantic definition of passive or active in general is undeniably inaccessible if only objective, truth-conditional factors are taken into account.

However, this problem can be overcome in the context of cognitive linguistics. For cognitivists (Langacker, 1987, 2006; Talmy 2000a, 2000b; Taylor 2002), this bounded-boundless relationship between the binary concepts in a grammatical category is pertinent to discrete and continuous features in the external world. It has been claimed that discreteness and continuity are two concepts that reflect two different ways for people to observe and understand the world. A quantity is composite or (internally) discrete if it is conceptualized as having breaks, or interruptions, through its composition. Otherwise, the quantity is conceptualized as (internally) continuous (Talmy 2000a: 55).

According to Langacker (2006: 108), we experience our world as being occupied (if not constituted) by bounded objects (like *a dog*, *a house*, *or a tree*), by continuous substances (like *water*, *soil*, *or plastic*), and by collections of discrete entities (like *people*, *books*, *or peanuts*). Whether something is viewed as an object, substance, or collection depends as much on perspective and purpose as on its inherent nature. The basic ability to compare two experiences and register any discrepancy between them resides in everyone in society. Discreteness depends on there being a discrepancy between a standard and a target of comparison, in some domain or at some level of organization. Continuity occurs when matching the standard to the target reveals no disparity. The issue of discreteness and continuity has come into full play in all domains and at multiple levels of linguistic analysis.

Another point to be made here is that there are some features or concepts that are closely interconnected with discreteness and continuity. There seem to be significant parallels between the features involved in discreteness on the one hand, and continuity on the other hand.

A seminal contribution is made by Talmy (2002) in what he calls as the configurationally structure, which denotes the way by which entities contained in the meaning of the sentence are structured. Within this framework, he claims that the mass versus count distinction is too simple to convey the semantic features of the grammatical category. Tamly (2000a: 47) claims that configurational structure system consists of "geometric delineations in space or time or other qualitative domain that closed-class forms can specify." Within this system, the three most pivotal categories—plexity, boundedness and state of dividedness—are given priority. Plexity refers to a quantity's state of articulation into equivalent elements. Two values are involved in plexity: uniplex where the quantity is conceptualized as a single unit and multiplex where the quantity is visualized mentally as a group of units. These two values often surface in both lexical items and grammatical elements. We can examine them in terms of the following contrast between matter and action in the following examples. As illustrated in (1)a, the uniplex referent bird represents matter while sigh represents an action. Both of them can occur with grammatical elements that specify themselves a uniplexity as in (1)a. However, they can also go with grammatical elements that specify a multiplexity as in (1)b. This operation principle corresponds to the cognitive operation *multiplexing* in which single unit duplicates into various points in space time resulting in a multiplex referent that is unbounded, *birds* referring a flock of birds and *to sigh* referring to producing a series of sighs.

(1) a. Uniplex: A bird flew in./He sighed.

b. Multiplex: Birds flew in./He kept sighing.

(Tamly 2000a: 48)

Another category that is closely related to plexity is the state of boundedness, which involves two values, (1) unboundedness where a quantity is visualized as an entity without intrinsic bound that is continuing; and (2) boundedness where a quantity is conceptualized to be discriminated as a single unit entity. A concrete understanding can be obtained from the examples below. As shown in example (2)a and (2)b, *water* and *sea* denote matter as lexical items in English whereas *sleep* and *dress* indicate action as lexical items in English. Both the water and *sleep* possess unbounded value while *sea* and *dress* convey bounded value. These lexical features project onto the grammatical elements, bringing about the unacceptability or ungrammaticality of sentences in (2)a and the other way round in (2)b.

(2) a. (Unbounded)*We flew over water in one hour.

*She slept in eight hours.

b. (Bounded) We flew over a sea in one hour.

She dressed in eight minutes.

(Tamly 2000a: 51)

In addition, the state of dividedness, as the third category present by Tamly (2000a), tells of a quantity's internal segmentation. Two values are included in this category, i.e.

discrete where an entity is envisaged as having breaks, or a break, and continuous, or vice versa. It can be shown that there is some overlap between the notion of boundedness and dividedness. In practice, they can be different when you have a close look at (3)a and (3)b. As can be seen, examples in (3)a are singular multiplex nouns, which are more likely to elicit a conceptualization of their referents with a degree of obscuring and merging across their component elements. Reversely, examples in (3)b are the equivalent plural uniplex nominals, which sustain the visualization in terms of a demarcated composite.

(3) a. foliage, timber, and furniture

  b. leaves, trees, and pieces of furniture

Moreover, two opposite features still need to be taken into consideration. One is homogeneity and the other is heterogeneity. According to Langacker (1987a: 258), homogeneity indicates that the component states of something are viewed as effectively identical or alike while heterogeneity refers to a set consisting of entities that are dissimilar. Usually, mass nouns in (4)a are typically homogeneous while count nouns in (4)b are typically heterogeneous. But these features do not rely on necessary and sufficient conditions; they are good examples and bad examples. For example, *bicycle* may be the best example of heterogeneous feature in that bicycle has definable subparts while *pond* is not. *Oxygen* is a good example of homogeneous feature whereas *furniture* is not.

(4) a. oxygen, water, air, furniture

  b. bicycle, cat, piano, pond

 The last pair of features concerning discreteness and continuity is determinacy and indeterminacy. The former indicates that we can give a definite and precise specification of the elements and how they are connected to each other while the latter is the other way around. The former is widely applied in generative grammar and truth-conditional semantics while the latter comes into the fore due to the emergence of the cognitive linguistics. According to Langacker (1998), in describing grammatical relationships, vagueness or indeterminacy among the entities or elements occurs more commonly than the precise and determinate connections between specific elements, for it often denotes a special or probably uncommon case.

 In the main, the notion of discreteness and continuity will be used to analyse the categorical features of each type of voice and the relationships between the different voice categories. Special values, such as uniplexity and multiplexity, unboundedness and boundedness, the state of dividedness, homogeneity and heterogeneity, determinacy and indeterminacy will be taken into account.

2   Categories and Categorization

The above discussion leads us to believe that the notion of discreteness and continuity will be useless without examining the concepts of category and categorization. Category and categorization often go hand in hand.[①]

Categorization is the process in which ideas and objects are recognized, differentiated, and understood. Categorization implies that objects are grouped into categories, usually for some specific purpose (Cohen and Lefebvre 2005). It should never be taken lightly. There is nothing more basic than categorization to our thought, perception, action, and speech (Lakoff 1987: 5). We categorize not only concrete things but also abstractions. In most cases, it is subconscious and automatic in that it has become one of our internalized abilities. Jackendoff (1985) points out that categorization is the outcome of the juxtaposition of two conceptual structures. Ungerer and Schmid (1996) maintain that categorization is the mental process of the classification of different things as examples of the same category. In brief, categorization is one of the basic ways for human beings to know the world.

Category and categorization have been never-ending topic of discussion since Aristotle's time. In this section, an overview of the cognitive approach to categories and categorization will be presented by making comparison between prototypical view and classical view. Moreover, we introduce the theory of ICM as a supplement for prototype theory. By virtue of this, we put the study of category in both a historical and cognitive context and provide sufficient evidence to show why the cognitive approach offers a more viable and adequate alternative for description.

2.1   The Classical View

It seems natural that we tend to categorize things by common properties not only in our everyday folk theory but also in the principal technical theory. This evidence reveals that how entrenched the classical beliefs are, and why they have prevailed for more than two thousand years. It is classical, as put by Taylor (2003), in two senses, first, that it can be traced back to Aristotle and Greek antiquity, and second, that it has loomed large in philosophy, psychology and linguistics (among structuralists and generativists in particular) throughout 20th century.

The basic assumptions of the classical approach can be summarized as follows: (ⅰ) Categories are defined in terms of a conjunction of necessary and sufficient features. (ⅱ) Features are binary: X, or Not X. (ⅲ) Categories have clear boundaries, which means that

---

① See Labov (1973) and Geeraers et al. (1994) for more information.

something is in the category or it is not; (ⅳ) All members of a category have equal status, which means every instance of a category represents that category equally well.

There is no denying that the classical view has made a great contribution to linguistic study for it is not entirely wrong. However, some problems or inadequacies arise when it is examined and explored with acute insight. Three problems involving the classical view are revealed by Evans and Green (2006), i.e. (ⅰ) The definitional problem: sometimes even the exhaustive exploration of necessary and sufficient conditions is still insufficient to define a category. For example, the category of *game* as shown by Wittgenstein (1953).[①] (ⅱ) The problem of conceptual fuzziness: not all categories have clear boundaries. For example, table and chair can be the concrete instantiations of the category of *furniture*. The interesting question posing here is that when we deal with *carpet*, the perplexity arises naturally. (ⅲ) The problem of typicality: there are asymmetries between category members in categories not only with fuzzy boundaries but also with clear boundaries. For example, in the *bird category*, *robin* may be a good example of that category while *ostrich* is not. In the category of *even number*, though it has a clear boundary, as Armstrong et al. (1983) suggest, *2*, *4*, *6*, and *8* are better examples of the category than, say, *98* or *10002*. Targeting the above problems, Rosch (1973, 1975, 1978) and her colleagues present a new approach categorization based on large number of experimental findings.

2.2   The Prototypical View

While the classical view has been assumed an unquestionable truth over the centuries, thanks primarily to the ground-breaking work of Ludwig Wittgenstein and Eleanor Rosch, category and categorization studies have launched an upsurge of interest in a wide range of disciplines. The epoch-making assumption that categories have "best examples" called prototypes played a pivotal role in changing our idea about the most fundamental human mental processes and sent shock waves throughout the cognitive sciences.

Most of the deficiencies of the classical theory of category are anticipated by Ludwig Wittgenstein. He presents the concept of family resemblance to solve the first problem mentioned in last section. On a somewhat more abstract level, the principle of family resemblances has been defined as—a set of items of the form AB, BC, CD, DE, that is, each item has at least one, and probably several elements in common with one or more other items, but no, or few, elements are common to all items (Rosch and Mervis 1975: 575). The arising of the theory of family resemblance gives inspiration and revelation to many scholars among whom Rosch is a vanguard who made the study of category and categorization priority. The

---

① According to Wittgenstein (1953: 66-71), a category like game does not fit for the classical mold, since there are no common properties shared by all games. For example, chess and poker both involve competition. Poker and old maid are both card games, but they are similar to one another in a wide variety of ways.

contribution work of Berlin, Kay, Labov, Mervis and Brown cannot be neglected either for all their efforts to develop the notion of family resemblance further develop into the prototype category, causing it to supersede the classical view as the leading approach in dealing with category issues.

Many cognitive linguists involve themselves in the study of prototype. Their definition of prototype varies but they are in essence similar to each other. Langacker (1987a: 371) argues that a prototype is a typical instance of a category, and the other elements are assimilated to the category on the basis of their perceived resemblance to the prototype. Taylor (1989: 59) maintains that the prototype can be understood as a schematic representation of the conceptual core of a category while Ungerer and Schmid (1996: 39) define the prototype as "a mental representation, as some sort of cognitive reference point".

A generalization of the prototypical approach to categories can be summed up as follows: (i) Categories are defined in terms of family resemblance rather than the means of a set of necessary and sufficient features. (ii) Membership in a category is determined by the perceived distance of resemblance of the entity to the prototype. (iii) Membership is not a matter of all or none. The basic assumptions of prototype theory are as follows: (i) A category may have fuzzy boundaries. (ii) A category may merge with neighbouring categories. (iii) There are degrees of membership in the category. (iv) Categories may be acquired from the prototype outward, perhaps with a stage of overextension. (v) Knowledge of features does not have to precede the learning of the category. (vi) Categories can be flexible, and are able to accommodate new experience.

In brief, the prototype theory is considered not so much a theory of knowledge representation as a series of experimental findings that provide extraordinary forward-looking enlightenments into human categorization. In spite of this, the prototype is far from being perfect after being closely scrutinized.

As stated by Evans and Green (2006: 268), four problems with the prototypical view of categorization are proposed. The first one goes to the problem of prototypical primes concerning the study of odd numbers which shows even a "classical category" of this nature exhibits typicality effects. Moreover, similar to classical theory, as criticized by Laurence and Margolis (1999), prototype theory is also subject to the problem of ignorance and error. The underlying assumption is that prototype theory may be unable to explain a concept with a prototype structure, without knowing or mistakenly counting out instances that fail to exhibit any of the properties that typify the prototype. According to Laurence and Margolis (1999), the third problem concerns the "missing prototypes" problem, which shows that the description of a prototype for some categories is often unfeasible. The last problem is the compositionality enunciated by Fodor and Lepore (1996), revealing that prototype theory may fail to offer explanation for the fact that complex categories do not reflect prototypical features of the concepts that contribute to them.

Despite the problems with prototype theory, its progressive enhancement in categorization aids significantly in linguistic analysis. In line with Lakoff (1987), it is uncontroversial that typicality effects are "real" in the sense in that they are based on empirical findings. However, assuming that prototype or typicality effects are virtually on a par with cognitive representations would be untenable or mistaken. Aiming to solving the problems arising in prototype theory and fill the gap uncovered by Rosch and others, Lakoff (1987) presents the theory of *idealized cognitive model* which avoids the problems discussed above and serves as an effective supplement for prototype theory.

2.3   The Theory of Idealised Cognitive Models (ICMs)

According to Lakoff (1987: 68), human beings organize knowledge by means of structures called *idealized cognitive models* (*ICMs*), and that category structures and prototype effects are by-products of that organization. As one of the leading frameworks in cognitive semantics, ICMs represent the cognitive model that is "idealised" in that the model is extracted from a range of experiences rather than restricted instantiation of a given experience. Lakoff suggests that ICMs guide cognitive processes like categorisation and reasoning, and are closely interconnected with categories. The typical effects of categories which are unable to be explained by prototype theory can be accounted for by virtue of ICMs.

In Lakoff's view, the typicality effects can occur in a variety of ways from numerous different sources. In the main, Lakoff offers four approaches to typicality effects:

(1) Mismatches between ICMs. For example, there is a mismatch between the ICM against which *bachelor* is understood. In terms of marital status, the *Pope* is a bachelor but does not satisfy the attributes of bachelor precisely.

(2) Cluster Models. These cognitive models are more complicated since they consist of a number of distinct subcategory models in which one subcategory is always considered to be more salient than the others. For example, the category *mother* may have birth model, nurturance model, genetic model, etc. When the cluster of models that jointly characterize a concept diverge, there is still a strong pull to view one as the most important (Lakoff 1987: 75), and hence, many dictionaries treat the birth model as primary.

(3) Metonymic ICMs. It holds that these ICMs are virtually hinged on exemplars that represent the category as a whole. Typical metonymic models can function as a cognitive reference point and fall into six types as described by Lakoff: stereotypes, typical examples, ideals, paragons, generators and salient examples.

(4) Radial Categories. In this approach, some subcategories are seen to deviate from the

composite prototype, but the operating rules say that members of a radial category exhibit degrees of typicality depending on how close to the composite prototype they are.

Following the theory of ICMs, let us see how the problems with the prototype theory can be solved.

First, concerning the prototypical primes, the typicality effects exhibited by classical categories can be interpreted by analyzing the nature of the cognitive model underlying them.

Second, as for the problem of ignorance and error, it maintains that this problem only occurs providing that typicality effects are identical to cognitive representation. In fact, both correct and incorrect instances involved in categorization naturally lead to miscategorisation if we follow typicality of attributes with ICM.

Next, with regard to "missing prototypes", it still can be attributed to the reason that typicality effects are assumed to be equivalent to cognitive representation. It is said that ICMs are established in repeated experiences, thus non-existent and heterogeneous categories will be naturally unable to exhibit typicality effects.

Moreover, the problem of compositionality is based on the assumption that there is always a straightforward composite of the meanings of the two conceptual categories. But the truth is that the composite category expresses one concept actually possessing two independent category structures which are related.

3 Schema Theory

Centering on the topic of categorization and categories, various linguists have been making unremitting efforts in exploring the very nature of them. The prototype theory has been seen as a good alternative to classical theory. In addition, the theory of ICM also refreshes the prototype theory with some new explanations. Still, there are two sticking points concerning prototype theory. For one, it tends to neglect human beings' abstraction ability, for it categorizes things based on observation of their similarities. For another, it may blur the distinction and individuality of instantiations in the same category. Thus, a schema gives rise to illustrate the relationship between prototype and instantiations as a more general and abstract model.

The schema is not a new concept and its origin can be traced back to the 18th century when Kant first presented the concept of cognitive schema. It was Bartlett in 1932 that developed schema theory and applied it to explain the experimental data on perception and memory in modern psychology. For Bartlett (1932), the schema is loosely defined as "a structure which captures our knowledge and expectations of some aspect of the world".

Rumelhart and Ortony (1977) liken a schema to a play in that there are correspondences between the internal structure of the schema and the script of the play. In addition, they also generalize four essential characteristics which are essential in representing knowledge in memory. i.e. (ⅰ) Schemas have variables. For example, a schema for the word give may involve three variables: a giver, a gift and a recipient. In different contexts and situations, the three variables will reflect different values. (ⅱ) Schemas can embed one within the other. For instance, the face schema consists of many such constitutes as *mouth*, *nose*, *ears*, *eyes*. etc., and it offers specification of these subschemas and relationship between them. Whereas, constitutes part, such as *pupil*, *iris*, *eyelid*, etc., serve as subschema for eye schema that embed in face schema. (ⅲ) Schemas represent generic concepts and vary in their levels of abstraction. For example, the lower level *do* schema is more abstract than those higher level *give* schema or *break* schema. (ⅳ) Schemas represent knowledge rather than definitions. Schemas possess more flexible and variable constraints than that of definitions in that to some extent schemas tolerate some distortions and deviations just as knowledge does. For example, a dead animal is still an animal, and a three-eared cat is still a cat. Schemas stand for knowledge allowing for certain degree of vagueness, imprecision and quasi-inconsistencies. Later, the schema theory was further developed by Rumelhart and Nroman (1985: 36) who generalize schemas as packets of information that contain a variable.

In cognitive linguistics, Talmy (1978) maintains that space and the things in it are schematized through perception and cognition, as well as in language. Lakoff (1987) holds that schema is a significant approach to construct and construe metaphor. However, he scarcely uses schema but image schema which is often in more restricted sense and refers to the simple structures that constantly recur in our daily physical experience.

Admittedly, Langacker's (1987a, 2000, 2009) works shed more light on the understanding of schema theory. As put by Langacker (1987a), there are three models of categorization, the classical one which was defined as strict criteria-attribute model is questionable in serving as the basis for language structure. The other two alternatives—the prototype model and the schema model (a model based on schematicity) which take root in cognitive science—have gained wide acceptance due to their adequate accounts of linguistics categorization based on empirical data. The last two models are intrinsically irreconcilable but both are regarding as indispensable and reliable ways to describe natural language.

As shown in the last section, a prototype serves as a most typical instance of a category and other instances are integrated into the category based on similarity to the prototype. The degree of membership varies according to the degree of resemblance. Conversely, a schema is an abstract characterization that is fully compatible with all of the members of the category it defines (Langacker 1987: 371). There is no degree variation in membership. In addition, a schema functions as a unified structure that reflects the universality of its members, which are not simple conceptions but involving greater specificity and detail. In other words, a schema is the commonality that emerges from distinct structure when one abstracts away from their points of difference by portraying them with lesser precision and specificity (Langacker 1999: 93).

According to Taylor (1995), prototype can be understood in two approaches, one is regarded as the central member of a category, and the other is taken as a schematic representation of the conceptual core of a category. In line with the second approach, it is generally accepted that a particular entity instantiates the prototype. As stated by Langacker, three factors contribute to the understanding of the schema category. As Figure 6 shows, schema is the cognitive model which is generated from the instantiations of the category. It denotes the commonality of every member of the category and blurs the differences of them. Therefore, schema can surface both on the prototype and peripheral members (thus why Langacker adopted the solid line). Prototype and instantiations are in linear order where the prototype serves as the exemplar while instantiations are constrained by the schema on the one hand, and influenced by the prototype on the other hand.

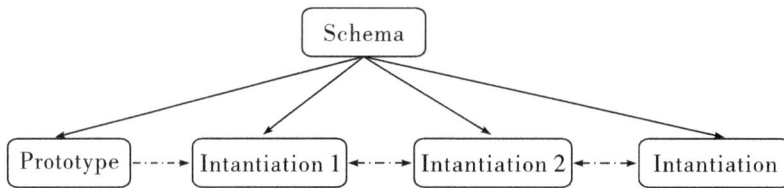

Figure 6   The Relationship among Schema, Prototype, and Instantiations

As claimed by Tuggy (2007), all human concepts show schematic features to some degree. The inherent imprecision and flexibility make language a feasible tool of thought and communication. Since schematicity is gradable at different levels, and a range of variations are allowed, hierarchies of schematicity naturally occur. As can be seen in Figure 7, the abstractness of a schema is relative to its instantiations within different levels of specificity. Precision of specification varies and constrains by different parameters. In Figure 7, from the concept *tall* to the concept *exactly six feet five and one-half inches tall*, the degree of specification is increasing while the abstract feature is decreasing. Comparing the concept *tall* and *over six feet tall*, we can arrive at the conclusion that the former characterizes a more abstract schematicity in contrast to the more precise specification of the latter. Some additional points need to be noted here. Through the characterization of schematicity, we can see that full precise description of linguistic expressions is hardly available, schematicity is a relative matter and the range of values permitted by a particular schema can be restricted in numerous mutually inconsistent way (Langacker 1987a: 133).

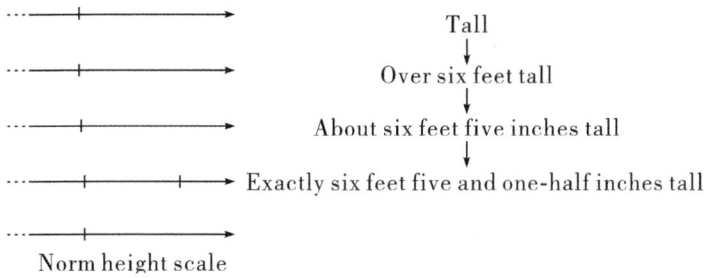

Norm height scale

Figure 7   Hierarchies of Schematicity (Langacker 1987a: 133)

Reumehart (1980) contends that the schema serves as the building block of cognition on which all information processing depends. The supporting evidence underlying this argument lies in the fact that there are some advantages concerning the schema. For one, a schema is abstracted from the repeated experience and whole schema can be activated by the partial features of the schema entrenched in the memory. For another, the schema embodies itself through a multilevel network in which different levels of schemas interact, imbed, supplement, and revise dynamically with each other.

The research on schema theory has been illuminating in explaining language decoding and reading comprehension. It is said that the reader's prior knowledge determines the way in which the new information is understood and this proposition has been validated in a large amount of research. One of the revelations is that the acquisition of English voice categories has been correlated with a learner's prior knowledge of grammatical structures, and if there are not enough schemas about a certain type of voice, it will be hard to get a good command of the English language. Therefore, a schematic view is adopted here to interpret English categories, aiming at giving a holistic abstraction of English voice. In order to look into the underlying operation mechanisms between the cognitive and schematic representation, we have to resort to another concept from cognitive grammar, i.e. construal. In next section, special efforts are made to explain what construal is and how it works in facilitating our cognition.

4   Construal

As maintained by Langacker (2008), the reason why there is a consensus among linguists that grammar is extremely complex and hard to describe properly is that grammar is meaningful. A central claim in cognitive grammar is that there are two variables serving as determinants in meaning analysis. One is conceptual content, the other is how we construe the content in an alternative way. Cognitive linguists perhaps have been the most preoccupied with the idea of construal. Construal[①] is our ability to conceive and portray the same situation in

---

① The term construal is preferable to imagery, used in certain earlier works of Langacker, but we prefer the former in this study.

alternate ways (Langacker 2008b: 43). It plays a pivotal role in both semantic and grammatical structure. Every lexical and grammatical element embodies not only the inherent aspect of its meaning but also a certain way of construing the conceptual content evoked. In order to make our discussion more concrete, let us use Langacker's example to illustrate what construal really is.

Just as Figure 8 shows, picture (a) designates the exact content we want to describe, that is, a glass containing water occupying just half of its volume. An interesting question to ask at this point is how we can express the meaning of this content. It is assumed to be easy to describe it in a very objective way. But we tend to add some note of subjectivity while we try to convert the picture into linguistic expression. Pictures (b) to (e) illustrate four options matching with four distinct expressions with different perspectives and different salient features. The heavy line is used to accentuate the focus within the conceived situation: Picture (b) lays emphasis on a glass functioning as container for water. Picture (c) brings attention to the liquid the glass contains. Picture (d) emphasizes the half-full relationship wherein the volume occupied by the liquid is just half of its potential volume, and picture (e) is just the opposite, it highlights the half-empty relationship wherein the volume occupied by the void is just half of its potential volume.

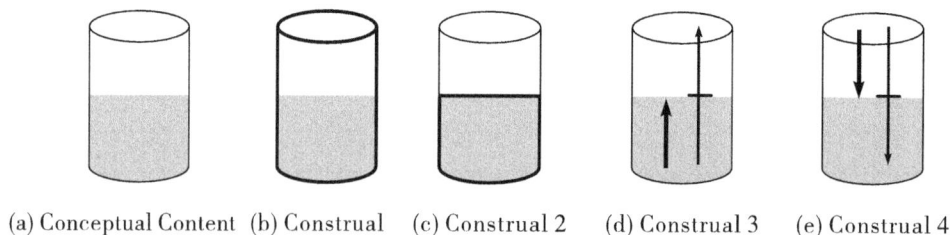

(a) Conceptual Content (b) Construal (c) Construal 2 (d) Construal 3 (e) Construal 4

Figure 8 The Conceptual Content and Ways of Construal (Langacker 2008: 44)

In line with above analysis, it is clear that both the conceptual content and construal are running neck and neck in the meaning interpretation. Reading through Langacker's (1991b: 4; 2000: 5; 2008: 55-85) many substantial works, we find that his theory of construal is constantly in a state of adjustment. Originally, imagery is used rather than construal. Later, construal is adopted while imagery is abandoned totally. Despite the variation, construal is described as a multifaceted phenomenon whose various dimensions reflect some of the basic cognitive abilities. Although the factors vary in different works, in this dissertation, we assume there are five factors that influence the description of construal. Let us look at them in turn.

4.1 Profile and Base

The first dimension of construal we tend to impose while interpret meaning in every linguistic predication is the contrast between base and profile. The former refers to the domain of a predication (or each domain in a complex matrix), the latter denotes a substructure which is elevated to a special level of prominence within the base (Langacker 1991b: 5). Some examples presented below will demonstrate how the base and profile work. Just as examples show in Figure 9, the heavy lines are applied to signify the profile. As can be observed, in picture (a) the hypotenuse elevates as a profile by taking the right triangle as the base. In picture (b), the characterization of the tip is the conception of an elongated object, whereas uncle serves as profile by taking a set of individuals who share kinship relations with him, as in picture (c). As stated by Langacker, the base is a must-have in deciphering the semantic value of each predication, but its value can only be achieved by interaction with the profile. In addition, the profile must be put within the base. Only by dealing with the relationship between the base and profile can the sematic value be vital.

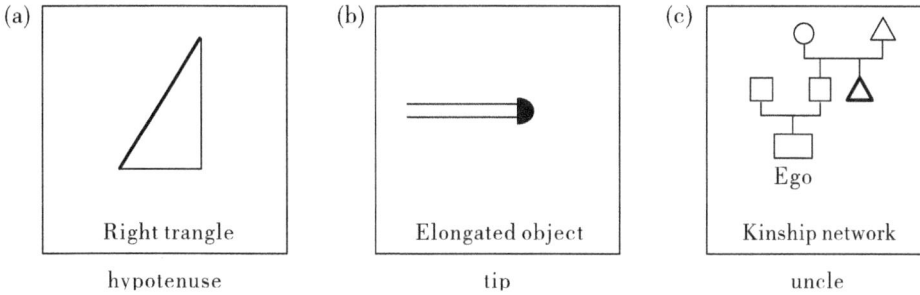

Figure 9   The Contrast Between Profile and Base (Langacker 1991b: 6)

4.2   Specificity

The second dimension of construal concerns specificity, which reflects our capability to perceive and characterize an entity at varying levels of precision and detail. As can be seen in (5), under proper condition, the same entity, temperature might be specified by any of these expressions below. There is hierarchical relationship ranging from (5)a to (5)d. The description becomes more precise and meticulous from (5)a to (5)d, and the specificity of the temperature increases accordingly. By contrast, schematicity, as discussed in the previous section, takes the opposite path, the degree of schematicity enhances from (5)d to (5)a.

(5) a. It is cold.

   b. It is in the minus 20 s.

   c. It is about minus 25 degrees.

   d. It is exactly minus 25.3 degrees.

Two other alternate terms—granularity and resolution—are also introduced by Langacker

(2008) to elaborate the concept specificity. Most of the time, fine-grained detail with precise features and a discrete perspective goes into the highly specific expression when describing an entity, while more coarse-grained observations are used in less specific descriptions. Therefore, the more specific an expression is, the higher the resolution is. On the contrary, the coarse-grained account with gross features and global organization often goes hand in hand with a highly schematic expression while giving a description of an entity and the fine-grained depiction take a converse path. Consequently, the more schematic an expression is, the higher the granularity is.

In line with above analysis, as can be seen in example (6), animal is schematic vis-à-vis mammal, and mammal is schematic in regard to dog. Dog is schematic with respect to Chihuahua, and Chihuahua is schematic with regard to the female Chihuahua, etc. Langacker commonly employ a solid arrow to illustrate this elaborative relationship. The notation is A→B.

(6) Animal→Mammal→Dog→Chihuahua→female Chihuahua

To sum up, the schematic account of any entity (lexical items, expressions of any size) can be realized by any number of instantiations with different degrees of specification serving to elaborate its schematicity. Specifications and schemas are not only quintessential in every aspect of language structure, but also fundamental to our cognition for they seem to be constantly involved in every realm of our experience. By adopting these two approaches, we can make our expression more specific or more concise, or be of any length under appropriate circumstances. In dealing with English voice category, both specific descriptions and schematic accounts are needed when it comes to something intricate or unsophisticated.

4.3   Scope

The third dimension of construal is concerning scope which refers to "array of content a predication specifically evokes for its characterization" (Langacker 1991a: 4). Part-whole relationship is omnipresent in our conceptual system. Human beings tend to address particular part of an entity through linguistic expressions. This special habit can be attributed to the focusing view or the attentional view[①] in cognition. Focusing always involves selecting a proper expression in contrast to array of content available in the domains accessed. Usually,

---

[①]   According to Ungerer and Schmid (1996, 2006), essentially, cognitive linguistics consists of three main overlapping and interlocking approaches to language via its relation to the world around us, that is, the experiential view (attributes including associations and impressions which are part of our experience), the prominence view (How the information in a clause is selected and arranged) and the attentional view (What we actually express reflects which parts of an event attract our attention).

one part of these domains will serve as the focus for linguistic presentation while the extent of its coverage will function as the scope.

The notion of scope is entrenched in our cognition. We are mortal as human beings, the time we possess is only within the scope of being alive. Though we are eager to see things in a far-away place, the visual apparatus naturally restricts our scope to see only one thing at a time. As maintained by Langacker (2000, 2008), an expression's scope is always conceived as being bounded, which refers to having only limited expanse even though there are cases in which the line of demarcation is blurry or hard to draw. Taking the entity of *Tomorrow* as an example: the temporal scope of it is supposed to include the time of speaking and the next day instead of eternity.

However, the notion of bounding applies not only to the objectively discernible boundary but also to a hinted, indiscernible boundary exerted by the subjective viewing frame that is constant in size and may subtend a region of almost any objective size in the domain being viewed. For example, we can use the word car not only to denote a real vehicle entity of normal size, but also to epitomize a small model toy car or to designate gigantic transformers in fiction. It seems that the same expression *car* is workable in several conditions at any scale. The reason behind it is that there always exists a subjective constancy which has nothing to do with the variation in scope. Because of this, human beings are inclined to neglect gross discrepancies in size when characterizing an entity, which is remarkably consequential in expression selection.

In addition, two types of scope—maximal scope and immediate scope—are introduced by Langacker (2008) in contrast to background and foreground. The former refers to the full extent of its coverage of an expression while the latter refers to the portion directly relevant for a particular purpose. It claims that the immediate scope is often foregrounded with regard to the maximal scope. In order to facilitate our understanding, let us illustrate them below.

As can be seen in Figure 10, picture (a) designates the notion of *elbow*. For the word *elbow*, the full extent of its coverage should be the conception of the *body*. However, the *body* consists of several major parts, two of which are the arms that are most directly relevant to the *elbow*. Therefore, in the conception of elbow, the *arms* always precede the body, for the elbow is the first and foremost part of the *arm*. Hence the conceptual hierarchy occurs in the sequences like: body > arm > elbow, which means *body* figures directly in arm, and *arm* in turn to *elbow*. But *body* can only indirectly figure *elbow* via *arm*. Accordingly, the *body* is said to serve as maximal scope of the elbow while the *arm* functions as immediate scope. In the same vein, for the word *hand* designated in the picture (b), the sequence of conception should be like this: body > arm > hand. The conception of an *arm* is regarded as the immediate scope for *hand* while the *body* is the maximal scope for hand.

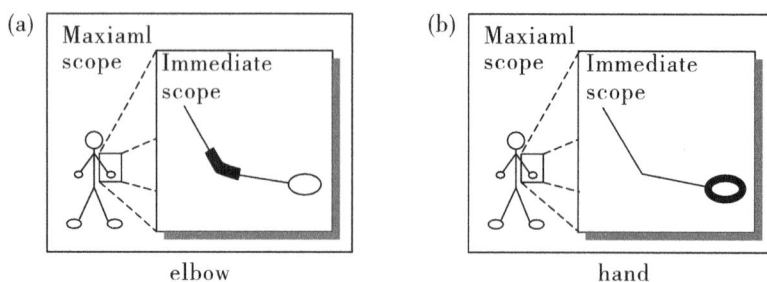

Figure 10 The Contrast Between Immediate Scope and Maximal Scope
Exemplified by Elbow and Hand (Langacker 2008: 64)

4.4 Foreground and Background

The fourth dimension of construal pertains to background and foreground, concepts that are akin to the notion of maximal scope and immediate scope. In order to characterize an entity, we not only need to select the conceptual contents, but we also need to arrange them in the proper order, which gives rise to the assumption of background and foreground. Following the encyclopedic semantics' view,[①] two factors exert great influence on the arrangement of conceptual content. First, central domains are foregrounded in contrast to peripheral ones for they are more accessible. Second, domains that involve a high level of activation are usually foregrounded.

Many kinds of asymmetries lend support to the interpretation of foreground vs. background. Our capacity for construal of one structure in correspondence to another structure manifests in various ways.

4.4.1 Figure/Ground Organization

The most significant correspondence speaks to the inherent asymmetry of figure/ground organization. In order to have a better understanding of this notion, let us first come to the well-known face/vase illusion shown in Figure 11. It seems that there are always two alternatives in perceiving the picture, and though it is easy to shift from one to the other, it is impossible for us to discern the face and vase at the same time. This is due to the segregation of figure and ground.

Scrutinizing Figure 11 carefully, we notice that the figure and ground differ in shape, contour, and location. In terms of shape, it can be detected that the figure has form or shape, and possesses structure and coherence, while the ground is formless or shapeless, unstructured and uniform. With regard to the contour, it seems that only figure has that feature. As for the location, the figure seems to situate in front of the ground which appears to spread behind

---

① According to Evans, Vyvyan (2011: 75-76) encyclopedic semantics is one of main tenets of cognitive linguistics. It mainly consists of two parts: First, it claims that semantic representations in the linguistic system relate to or interface with representations in the conceptual system. Second, it holds that the conceptual structure, to which semantic structure relates, constitutes a vast network of structured knowledge, a semantic potential which is hence encyclopaedia-like in nature and in scope.

it in a continuous way. Just as put by Langacker (1987a: 120), the figure within a scene is a substructure perceived as standing out from the remainder (the ground).

Figure 11   The Face/Vase Illusion (Rubin 1921)

4.4.2   Trajector/Landmark Alignment

Langacker (2008) claims that relational predications reflecting an asymmetry in the portrayal of the relational participants can be attributed to an inherent discrepancy to figure/ ground organization. Usually there are two participants: the primary focal participant is elevated and functions as the figure called the trajector while the secondary focal participation is called the landmark. Generally, figure and ground organization are not intrinsically invariable for a given scene. In a normal manner, we can describe the same scene with alternate choices of figure. As shown in Figure 12. Taking a look at (7)a and (7)b, we find that the two sentences depict the same scene, but they differ in how they construe (7)a, *desk* serves as a point of reference, a landmark for locating the *lamp*, the trajector. Whereas in (7)b, the *lamp* functions as the landmark while the *desk*, the trajector.

(7) a. The lamp is above the desk.

b. The desk is below the lamp.

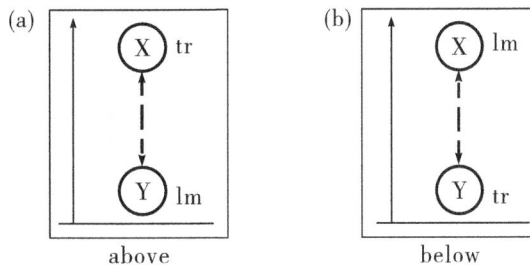

Figure 12   Trajector/Landmark Alignment Exemplified by above and below (Langacker 2008: 71)

In addition, the contrast between foreground and background can also manifest in many other ways. In cases of categorization, the categorizing structure functions as background, which is regarded as a preset basis for assessing the target in the foreground. In the same vein, the source domain of the metaphor, which is more concrete in reality, surfaces as the background for rendering help to understand the target domain, which is more abstract. Moreover, in discourse, the prior discourse often serves as the background to interpret the current discourse that figures in the distinction of given and new information structuring.

4.5 Perspective

The next dimension related to construal is the notion of perspective. Among the many factors included in this term, two are most discussed in cognitive grammar. One is a viewing arrangement which takes the vantage point as the core, and the other involves the dynamicity of processing time, which takes the mental scanning as core.

According to Langacker (2008: 73), a viewing arrangement is the overall relationship between the *viewers* and the situation being *viewed*. A vantage point, which is the actual location of the speaker and hearer in default cases, is often presupposed when conceptualization occurs. Admittedly, some lexical items possess inherent spatial vantage points in their unfolding meaning (e.g. *here*, *inside*, *downstairs*), and some have inherent temporal vantage points hidden in their meaning (e.g. *tomorrow*, *soon*, *Sunday*).

In most cases, for the same objective situation, the description and observation may vary accordingly if different vantage points are adopted. It naturally gives rise to the disparate construal which may pertain to different perspectives. Langacker (2008: 75) argues that a great number of expressions do undoubtedly elicit a vantage point as part of their meaning. Making a comparison between the words *in front of* and *behind* in (8), it seems that both words denote almost the same spacial relationship, but as Figure 13 shows, they actually start from different vantage points.

(8) a. Mary is standing in front of Tom.

  b. Tom is standing behind Mary.

To be specific, in both Figure 13 (a) and (b), VP designates the vantage point, and a dashed arrow indicates the viewer's line of sight. In Figure 13 (a), it is the trajector that first involves in the line of sight leading form the vantage point to the landmark. In Figure 13 (b), it is the other way around. The alternation of trajector and landmark in the two words indicate that they are semantically contrastive.

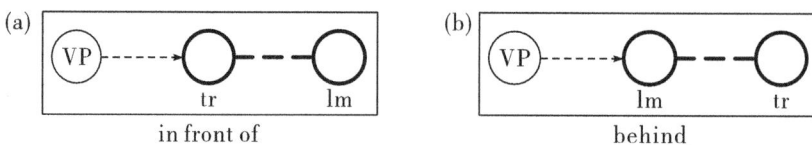

Figure 13　The Contrast of Vantage Point Exemplified by in front of and behind (Langacker 2008: 76)

In terms of perspective, the other two aspects of construal, subjectivity and objectivity, need also be taken into account since they are particularly associated with vantage point. The two notions indicate the relationship between a conceptualizer and the conception he entertains, also called the subject and object of conception. In terms of viewing arrangements, there is always an asymmetry between the viewer (the subject of the perception) and what is viewed (the object of the perception). Objective construal thus correlates with profiling and explicit mention, and subjective construal with an implicit locus of consciousness (Langacker 2008: 77).

As can be observed, the verb rise reflects the contrasting construal perspective in (9a) and (9)b. In (9)a, rise indicates a process in which the trajector balloon moves objectively through its landmark. By contrast, it seems that rise in (9)b is subjectivity-oriented. It appears that it is the conceptualizer who moves subjectively through the scene, therefore exerting a movement on the static situation.

(9) a. The balloon rose slowly.

   b. The hill gently rises from the bank of the river.

(Langacker 1991a: 218)

The next notion which pertains to construal is that dynamicity that resides in mental processes, indicating how a conceptualization unfolds through processing time. There is an entrenched idea among linguists that conceiving or processing time often goes with the order or the sequence of events. The sequencing is significant at the conceptual level but there are always covert elements that are not order-driven. Under these circumstances, Langacker (2000, 2008) introduces the notion of *mental scanning* to further interpret the perspective of construal, which can be exemplified by the difference in meaning between *rise from* and *fall to* in expressions like (10)a and (10)b. As can be seen, both (10)a and (10)b depict the same, static objective situation, but they reveal a discrepancy in the direction of mental scanning. In the process of conceptualization, the conceptualiser has two meaning choices while constructing an image of the hill. *Rises from* evokes an upward mental scan, and *falls to*, a downward scan. Their semantic difference resides in how the conceptualizer scans through the scene. In addition, we can see that the conceptualizer is construed subjectively in that it involves motion while the hill itself is static and construed objectively. In addition, mental scanning can follow a path that is either continuous or discrete. In (10)a and (10)b, the conceptualizer adopts a continuous path to forming the meaning while in (11)a and (11)b, discrete steps can be inferred from the process of conceptualization. It involves a specific method of scanning involving a reference relationship which is best reserved for discrete mental pathways, where each element can be addressed individually.

(10) a. The hill gently rises from the bank of the river.

　　b. The hill gently falls to the bank of the river.

(11) a. Gestation period varies greatly from one species to the next.

　　b. I'll never get into a size 8, and a size 9 is probably still too small.

All in all, the notion of construal seems to be complicated since Langacker introduces so many concepts, some of which seem very similar. Securitizing carefully, we can classify them into three categories: (ⅰ) specificity, (ⅱ) focusing and prominence (it mainly consists of foreground vs. background, scope, and profile vs. base), and (ⅲ) perspective (it includes view arrangement, subjectivity vs. objectivity, and mental scanning).

It is said that a scientific semantics is assumed to be objectivist in nature, and susceptible to discrete formalization. Therefore, it seems that conceptual account of meaning naturally renders interpretation impossible or necessarily unscientific. In fact, this is a stereotypical view that has become entrenched in semantic theory. One goal underlying the notion of construal is to provide evidence to get rid of this stereotypic view. Langacker utilizes the notions of base, profile, scope, vantage point, trajector, mental scanning, etc. to show that the cognitive semantic description can derive support from its efficacy as the basis for characterizing a grammatical structure, and that is also the position and principle we firmly uphold in this dissertation.

5　Force Dynamic Theory

It has been generally claimed that cognitive linguistics resides in a cluster of approaches rather than a single unified framework. No matter what approach is adopted, the underlying guiding assumptions of a cognitive approach to grammar is consistent. There are two central principles: one is the symbolic thesis, which avers that the fundamental unit of grammar is a form-meaning pairing or symbolic unit. The other is the usage-based thesis, which contends that the mental grammar of the speaker is formed by the abstraction of symbolic units from situated instances of language use (Evans and Green 2006: 476-478). Therefore, one distinctive feature of cognitive linguistics is that there is no principled distinction between knowledge of language and use of language, in contrast to generativists' belief that grammar is concerned with competence rather than performance.

One of the approaches representing the above notion is initiated and developed by Leonard Talmy, who maintains that grammatical units are inherently meaningful. Cognitive semantics is the study of the way conceptual content is organized in language (Talmy 2000a: 4). His model of the conceptual structuring system is influential in demonstrating the above notion. Force Dynamic theory is one subbranch of this system, which was first introduced by Talmy in1981 and then was further developed in Talmy (1985, 1988, 2000a, 2000b).

According to Talmy (1988), force dynamics is a semantic category that deals with how entities interact with respect to force. The recent few decades have witnessed increasing attention directed at force dynamics in cognitive linguistics. The semantic category of force dynamics permeates all levels of language. It not only has a direct grammatical representation as closed-class element, but also integrates in open-class lexical items or even in discourse. The main tenets include the exertion of force, resistance to such a force, the overcoming of such a resistance, blockage of the expression of force, removal of such blockage, and the like (Talmy 2000a: 409).

A natural question to ask here is what the origin of this theory is, since it is seldom seen before Talmy. In Talmy's view, force dynamics is a recapitulation the notion of the *causative* in traditional linguistics. What makes the force dynamics unique can be generalized in two ways. One point is that it takes advantage of physical force and transfers it metaphorically to understand the psychological relationship and social interaction in a semantic category at a conceptual level. Therefore, it works well not only for the expression of relationships between physical entities, such as *dragging* or *leaning*, but also for the psychological forces, such as, to *persuade* and to *urge*, or some other abstract concepts, such as *permission* and *obligation*. Another point is that it delineates the concept of *causing* in a finer style and enlarges its scope, ranging from the normal cases to some abnormal cases such as *letting, hindering*, and *helping*.

Talmy (2000a) claims that linguistic expressions can manifest force dynamic pattern or can be force dynamically neutral. As can see from the examples below, (12)a are force dynamically neutral in that there is no force exerting on each other. By contrast, (12)b typifies a force dynamic pattern. Obviously, *the window* is liable to open but there is some other force preventing it from being opened.

(12) a. The window is closed.

b. The window cannot open.

c. The window kept open despite the gale.

The basic characteristic of a force expression is to assume the presence of two entities that exert force. The forces possessed by two entities differentiate themselves by their roles in language. The entity that receives focal attention is called the *agonist* and the entity opposing it is called *antagonist*. Therefore, in (12)a, *the window* is the agonist and the force stopping the window from being opened is the antagonist.

In order to vividly show how force dynamics works in linguistics expression, Talmy uses a lot of diagrams in his works. Let's get familiar with these symbols, for we will use them in our explanation later. As we can see from Figure 14, the Agonist (Ago) is designated by a circle and the Antagonist (Ant) by a concave figure, as shown in Figure 14 (a). The entities usually possess an intrinsic tendency reflected in two ways: one is toward action, as shown in (12)b, the window has a tendency toward action. And the other is toward rest, as can be seen in (12) c, the window tends to toward rest though there are forces that want to change that situation. For the agonist, this tendency can be marked with an arrowhead or with a large dot to represent toward action or toward rest respectively, as in Figure 14 (b), and placed within the agonist's circle. Now that the antagonist has an opposing tendency, there is no need to have a marker.

Another factor is concerning the balance of the two forces. By default, we can assume that the forces are out of balance. One force thereby can be stronger or weaker than the other. An entity with a stronger force is indicated by a plus sign, a weaker force with a minus sign, as in Figure 14 (c). In addition, the opposing force entities have a tendency to yield a resultant due to the imbalance of strengths. There is also a two-way distinction, either toward action that will be indicated by line beneath the agonist bearing an arrowhead or toward rest represented by line bearing the big dot, as in Figure 14 (d).

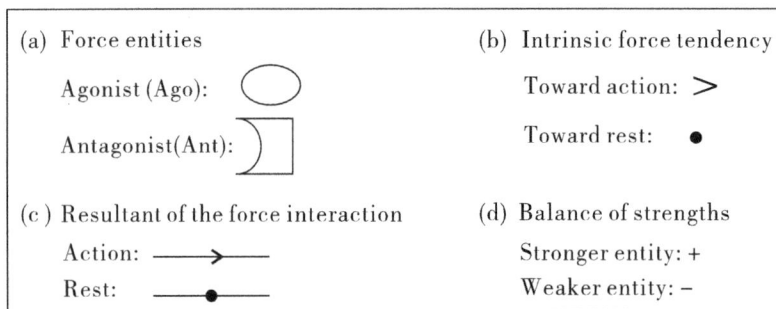

Figure 14   The Symbols Used in Force Dynamic Theory (Talmy 2000a: 414)

Based on above sign distinction, Talmy (2000a) illustrates the four most basic force-dynamic patterns (those entities involve steady-state opposition) by using the diagram as follows. The four corresponding examples are as follows:

(13) a. The ball kept rolling because of the wind blowing on it.

b. The shed kept standing despite the gale wind blowing against it.

c. The ball kept rolling despite the stiff grass.

d. The log kept lying on the incline because of the ridge there.

(Adapted from Talmy 2000a: 415)

As can be seen from Figure 15 and the corresponding examples, (13)a shows that *the ball* (the agonist) has an intrinsic tendency to rest, but it is overcome by *the wind* (the antagonist), which has a stronger force, forcing the ball have to move. Whereas, (13)b indicates that *the shed* (the agonist) has an intrinsic tendency to rest, and its resistance is stronger than the force exerted by *the wind* (the antagonist) that tries to move it, so *the shed* remains as it is. (13)c shows that *the ball* (the agonist) is inherently liable to move, although it is blocked by *the stiff grass* (the antagonist), *the ball* possesses more force than *the stiff grass*, and so it moves. (13)d designates that *the log* tends to move, but the motion is blocked by *the ridge* (the antagonist) which possess more force than *the log*, therefore, the log remains in place.

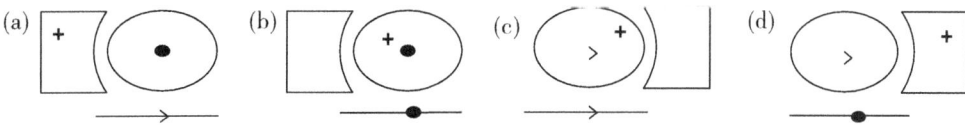

Figure 15　The Basic Steady-state Force-dynamic Patterns (Talmy 2000a: 415)

As Figure 15 illustrates, in terms the agonist's tendency, both Figure 15 (a) and (b) are toward rest while (c) and (d) are toward action. With regard to agonist's resultant, both Figure 15 (a) and (c) are toward action while (b) and (d) are toward rest. Comparing agonist's force with antagonist's force, the agonist's force is lesser in Figure 15 (a) and (d) and greater in both Figure 15 (b) and (c).

In addition to this basic steady-state force-dynamic pattern, Tamly also illustrates the force dynamic theory by gaining evidence from complex patterns, alternatives of foregrounding, and metaphorical extensions. We will not go into the details here. What we want to prove here is that psychological plausibility is the key element to make the theory striking. It vividly interprets the causation in language by mapping our physical experience with the psychological experience and social interaction. Therefore, force dynamic theory has been supported and developed by many other linguists of cognitive persuasion. Croft (1991, 1998) claims that the force dynamic structure of events plays a decisive role in the encoding of subject, object and oblique arguments of predicates. Jackendoff (1990, 1996) incorporates force dynamic theory into his system of conceptual structure. Talmy's account for modals by using force dynamic theory has inspired many linguists and brought about various studies. Further investigation into model meanings is launched by other linguists (Johnson 1987; Sweetser 1990; Langacker 1991). These studies vary in perspectives but they hold that force dynamic theory reflects a conceptual exemplification in mapping our physical force interaction with language structures.

Within the framework of cognitive linguistics, force dynamic theory has always had something to do with event interpretation. Let us consider the examples below. As can be seen, the choice of *for* in (14)a and *with* in (14)b can be attributed to different event structures combined with physical interaction. In (14)a *Lili* is the endpoint, serving as the beneficiary of the baking event, whereas the *drumstick* acts upon the drum and is an intermediate entity that participates in the force-dynamic chain.

(14) a. Tom baked biscuits for Lili.

      b. John beat the drum with the drumstick.

In addition, according to Croft and Cruse (2004: 66), the choice of verbs, voices, and arguments play a significant part in conceptualizing the force-dynamic structure of the event. Consider the following example, *open* serves as a transitive verb in (15)a and intransitive verb in (15)b. The choices of verbs indicate that (15)a describes an event caused by an external force while (15)b describes an event with a self-contained force.

(15) a. John opened the door.

      b. The door opened.

In addition to causation, force and resistance can also offer an explanation for deontic modals in (16)a and (16)b. *May* in (16)a can be construed as an absence of resistance while *must* in (16)b evokes the exertion of the force by some other factors.

(16) a. You may stay.

      b. You must stay.

In brief, force-dynamics has something to do with our experience of motion energy. Entities can serve as energy possessors or energy receivers. Based on this, Langacker (2002) proposes the prototypical action chain model in dealing with agent-patient relation. According to Langacker, the prototypical action is characterised in terms of the transfer of energy from agent to patient, resulting in a change of state of the patient (Evans and Green 2006: 545). In line with Langacker, both subject-object relation as well as active-passive relation can be explained by the prototypical action chain model. The prototypical subject can be interpreted as the volitional energy source, and the prototypical object serves as the passive energy sink. The alternation between active construction and passive construction involves a shift of attention from agent to patient within the action chain model.

6 Research Methodology and Procedure

Having determined our approach to the grammatical voice and reviewed the related theories we will adopt in this study, let us give a brief description about how the research will proceed with these theories at hand.

It goes without saying that the analysis of linguistic phenomena ineluctably involves linguistic data. Data collection, thereby, is a routine procedure for addressing the English voice category. Primarily, three options are available: (ⅰ) an intuition-based approach, (ⅱ) a dictionary-based approach, and (ⅲ) a corpus-based approach.

The first approach, also called introspective data collection, is to elicit data from one's own language intuition as a native speaker or create some examples to illustrate one's standpoint. Many linguists, especially generativists, often choose themselves as informants in collecting data. Nonetheless, this approach has been susceptible to heavy criticism from commentators inside and outside the circle of linguistics. Indisputably, personal introspection for the most part cannot be the only source of data for linguistic analysis. Still, the value of introspective data should not be discounted. Evidence supporting this method comes from Newmeyer (1983: 48), who claims that the use of introspective data hardly originated and is confined to generalists but, rather, is a widely-employed approach relied upon by many others. Abandoning such data is tantamount to dismissing work ranging from the ancient Sanskrit and Greek grammarians to every modern school of linguistics. Accordingly, in this dissertation, some introspective data will be used to facilitate our account. As we are not a native speaker of English language, some examples from related grammar or academic books, and articles written or compiled by native English speakers, will be adapted for proper use.

The general practice of the second approach is to take the examples below each lexical item recorded in the dictionary as the data. These data are also to some extent reliable. We may use some of them as our supporting data from current popular paper dictionary or online dictionaries. For one, they are usually authentic language data that commonly occur in English. For another, lexicographical evidence for changes in word formation and word meaning may be conducive to the process of conceptualization of each lexeme.

The third option, a corpus-based approach, is said to have undergone a remarkable revival in recent years. It is said that the significance of corpora in linguistic analysis is closely associated with more general-accepted empirical data which are appropriate for both qualitative and quantitative analysis. The number one reason behind the popularity of corpus-based approach is that empirical data enable the researchers to make objective statements based largely (though not absolutely) on language as it really is rather than relying on a subjective account derived primarily from personal introspective data. On that account, we intend to use examples from BNC[1] and COCA[2] to illustrate our points in this research.

---

[1]   British National Corpus (https://www.english-corpora.org/bnc/).

[2]   Corpus of Contemporary American English (https://www.english-corpora.org/coca/).

Except the data collection, this study also resorts to two other research methods. One is the convergent validation method, referring to taking two measurements of the same construct and showing how they are related. It is often employed to analyze different kinds of linguistic information if two similar constructs correspond with one another. The other is an introspective method, using this method, we can retrospect our own language learning and teaching experiences and refer to those of others so as to greatly facilitate the construction of the model.

As Figure 16 shows, in order to construct the network of a cognitive model of English voice category, we adopt the following procedures.

Initially, the idea of the study is sorted out from observing and investigating issues occurred in the process of grammar learning and teaching.

Secondly, the hypothesis is made based on the actuality of grammar learning and teaching. It aims at firding possible ways to establish a cognitive model or a cognitive network to connect all the possible knowledge points of English voice together.

Thirdly, in order to test the validity of the hypothesis, we collect data from native speaker's grammar or academic books, journals articles, dictionaries and English corpora such as BNC, COCA.

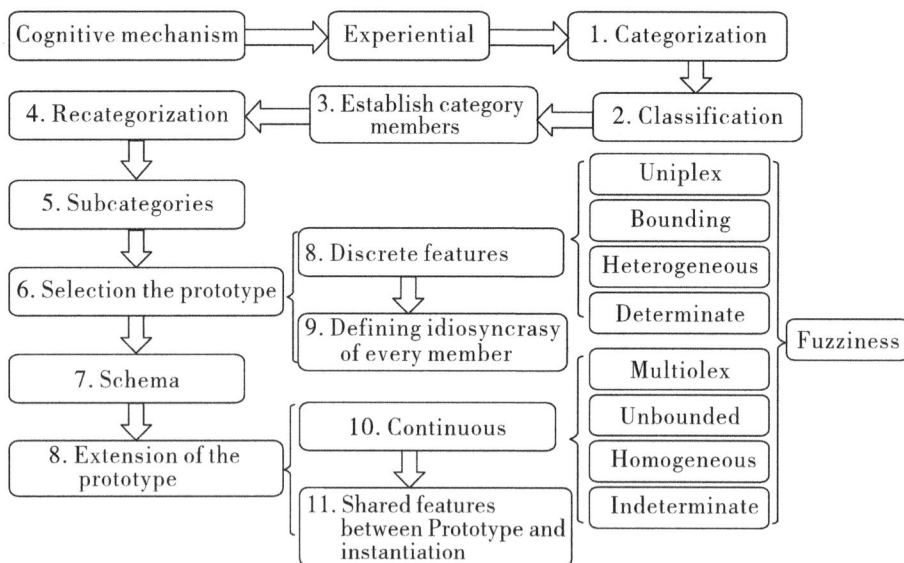

Figure 16　Research Procedure of This Study

Fourthly, we review the definition and classification of English grammatical voice and point out their problems, then classify the English voice according to prototypical prominence and establishing the main category members.

Fifthly, each member is described according to their schematic representation and the major category is reclassified into several subcategories according to the prototype and its instantiations.

Moreover, taking discrete schematic representation into consideration, the four features—uniplex, bounding, heterogeneous, determinate—are first addressed in detail and then the defining idiosyncrasy of each member is discussed.

Next, taking gradient continuity schematic representation into account, the four features—multiplex, unbounded, homogenous, and indeterminate—are elaborated respectively using examples. Then the features shared by prototype and instantiations will be examined.

Finally, the gradient schematic representation and discreteness schematic representation of every member in English voice category are combined together, and a cognitive network of English voice category is to be established based on these schematic representations.

7   Summary

In this chapter, we have provided an overview of the major theories underlying this study. We began by looking at the issue of discreteness and continuity in part one, arguing in particular that discrete and continuous features can be applied to interpret the inherent idiosyncrasy of each individual category and voice continuum formed in several voice subcategories.

In the next section, we introduce the notion of category and categorization and show how the understanding of these two notions has changed from the classical view to prototypical view, and then again in the ICM view. We maintain that prototype theory and ICM theory are based on empirical experiments and are more persuasive than the classical view. It has been claimed that prototype theory is employed as a pivotal principle to classify English voice category in this study and ICM approach to category will be integrated as a supplement in some special cases.

In section three, we extend our discussion to schema theory by elaborating the relationship between schema, prototype and instantiations. It is argued that schema is an abstract knowledge framework formed based on our experience and therefore it plays a significant part in language decoding. In order to help EFL learners and instructors facilitate the understanding of English voice category, the schematic representation of each voice subcategory is conducive to building the cognitive models of English voice system.

In section four, special effort is devoted to how grammatical phenomena are interpreted from the perspective of cognitive grammar, especially of the theory of construal. We contend that grammatical notion is not necessary objective or rigid in nature. The subjective notion held by cognitive linguists can also offer a more flexible explanation to grammar by adopting the notion of profile and base, specificity, scope, foreground and background, trajectory/landmark alignment, vantage point, and mental scanning. The study of English voice category will provide further evidence for this assumption.

In last section, we look briefly at the force dynamic theory and illustrate how it can be successfully applied to various grammatical issues in language. We propose that force dynamic theory can offer an accurate interpretation of causation in language. In addition, the notion that force dynamic theory has something to do with event model and energy motion in daily life undeniably provides a good explication for understanding the relation between agent and patient, the relation between subject and object and naturally the relation between the active and passive voices. Finally, we explain our research methodology and procedure.

Categorization of Grammatical Voice: Attributes and Taxonomy

It is generally said that grammatical analysis often starts from categorization without which there is no way to catch sight of recurrent patterns or regularities in language. In this chapter, we first look at the attributes of grammatical voice category in language by analyzing various definitions of voice given by different linguists, pointing out their problems and establishing our own definition. Next, our attention is devoted to the classification of voice across language, figuring out how many types of voice do we have in English. Finally, we establish the subcategories of English grammatical voice category in this study.

1 Attributes of the Grammatical Voice Category in Languages

It is clear that grammatical voice is one of the abiding topics in linguistic circles. It is no exaggeration to say that every grammar book devotes significant portion to them. Despite this, the definitions of voice used by different grammar books or different linguists vary greatly in that they observe and discuss voice from different perspectives. To learn the general attributes of grammatical voice category, let us look at some typical definitions.

(1) Transitive verbs have two voices or forms, the active and passive. In the active voice, the nominative does or directs the action; but in the passive, it suffers or receives it (Davidson and Alcock 1876: 47).

(2) By voice we mean different grammatical ways of expressing the relation between a transitive verb and its subject and object. The two chief voices are the active and passive (Sweet 1900: 112).

(3) Voice will be regarded as a grammatical system in the verbal group with two terms: active and passive. The active term and the passive term are in formal binary opposition and will be studied both at the rank of the finite verbal group and at the rank of the finite verbal clause, with regard to their internal relations as well as to their external relations (Svartvik 1966: 5).

(4) Voice is a strategy to move NPs in and out of the subject position (Barber 1975: 16).

(5) Voice is a grammatical category which makes it possible to view the action of a sentence in either of two ways, without changing in the facts reported. The active-passive relation involves two grammatical levels: the verb phrase, and the clause (Quirk et al.1985: 159).

(6) Voice is to be understood as a mechanism that selects a grammatically prominent syntactic constituent–subject–from the underlying semantic functions (case or thematic roles) of a clause (Shibatani 1988: 3).

(7) Voice, the grammatical category expresses the relationship between, on the one hand, the participant roles of the NP arguments of a verb, and on the other hand, the grammatical relations borne by those same NPs. In European languages, the most familiar voice contrast is that between active and passive constructions. Other categories of voice exist in some languages, such as middle, reflexive, causative and adjutative, to name a few (Trask 1993: 299).

(8) Voice refers to a grammatical category that expresses a way in which a predicate may alter the relationship between its arguments (Crystal 1991: 375; Spencer 1991: 236). Familiar voice categories include the active and the passive voice; others include the antipassive, applicative, causative, inverse, and middle voice, among others (Klaiman 1991; Palmer 1994; Spencer 1991: 237-254) (Melnar 1998: 161).

(9) Grammatical voice was originally understood as a system of alternating clause structures that cast different participants as subject: active voice clauses cast semantic agents as subjects, while passive voice clauses cast semantic patients as subjects. But it is now well known that not all languages distinguish a subject category comparable to that of Greek or English. Their numbers raise the issue of whether the notion of voice should be explicitly formulated to exclude them or generalized to include them (Mithun 2006: 195).

(10) Grammatical voice is a linguistic means of altering the perspective from which events may be viewed, providing speakers with a series of options for better approximating in language the infinitely graded spectrum of human conceptualization and experience (Woods 2008: 303).

(11) Voice, also known as diathesis, is a grammatical feature that describes the relationship between the verb and the subject (also known as the agent) in a sentence. More specifically, voice describes how the verb is expressed or written in relation to the agent. There are two main types of voice: active voice and passive voice. A third type of voice called "middle" voice also exists but is less commonly used (Herring 2016: 767).

Reading through the above definitions, we notice that, though the definitions of voice fluctuate every now and then, some generalization can be made. First, voice, together with mood, aspect, modality, and tense, incorporate the five major grammatical categories or functional categories of the verb. It is often defined morphosyntactically by marking the verb at phrasal level or at clausal level, as in (1), (2), (3), (5), (7), and (11).

Second, grammatical voice is very pertinent to the concept of valency; that is, the number of arguments for which a particular verb subcategorizes semantically, syntactically and morphologically, as in (4), (7), (8). The predicate can be semantically avalent (e.g. *snow*), momovalen (e.g. *cry*), bivalent (e.g. *kill*) and trivalent (e.g. *put*).

Third, voice is particularly concerned with the concept of transitivity; that is, it is often designated or closely related to different aspects of clauses, such as agency, affectedness and control. It is often used to characterize the relationship of the participants in a clause, as in (1), and (2).

Fourth, grammatical voice addresses and highlights the notion of diathesis, referring to any specific mapping of semantics roles such as agent, patient, theme, experiencer, or recipient. onto grammatical roles such as subject, object, other complements, or adjunct (Zúñiga and Kittilä 2019: 3), as in (2), (4), (6), (9), and (11). Next, the two-voice system seems to be most widely-adopted, as in (1), (2), (3), (5), but the existence of three-voice systems or multi-voice systems are not denied by many linguists, as in (7), (8), (9), and (11). Furthermore, voice is highly associated with perspective when viewing an event and it has its root in human experience and conceptualization, as in (10).

After making a generalization about various definitions in the current scholarship, let us try to schematize the basic attributes of grammatical voice systems across language by assuming that voice is a category which is equal to category in natural world when we conceptualize and understand the world. As Figure 17 shows, the schematic representation of voice is instantiated in at least six dimensions: grammatical category of the verb, valency, transitivity, diathesis, voice taxonomy, and perspective of viewing event. The solid arrows stand for the expatiation and propulsion of the voice schema, and the dashed arrows represent the extension from a more central feature to non-central features. And these features are not isolated but interact with each other in a dynamic way. In addition, a blank instantiation extension is inserted after the aforesaid six dimensions in that we assume maybe there are some unnoticed properties of voice. Since we only take some of the sample definitions of voice in literature, more elaborations will be added as our analysis goes further in the following sections.

Having considered how voice is defined by various linguists, let us now turn to look at how to fabricate a comprehensive definition of voice in this dissertation. With that schematic representation of voice in mind, the first problem to be solved here is to point out the issues with the above definitions. Only by doing so, can we flesh out the usage scenario of voice in this study.

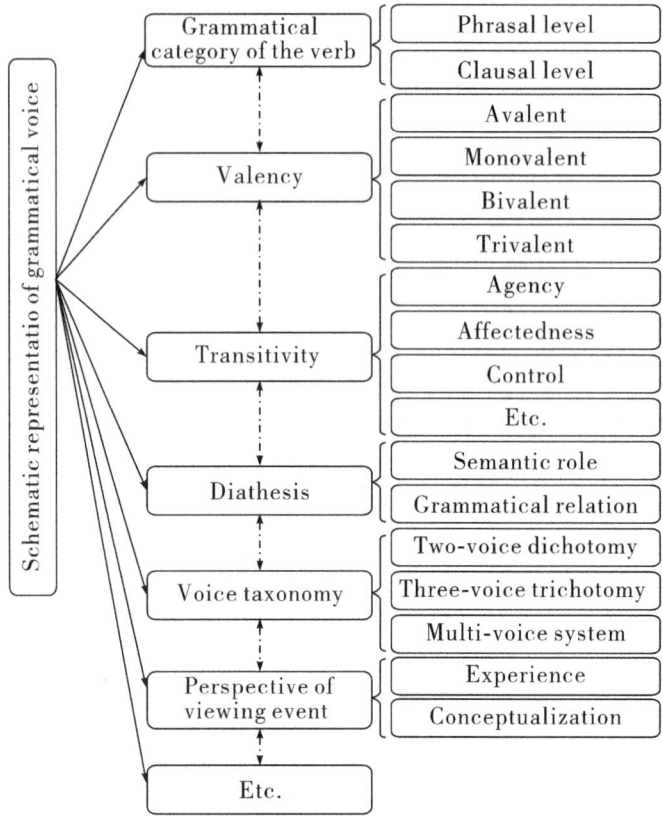

Figure 17   Schematic Representation of Grammatical Voice in Languages

With regard to the above definitions, whist essentially reasonable and accurate, they need to be polished and refined in one way or another. There are problems on several counts.

First and foremost, each definition is too limited because it only covers one or two properties of voice. Since different grammarians may embrace disparate approaches to grammatical analysis and view voice from divergent perspectives, their solutions may be reliable within their respective framework but it is hard to conceive a comprehensive definition as our schema shows. In line with the above analysis, this study will define voice from a cognitive dimension and try to take the aforementioned properties of voice into account. Therefore, our definition for voice is mainly based on Langacker, Lakoff, Talmy and Croft's generation. But before arriving at our definition, we have to look into how to deal with another problem that arises in various definitions above: that is, the taxonomy of the voice category.

As we can observe, researchers and linguists have never achieved a unanimous agreement on voice taxonomy in English. That is the second problem we can generate from the above discussion. A review of literature in Chapter II reveals that most grammarians (such as Davidson, Sweet, Svartvik, Quirk et al.) hold with a two-voice dichotomy in English: i.e. active voice and the passive voice constitutes English voice; some grammarians (such as

Herring), accept three-voice trichotomy in English, that is active voice, passive voice, and middle voice. There are still some other grammarians who approve of multi-voice system in English, (such as, Givón, Palmer, Klaiman, Spencer). Since we are dealing with the discrete features of English voice, we prefer to adopt the finer and more detailed multi-voice system in this dissertation. The toughest nut to crack is to determine how many types voice there are across language, and how many voices can be found in English? What is the best way to find out?

Let us first consider the concept of a two-voice dichotomy notion held by great the majority of grammarians. Incontrovertibly, we can make a tacit assumption that English has two major voices—active voice and passive voice, but this is complicated by the fact that we can also say that English transitive verbs have two voices or forms, the active and passive, only two corresponding voices in English. This view is held by Davidson and Alcock (1876), Svartvik (1966), and Quirk et al. (1985), early grammarians tend to present a very one-sided picture of the issue.

Quirk et al. (1985) among the first group of scholar who admit the problems inherent in the two-voice dichotomy, and their interpretation of English voice gives us a lot of revelations. They still claim that there is active-passive correspondence at the clausal level and even generate a formula for this correspondence. However, their definition is not always feasible because, as they admit, there isn't always a systematic correspondence between the active and passive sentences. To account this, they cite a lot of constraints blocking the passive-active conversion.

A set of "exceptions to the rule" which make the classification of English voice much more complicated. They designate these constraints in five ways:

Above all, the constraints on verbs are the first thing to be considered because voice is always marked by morphological changes in verbs. Verbs actually do not have as much freedom to occur in the passive as the active. In terms of transitivity, it seems that transitive verbs can show up in the passive freely in contrast to copular and intransitive verbs, but that is not the case.

Some stative verbs possessing the meaning of *being or having* have no passive counterparts, as illustrated in examples (1) and (2).

(1) a. Lee has a new cellphone.

   b.* A cellphone is had by Lee.

(2) a. John lacks courage.

   b.* Courage is lacked by John.

On the contrary, some verbs can occur in the passive, there are no active counterparts, as shown in (3) and (4).

(3) a. Mary was said to be a genius.

b. *They said Mary to be a genius.

(4) a. Tom was born in London.

b. Tom's mother bore him in London.

Preposition verbs can often occur in the passive, but their appearance is confined to an abstract passive subject rather than a concrete one, as shown in examples (5) and (6).

(5) a. The engineer arrived at the conclusion.

b. The conclusion was arrived at by the engineer.

(6) a. The couple arrived at the meeting room.

b.*The meeting room was arrived at by the couple.

As for the object constrains, the passivisation is unlikely or restricted in the following cases:

Transitive verbs with reflexive objects do not occur in the passive. The reason why (7b) and (8)b are unacceptable is that the reflexive must follow its antecedent.

(7) a. Bobby enjoyed himself.

b.* Himself was enjoyed by Bobby.

(8) a. We pride ourselves on our achievements.

b. *Ourselves are prided on our achievements.

In the same vein, transitive verbs with reciprocal objects have no way to be passivized, as in (9) and (10), both *one another* and *each other* serve as accusatives and reciprocal, therefore they do not passivize.

(9) a. Aaron and Adam slapped each other.

b. *Each other was slapped by Aaron and Adam.

(10) a. They treat one another kindly.

    b. *One another was treated kindly by them.

In addition, clausal objects are to some degree restricted in contrast to phrasal object, as in (11), where a finite clause functioning as object cannot be necessarily passivized whist in (12), the participle *watching* serves as the object of the verb *enjoy*.

(11) a. We consider that foreigners are guilty of looting historical relics.

    b.That foreigners are guilty of looting historical relics are considered.

(12) a. I enjoy watching the world going by.

    b.* Watching the world going by was enjoyed by me.

The Agent plays different parts in the active and the passive. The agent that serves as the subject in the active is compulsory while the agent which functions as an oblique in a by-phrase is non-mandatory, in most cases due to it is being irrelevant, its being unknown or to avoid redundancy. As illustrated in (13)a, the agents of the *mugging*, supposing to be *some louts*, have been omitted. In (13)b, the agent who allocates *the land* is of no need to be mentioned. Just as put by Svartvik (1985: 141), of the agentive[①] passives in his collected material, 80 percent are agentless.

(13) a. Carlo was mugged on his way home.

    b. Most of the land had been allocated to the refugees.

Next, some active sentences can be converted into a passive form, but there is no corresponding propositional meaning between the two sentences. This can be attributed to meaning constrains, as illustrated in (14) and (15) as follows. (14)a implies that each student read at least one book or other while (14)b indicates that there is one particular book that is read by every student. In English, model auxiliaries may cause the change in meaning in the process of voice conversion. As we can see in (15), the can in active voice always indicates ability, as in (15)b, which means *his parents* are unable to instruct *Adam*. Whereas it designates possibility in the passive form as in (15)a which implies that it is not possible to instruct *Adam*.

---

①   Agentive and agentful are two terms used alternatively in the literature. Both refer to the passive without omitting the agent in the clause. In this dissertation, we prefer the latter.

(14) a. Every student read at least one book.

　　b. At least one book is read by every student.

(15) a. Adam cannot be instructed by his parents.

　　b. His parents cannot instruct Adam.

Furthermore, the two voices also have restriction to the type of discourse or text they can be used in. As suggested by Quirk et al. (1985: 166), the active is used more commonly than the passive, with considerable variation among individual text types. The passive is more restricted, confined to informative writing, occurring much more frequently in scientific articles and news reporting.

A second problem of the two-voice dichotomy is that there are several constructions in English that may not meet the full standard of passive at all based purely on formal definition in English. These marginal cases are not fully identified or often cause confusion in the voice system in that they differ from the active and the passive to some degree but still relate to them, a situation which renders the two-voice dichotomy ineffective to some extent. Let's have a brief look at these cases using concrete examples.

In accordance with the formula identified by Quirk et al. (1985), the be+V-en construction is the most typical pattern of passive at the clausal level, that is the central passive or true passive, as they called it. There are two types of true passives. One is the agentful true passive in which the agent is introduced by the oblique by phrase, as in (16)b which is opposed to its active counterpart (16)a. The other is agentless true passive in which agent is often omitted, as in (17)b which has its active counterpart in (17)a.

(16) a. A man made the discovery yesterday.

　　b. The discovery was made by a man yesterday.

(17) a. You must keep the dog on the leash.

　　b. The dog must be kept on the leash.

The first type of passive that deviates from the central passive is called by semi-passive in Quirk et al. (1985). The constructions within this group often possess both the verbal and adjectival properties. In (18)a, it seems that *be encouraged* is more verbal-like but it has adjective attributes. As in (18)c, *encouraged* can be coordinated with the adjective or be modified by quite as in (18)d. In the same vein, (19)a shares the same attributes with (18)a, except that one preposition *about* is added, which introduces the agent-like phrases equivalent to an agent by-phrase.

(18) a. Farmers are encouraged to grow other crops.

b. The government encouraged the farmers to grow other crops.

c. Farmers feel rather encouraged and happy.

d. Farmers seem quite encouraged to grow other crops.

(19) a. We are worried about international terrorism.

b. International terrorism worries us.

Another type of passive is defined as pseudo-passive, or statal passive, which has neither a corresponding active transformation nor processes the possibility of agent addition (Qurik et al. 1985; Palmer 1987). In (20)a, *situated* does not have any properties of an adjective. It cannot be modified by very, nor can it modify a noun. In addition, be cannot be replaced by *seem*. The same rule applies to (21)a too.

(20) a. Anthem villa was situated on the hill.

b. *Very situated/*A situated villa/*The villa seems situated.

(21) a. Students are not supposed to be here.

b. *Very supposed/*supposed students/*students seem supposed

In addition to the aforementioned formal departure from the formula of the active-passive transformation, there are some additional special cases. For instance, in sentences with verbs followed by a gerund, the construction is active in form but passive in meaning, as illustrated in (22)a and (22)b.

(22) a. The office needs cleaning.

b. The manager deserves praising.

Furthermore, some transitive verbs in English have a tendency toward intransitivity. Middle verbs, such as *wash* (23) and *peel* (24), cannot be passivized.

(23) a. The coat washes well.

b.*The coat is washed well.

(24) a. The banana peels easily.

b. *The banana is peeled easily.

To sum up, the asymmetry between the passive and active voice is commonly seen in English. Some of the intricate and complicated issues within the scope of the active-passive framework are hard to handle actually. The great discrepancy between the active and passive in English and the many constraints and exceptions make the active-passive dichotomy untenable. As a result, it is plausible and, in fact, necessary, to resort to a more nuanced and refined classification of voice. As we discussed above, the reflexive and reciprocal construction are assumed to be two different subclasses of voice by some linguists, and the middle verbs are also given a separate subclassification as well. Based on this analysis, this study will adhere to multi-voice system in English. The next question is to determine how many voices are there in English.

2   Taxonomy of the Grammatical Voice Category in Languages

In this part, we mainly deal with the multi-voice system across languages and try to identify the voice types confined to English. There are some representative typological studies of the grammatical voice, so we will examine their classifications systems first, then establish our own members in English voice category.

According to Shibatani (1988: 3), discussions of voice phenomena in the literature have generally suffered from the absence of a clear general concept of grammatical voice. Some researchers only focus on the English two-voice system, and others go in for a finer classification of voice systems typologically across language. It is generally claimed that voice forms are easy to deal with in formal syntax since formalists only deal with indisputable voice types in English. However, distinguishing between different voice forms is not easy for topologists since, as we have seen, there are a number of variations in voices forms in English and other non-ergative languages in contrast to ergative languages, where there are few or none. Despite these difficulties, some linguists attempt to classify voice from different perspectives.

First, Klaiman's (1991) typological study of grammatical voice is of great significance. He points out that, among the five function categories of the verb, voice is likely to be the most complicated and intricate one in contrast to tense, aspect, modality and mood in that it often manifests in multifarious ways. As he put it, since most previous studies lay emphasis on certain specific voice types, passive in particular, there is a great necessity in conducting a further study on voice systems hinged on probe across languages.

Figure 18 shows the three-way taxonomy of voice types proposed by Klaiman (1991).

First, taking the criterion of passivization, the active-middle systems are regarded as a basic, unmarked voice while derived voice has the property of passivization, which is non-basic and marked. Secondly, the pragmatic voice is distinguished by relying on the inverse system and information salience in a sentence, that is, assignment to some sentential arguments of some special pragmatic status or salience (Klaiman 1991: 24). Indeed, Klaiman's classification of voice category is a good attempt to deal with voice in a refined way. It can provide some references for our classification in this study. However, some explanations are still too general to include the diverse configuration of voice in English and in other languages.

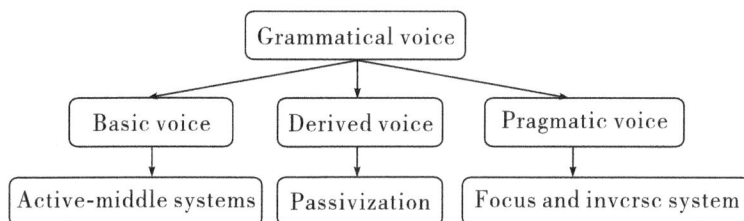

Figure 18   Taxonomy of the Grammatical Voice Category by Klaiman (1991)

Next, let's recapitulate Givón's (1993) classification of voice category. Givón's perspective on voice is really intriguing. He takes transitivity as the main criterion to distinguish between different clauses and regards transitivity as a category within which there is a prototype-like member and also some peripheral members that share more or less the same features with the prototype. The active-transitive clauses are taken as the prototype of the voice category. Those clauses that deviate from simple transitive clause he regards as a de-transitive voice. As stated by Næss (2003), transitivity can be defined as a type of grammatical relationship encoding the distinctness of participants in a situation described by the clause. It is an essential issue but to some extent a sticky one in that it is a rudimentary approach to the structure of major clause types on the one hand, and a complex, clause-level occurrence with a lot of configurations on the other.

Hopper and Thompson (1980) pay high heed to transitivity in grammar and discourse across languages. They point out that transitivity concerns an activity that is transferred from an agent to a patient, as naturally there are two participants involved. A set of parameters of transitivity are identified. As can be seen from Table 3, each parameter offers a scale from high to low based on which clauses can be ranked. A and O represent Agent and Object respectively in the clause. Patient serves as the actual receiver of the action referred to by O.

Transitivity shows continuous features rather than being dichotomous. So many facets of the effectiveness or intensity are designated. It involves a number of factors. (i) In terms of participants, it takes two participants to care out the transfer. (ii) Kinesis designates that transfer from one participant to another renders to action but it doesn't apply to state. (iii) Two types of *Aspect* are involved here: telic action and atelic action. The former views an action from its endpoint, therefore transference is executed more adequately than in the latter where no endpoint is offered. Therefore, the activity is not complete, and transference is only partially fulfilled. (iv) Punctual action always occurs instantaneously; that is, the action happens very quickly and we cannot observe the transitional phase from the beginning to the end. By contrast, unpunctual action may experience some temporal duration varying from a short span to a long span. (v) Volitionality is the criterion to gauge whether the subject or agent of a particular sentence is volitional or non-volitional. Volitional action is done consciously, an intended action without the influence of external factors. Non-volitional is the other way around. Hence, the more intention the agent acts under, the more apparent the effects the patient. (vi) If the sentence structure is affirmative, it may have a higher degree of transitivity in contrast to negation which has a lower degree of transitivity. (vii) Mode involves the encoding of events in a realis or irrealis ways. The former refers to actualized or real events which is apparently more effective than the latter which indicates non-actualized or hypothetical events. (viii) Agency refers to the potency which the participants possess, a capacity which will have an impact on the transference of an action; the higher potency the participants have, the more impact on the action of transfer. (ix) Affectedness of an object refers to its aspectual property; how completely that patient is affected is correlated to the degree to which an action is transferred to patient. There is a continuum from totally affected to non-affected. (x) Individuation of object concerns both the distinctness of the patient from the agent and its distinctness from its own background. Referents of nouns with the properties of being *proper*, *human*, *animate*, *singular*, *count*, *referential*, *definite* are regarded being highly individuated while the referents of nouns with the properties of *common*, *inanimate*, *abstract*, *plural*, *mass*, *non-referential* are regarded as non-individuated.

Table 3   Parameters of Transitivity (Hopper and Thompson 1980)

	High	Low
A.Participants	2 or more participants, A and O	1 participant
B.Kinesis	Action	Non-action
C.Aspect	Telic	Atelic
D.Punctuality	Punctual	Non-punctual
E.Volitionality	Volitional	Non-volitional
F.Affirmation	Affirmative	Negative
G.Mode	Realis	Irrealis
H.Agency	A high in Potency	A low in Potency
I. Affectedness of O	O totally affected	O not affected
J. Individuation of O	O highly individuated	O non-individuated

The parameters of transitivity are conducive to the understanding of the concept of de-transitivization. According to (Givón 1981: 168), de-transitivization occurs as the clause becomes semantically less-active, less-transitive, and more-stative. He gives three criteria to designate the semantics of de-transitivity and points out that constructions that reflect a decrease in (i) the agentivity of the agent, (ii) the affectedness of the patient, or (iii) the compact, bounded, sequential or realis-like nature of the verb can be defined as de-transitivization (Givón 1993: 46).

Therefore, the six types of voice—passive, impersonal, antipassive, reflexive, reciprocal and middle—are all defined as de-transitive voices in contrast to the active-transitive voice. In addition, a great number of examples form English are given to illustrate the semantic and pragmatic features of these voice types. In line with Givón's view, we can expand the two-member voice category to a seven-member voice category.

Therefore, the six types of voice–passive, impersonal, antipassive, reflexive, reciprocal and middle—are all defined as de-transitive voices in contrast to the active-transitive voice, as illustrated in Figure 19. In addition, a great number of examples form English are given to illustrate the semantic and pragmatic features of these voice types. In line with Givón's view, we can expand the two-member voice category to a seven-member voice category.

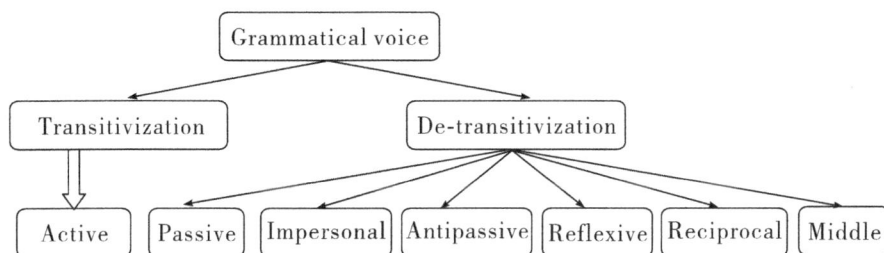

Figure 19   Givón's (1993) Classification of Grammatical Voice across Languages

In contrast to Givón's view, Palmer (1994) discusses the voice category in considering the relationship between grammatical roles and grammatical relations. Firstly, he maintains that sentences pairs like (25)a and (25)b are traditionally regarded as being active and passive respectively. They vary grammatically in the marking of the arguments but with little change in terms of meaning. In accusative systems such as English, the primary term subject serves as the agent, the secondary term object functions as the patient. The conversion from (25)a to (25)b involves the demoting the primary term and promoting the secondary term with passivization.

Sentence pairs like (26)a and (26)b are defined as ergative alternation or ergative pair. In (26)a, *the bell* serves as an affected object of a transitive clause, whereas in (26)b, it functions as the affected subject of an intransitive clause. Sentences in (27)a and (27)b stand in stark contrast to sentences (28)a and (28)b. The former shows that in English the single argument *he* of an intransitive sentence (27)a has the same grammatical marking as the agent *he* of an active transitive sentence (27)b while the latter reflects a different phenomenon.

Among languages such as Dyirbal in Australia as in (28)a and (28)b, the single argument *ŋuma* is identified not with the *agent*, but with the *patient* of the active transitive. In line with this analysis, assuming agent as being the subject and patient as being the object may not seem to be feasible in ergative languages though many researchers retain the term. For Palmer (1994), a remedy for this problem is to use the terms *ergative* for agent and *absolutive* for patient if a single argument is identified with the patient, taking the names of the two relations from the cases which mark them. Accordingly, the primary term in ergative systems is the absolutive (single argument equals patient), the secondary term is the ergative agent. As can be seen in (28)c, *ŋuma (father)* is promoted from the status of secondary term ergative to primary term absolutive, while *yabu (mother)* is demoted from primary term absolutive to the status of an oblique term, marked by the dative. For this type of conversion, it is generally regarded as the antipassive in ergative languages in contrast to its counterpart passive in accusative systems. Although Parmer (1994) didn't mention whether English has an antipassive voice or not, we have confirmed from other works that give evidence to support that there are antipassives in English.

(25) a. The boy chased the dog.

    b. The dog was chased by the boy.

(26) a. We rang the bell.

    b. The bell rang.

(27) a. He smiles.

    b. He likes them.

(28) a. ŋuma banaga-ɲu.

      father + ABS return-PAST

      Father returned

    b. yabu ŋuma-ŋgu bura-n.

      mother + ABS father-ERG see-PAST

      Father saw mother

    c. ŋuma bural-ŋa-jiu yabu-gu.

      father + ABS see-ANTIP-PAST mother-DAT

      "Father saw mother"

(Adapted from Palmer 1994: 12-18)

In addition to active, passive, and antipassive, Palmer also maintains that there exists a middle voice in languages, taking classical Greek and Sanskrit as archetypes. It is claimed that the middle stands out as a contrast with the active morphologically on the one hand, but it lacks the demotion or promotion of grammatical roles of the passive on the other hand. For Palmer, middle is more apparently to be used to refer to actions that are done by subjects themselves.

Unlike Givón's (1993) classification, Palmer (1994) also introduces the applicative as another voice type. It is claimed that some languages have the feature of promotion not to subject but to object. Though it has implications for passivization, it differs from the passive and should be considered an independent voice system. He draws a great number of examples from several languages such as Kinyarwanda, Bantu, Chichewa and Fula, to illustrate the diverse features of the applicative voice. In addition, he claims that though English does not have clear applicative voice, it has similar constructions. For example, one interpretation for the following sentences is that (29)b is derived from (29)a in that the indirect object *John* is promotes to object in (29)b, and that, therefore, in both (30)a and (30)b, it is the object that is promoted to subject by passivization.

(29) a. Mary gave a book to John.

   b. Mary gave John a book.

(30) a. A book was given to John by Mary.

   b. John was given a book by Mary.

Another voice category discussed by Palmer (1994) is the inverse voice, he claims that both the inverse and passive are essential features across languages. Though they vary in degrees, a distinction can be made in extreme cases. In term of demotion, the agent of the inverse voice is not overtly demoted while the agent of the passive is overtly demoted. In addition, the empathy hierarchy is of great importance in the inverse voice whereas it is of no value for the passive voice.

Another difference between Givón's (1993) classification and Palmer's (1994) is that the latter also incorporates causatives as one member of the voice category. It is argued that causatives are common across languages, serving as a grammatical or semi-grammatical device for expressing the general notion of causing someone to perform a certain action (Palmer 1994: 214). Causatives are similar to passives in that both voices can be viewed as derived from a simple active sentence. What make the causative differ from the passive is that the former introduces a new argument that represents the notional cause while the latter promotes an argument. It is also contended that English doesn't seem to have a grammaticalized causative construction. However, using some specific verbs such as *make*, *get*, and *cause* to express the causative makes English causatives of special interest in voice exploration.

In the main, Palmer (1994) takes the correspondence between the grammatical role and grammatical relations as the criteria for classification of English voice. That is what have termed diathesis in previous sections. As illustrated in Figure 20, Palmer's (1994) classification of the English voice category can be summarized as Figure 20. We can see there are mainly eight voice types in the category of grammatical voice. Five of them overlap with Givón's classification, that is, active, passive, antipassive, inverse, and middle. Three are added by Palmer. Combining Givón's classification with Palmer, we now have 11 members in grammatical voice category.

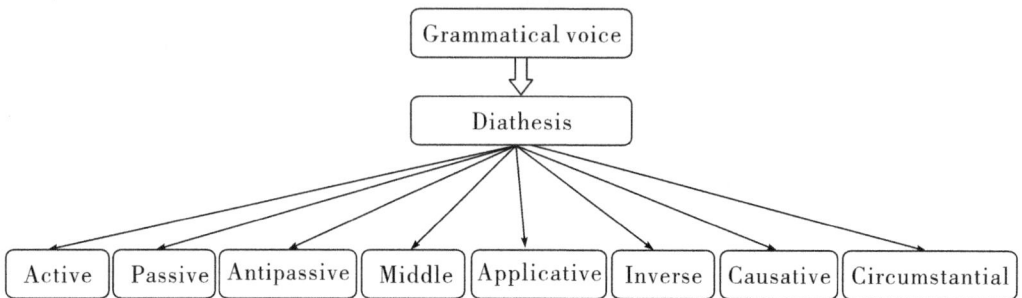

Figure 20　Palmer's Classification of Grammatical Voice Across Languages(1994)

In addition to Klaiman, Givón's and Palmer's classification of voice category, Trask (1993) proposes an even more comprehensive classification of the voice category. Since Trask's (1993) purpose is to list all the related voices in scholarship and converts them into linguistic terms, his classification is introductory rather than typological-oriented. Let's look at how he deals with voice, as illustrated in Figure 21.

Firstly, Trask (1993) claims that the most familiar voice contrast in European languages is that between active and passive constructions. Namely, active and passive serve as the two leading subcategories of grammatical voice category.

Second, he maintains that other types of voice can be found in some languages. On the left side, five voice types are branched: middle, reflexive, causative, reciprocal and impersonal passive. On the right side, five other voice types are also introduced: adjutative, applicative, antipassive, inverse, and circumstantial. These terms seem less familiar to us. In the main, we have altogether 12 voices types cited by Trask. What is new to this classification is that two different voice types are added to Palmer's taxonomy of voice: the adjutative, and impersonal passive. In fact, adjutative is mentioned by Palmer (1994), but he incorporates it into the subcategory of causative voice. The impersonal passive is included in the passive category in Pamler (1994).

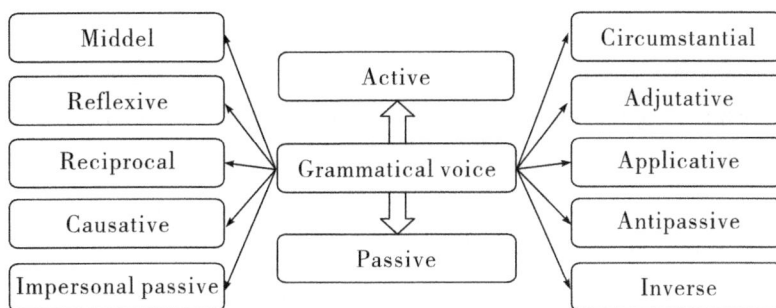

Figure 21   Trask's (1993) Classification of Grammatical Voice Across Languages

Following above analysis, a rough conclusion to be drawn is that there are 12 voice types cited in the aforementioned studies: active, passive, middle, reflexive, causative, adjutative, applicative, antipassive, inverse, circumstantial, reciprocal, impersonal passive. In addition to above voice types, Zúñiga and Kittilä (2019) also introduce the acticaustive as one of the voice types in languages. This study will take anticaustive as one type of voice in English though some researchers think it is not well-established.

The line of argument taken by typologists is that voice is language specific. Typologically, languages of the world can be classified in terms of how the subject and object noun phrases are marked in a sentence. There are two essential typological groupings of the world languages, nominative-accusative languages like English, and ergative-absolutive languages like Bandjalang in Australia. In the former, transitive subjects and intransitive subjects are generally marked or treated in the same way for grammatical purpose in contrast to direct objects of transitive verbs that are differentiated or treated differently. In the latter, however, intransitive subjects and transitive objects are generally treated in the same way for grammatical purpose as opposed to transitive subjects that are marked or treated differently.

The two types of language are differentiated by morphological case and word order. For nominative-accusative languages, both the transitive and intransitive subject are regarded as nominative noun phrases, or in other words, they are marked with nominative case, while the direct object is assumed to serve as an accusative phrase or marked with accusative case. Word order can play a part when case marking is not available, just as in English, where the basic language structure is SVO: that is, the subject usually comes before the verb while the object follows it. On the contrary, for the ergative-absolutive languages, both the object of a transitive verb and the subject of an intransitive verb are assumed to be absolutive noun phrases, or, to put it another way, they are marked with the absolutive case. The transitive subject is said to be the ergative noun phrase or to be marked with the ergative case.

Word order is preferred if there is no case marking available. It is said that the absolutive argument usually comes before the verb and the ergative argument follows it.

Admittedly, Klaiman (1991), Givón (1993), Trask (1993), and Palmer (1994) all agree that certain voice is language specific. Both accusative and ergative languages manifest their ways and means to assign the syntactic functions of arguments to particular thematic roles. It is said that the passive is a common device found in accusative languages while the antipassive is assumed to be the counterpart of passive in ergative languages. It can be seen from the above analysis that the aforementioned researchers primarily employ the functional and typological approach to voice phenomena based on a Multilanguage study. Their studies have fabricated a rough network for the operation of grammatical voice across languages and paved the way for our current study for sure. However, they have necessarily been forced to oversimplify voice issues in English because of the wide scope of their studies. Given this, we will define the grammatical voice from cognitive perspective and confine the taxonomy of grammatical voice to English.

3   Definition and Subcategories of Voice in English in this Study

In this section, our discussion will be devoted to giving a comprehensive definition of voice by employing the cognitive approach and reclassifying the English grammatical voice types according to the discrete and continuous features of languages.

Following a cognitive approach (Langacker 1987a, 1987b, 1991a, 1991b, 2000, 2001, 2004a, 2004b, 2008a, 2008b), the grammatical voice can be defined from several aspects as follows:

First, the grammatical voice is a symbolic unit residing in the symbolic relationship between a semantic unit and phonological unit. It is a grammatical category formed from schematizing and categorizing the usage events (actual instances of language use in all its complexity and specificity) by the speaker and hearer. It is generally held by cognitive grammarians that lexicon, morphology and syntax form a continuum of symbolic units, with varying complexity and specificity in conceptualization and linguistic coding. Not only the morphosyntactic properties alone, but also the semantic and pragmatic functions of grammatical voice in diversified contexts embody the very nature of the voice.

Second, in dealing with new expression concerning voice, analyzing its main properties and categorizing it according to the basic schema of the voice category are the first concern. We may have active voice, and passive voice in some languages that are fully manifested in the schema of grammatical voice without distortion and instantiate the schema fully on the one hand. It can be defined as the prototype of the voice category or use the term we have chosen, ICM of the voice category. On the other hand, we also have other voice types that only partially fulfill the schema. They can be defined as extensions of the prototype or peripheral members of the voice category or deviations from ICM or flexible applications of the ICM. Therefore, grammatical voice is a category that is not always well-demarcated but it is still structured around prototypes.

Third, a cognitive interpretation of the linguistic meaning of grammatical voice relies not so much on objective denoting of the object as it is based on the subjective construal that characterizes the interplay of the interlocutor's mind with the world around them. Verbs in human language designate an ICM of events as suggested by Croft (1990, 1991). It is said that verbs represent self-contained events. Subjects and objects represent the starting point and endpoint respectively of the segment of the causal network that is represented by the verb. Oblique NPS represent other entities involved more or less directly in the causal segment denoted by the verb (Croft 1994: 92). It is assumed that events are construed as having a tripartite internal structure, showing in the sequence of *cause, become, state* and dovetailing with *causative, inchoative*, and *stative* verbs or event views. These three types of verb forms seem to match with transitive verbs, intransitive verbs and stative verbs (or adjectives) successively and accord with the active, the middle and the passive/resultative basic voice types consecutively. However, it has to be admitted that *causative, inchoative and stative* can only represent the ICM for each of those verbal types that are usually unmarked. In practice, a great deal of flexibility will be involved in any application of event views. This is very natural, as we know, because ICM is only an idealized way of conceptualization, and deviation will always exist. Therefore, the active, middle and passive voice can be treated as the ICM of the voice category. Some other voice alternations reflect the disparity of ICM to some extent.

Fourth, as suggested by cognitive grammarians, a verb usually characterizes a type of process and heads a clause that conventionally encompasses nominals representing participants in the profiled relationship. Clausal organization concerns how the semantic roles of the participants such as agent, patient, instrument, etc. map onto grammatical roles such as subject and object. These participants interact with one another and these interactions are a natural part of billiard-ball model in our conception within which objects may move and impact each other through physical contact. Some objects may offer the needed energy through their own internal resources; others may merely transmit or absorb it. An agent is regarded as an energy source and the initial participant in an action chain, and the patient is taken as an energy sink and the final participant in an action chain, which make changes because of being affected by outside forces. In this study, we maintain that voice is the device responsible for aligning participant roles of an event with syntactic functions and the notion of asymmetrical force or energy transmission among the event participants is rooted in human experience and cognition.

Fifth, as we discussed above, topologists and functionalists' voice types are language specific, in that ergative languages and accusative languages show different preferences for certain voices. In line with cognitive grammarians, we maintain that languages are not ergative and accusative per se, and so does grammatical voice. Instead, to designate a language as ergative or accusative is only to reveal what strategies, either ergative or accusative, will be adopted to construe event. In fact, accusative languages, though they may have cardinal accusative patterns, also exhibit ergative properties to some extent, and the inverse is true of ergative languages. Voice patterns, thereby, are determined by the strategies used to construe an event construction within which the notion of a starting point that refers to the specific part of the event from which we begin construing a scene takes a predominant position. As put by Maldonado (2007: 831), starting points operate at three levels: prominence (the hierarchy of participant prominence), inductivity (the hierarchy of participants organized according to their capacity to initiate an event as determined by the conceptual content of verb) and case marking (the association between prominence and inductivity). In accusative languages, construal leads from the agent to the core of the event in which agent is regarded as the event-initiating participant and the patient is lower in capability in the hierarchy to initiate an event. Whereas in ergative languages, the theme is regarded as the most salient participant, and under most circumstances the agent is either neglected or is marked as an oblique.

After redefining the voice from the cognitive perspective, what we need to do next is to reestablish the voice types in English in this study regarding the continuous and discrete features of language.

With regard to discrete features, every voice type should be regarded as being individuated, possessing features like, uniplex, bounding, heterogeneous, and determinate. Just as Figure 22 shows, the functions or meaning of the finite verb group in English are diverse. Several functional categories can be associated with the verb groups, tense, aspect, mood, modality and voice. In English, it is argued that there are nine types of voice: active, passive, middle, antipassive, applicative, causative, anticausative, reciprocal and reflexive.

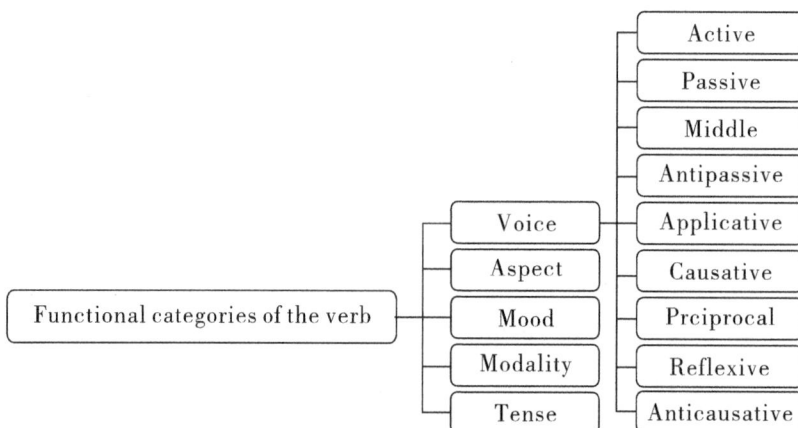

Figure 22   The Classification of Grammatical Voice in English According to Its Discrete Features

In terms of continuous features, we maintain that there are three major subcategories of voice groups in English. As shown in Figure 23, active and passive are two major voices. In addition, there is an intermediate voice type inserted between the active and passive, and it is defined as the medial voice. In fact, the medial voice itself is not a type of voice; it is only a schema and has many variations that are represented as the middle, causative, anticausative, reflexive, reciprocal, antipassive and applicative. These voice types resemble active or passive in one way or another and form, therefore, a continuum between the active and passive, and all the voice types together instantiate the category of English voice.

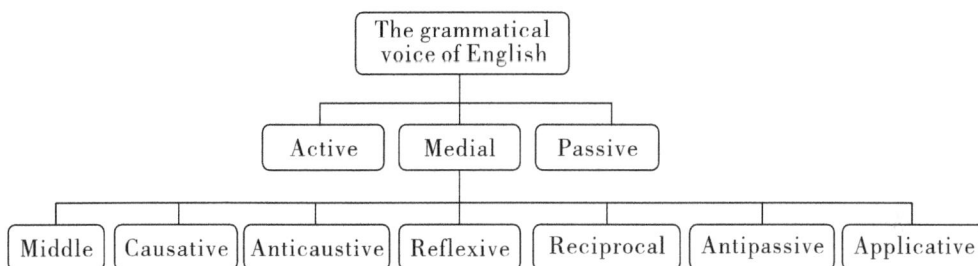

Figure 23   The Classification of Grammatical Voice in English According to Its Continuous Features

As discussed above, discreteness and continuity are two inseparable concepts in language study, which reflect different ways in which people view and understand the world. The former indicates features such as, individuality and dividedness, which are rooted in the uniplex, bounded, heterogeneous and determinate law of universe. The latter reflects features such as, the connectedness, isomorphism congeniality, which are rooted in the multiplex, unbounded, homogeneous, indeterminate laws of the universe. Without discreteness, there are no differences between language structures. Without discreteness, there are no boundaries between categories. Therefore, it is necessary to designate the discrete features of each subcategory of grammatical voice. In the following sections, we begin by examining the discrete features of the active voice, and then passive voice, and finally take a look at the discrete features of the medial voice, which can be subdivided into middle voice, causative voice, anticaustive voice, reflexive voice, reciprocal voice, antipassive voice and applicative voice.

4   Summary

To sum up, this chapter began with a discussion the attributes of the grammatical voice by resorting to diverse definitions from different linguists. Then we investigated the diverse voice types in languages. Based on these analyses, we have arrived at a more nuanced definition of voice from the perspective of cognitive linguistics. It is claimed that voice is a grammatical category denoting an interlocutor's subjective construal of usage events. It unavoidably involves schematizing and categorizing the actual examples of language use, taking all its complexity and specificity into account. In addition, we argue that though we divide English voice into different types, there is a voice continuum among various voice types due to the fuzziness of the category boundaries. Based on the above analysis, in the next chapter, we will analyse the morphosyntactic, semantic and pragmatic features of each category and to see how different voice types are related in one way or another.

V

The Fuzzy Feature Shown in the Categorization of Active Constructions and Their Cognitive Model

In this chapter, we attempt to deal with fuzzy the feature of the English active voice category in two aspects: one which concerns the discrete features of active constructions, and another which involves the continuous features of active constructions. Using the theoretical framework set up in Chapter III, we begin by selecting the prototype of active constructions through explicating morphosyntactic, semantic, and pragmatic features of different members. We then go on to flesh out the category by introducing the other instantiations or the non-prototypical members to see how every member of the subcategory of active voice are related in one way or another. Furthermore, we abstract the schema of the active voice category from the prototype and non-prototypical members and establish its cognitive model by combining the prototypical model, construal model, and force-dynamic models together.

1 The Active Prototype and Its Discrete Characterization

According to Ungerer and Schimid (1996, 2006), cognitive models are all the stored cognitive representations/knowledge bases that belong to a certain field. In order to establish a cognitive model of the active category, the inner structure of it needs to be clearly designated. However, the discovery that variations in language data do not always fall neatly into a simple grammatical system, as suggested by Klammer and Schulz (1992), has resulted in an approach involving prototype theory, which is feasible and practical in understanding the nature of grammatical relationships within a category. As one part of grammatical system, we posit that English actives as a category has diverse members. The membership of the active category is a matter of degree rather than being binary. The member with the most typical features should be regarded as the prototype of the active category and the peripheral members can be defined according to how many features they share with the prototype. In Chapter III, we discussed alternative models of categorization from a cognitive perspective. In addition to the prototype model which serves as the most typical exemplar of a category, a schema model which denotes the commonality of every member of the category is also worth our attention. At this connection, three natural questions to ask here are: (ⅰ) What is the schematic cognitive model of the active category? (ⅱ) What is the prototypical cognitive model of the active category? (ⅲ) How do the related constructions deviate from the prototype?

To answer above three questions, therefore, as Figure 24 shows, the prototype of active constructions will be analyzed first. Taking the morphosyntactic, semantic, and pragmatic features into account, the prototypical model, construal model and force dynamic model of the active voice will be illustrated. Based on these models, the idealized cognitive model can be generalized. However, according to the prototype theory, the members in the active category do not have equal status; there are always deviations from the prototype. Taking the prototype as the core, we compare and contrast them with other peripheral members of the active voice and generate the schema of the active voice category. Combing the ICM with the deviations of other instantiations, we finally attempt to arrive at a complete cognitive model of the active voice.

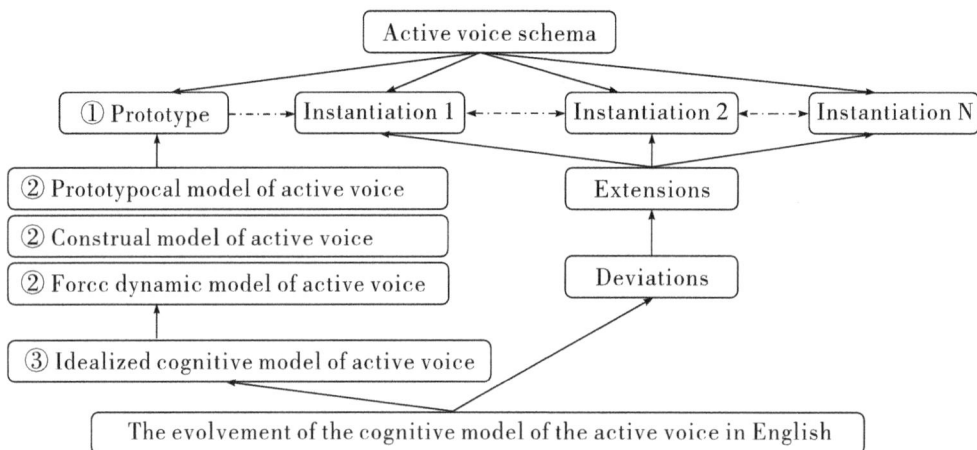

Figure 24   The Evolvement of the Cognitive Model of the Active Voice in English

1.1   Active Prototype Selection

In order to define the prototype of the active voice, it is instructive to resort to the research of other linguistic schools on the active system in that the research tends to lay emphasis on the most essential parts of the active in English and naturally shed light upon our current discussion. Therefore, two approaches to active prototype are to be analyzed in this part.

1.1.1   General Approach

A review of the literature reveals that many traditional grammarians (Sweet 1892; Jespersen

1924; Poutsma 1926; Svartvik 1966; Quirk et al. 1985) tend to define the active voice in terms of its relations to the passive voice. For instance, Sweet (1892) claims that the active and passive present different grammatical ways of expressing the relation between a transitive verb and its subject and object. Jespersen (1924) and Poutsma (1926) use *turning* and *conversion* respectively to distinguish the verb forms of one voice from another.

Though there are divergences in view, grammarians from different schools have one thing in common: the active is the primary, central, underlying feature of the verb or clause in contrast to other voices in English. Kruisinga (1927) considers the active is the primary form of the verb while passive, which is the secondary and derivative form, depends upon the active. Both Chomsky (1957) and Lees (1957) took actives as kernel sentence and hold that passives are less central than actives in that it involves less complexity and fewer rules when we transform an active into passive and, conversely, more complexity and more rules when we change a passive to an active. In the same vein, Svartvik (1966) maintains that passives, being less central than actives, are then best derived from actives. According to Givón (1993a), it is instructive to describe the grammar of any language as a logical progression from simple clauses to complex clauses. In addition, the simple clauses are likened to a theme on which complex clauses are the variations. The prototypical theme clause is a main, declarative, affirmative, active clause in contrast to dependent clauses, non-declarative (interrogative or imperative) clauses, negative clauses and passive clauses.

Despite this, some grammarians give clear independent definitions of the active voice, which can lend support to our current study. For instance, according to Michael (1970: 374-375), the active voice is said to encode the doing of an action that notionally devolves from the standpoint of the most dynamic, or active, party involved in the situation, typically the agent. Herring (2016: 770) claims that the active voice exhibits itself in two interconnected ways. One is that the subject of a sentence is also the agent of the verb—that is, it performs the action expressed by the verb. Another is that the agent always comes before the verb. According to Trask (1993), an active (of a clause) is used to denote a construction, usually involving a transitive verb, in which the grammatical subject of the verb typically (though not without exception) represents the agent performing the action with the direct object representing the patient.

In line with the above analysis, the typical active construction consists of the following features as shown in Figure 25. (i) In terms of the status, the active voice serves as the default voice in English, which means that verbs appearing in the active voice reflect zero inflections, and are unmarked. (ii) With regard to pattern of manifestation, voice is generally regarded as a function of a verb, and to be exact, a transitive verb. However, the verb itself cannot be sufficient to make a verb active in that the transitivity of the verb involving the global properties of an entire clause is such that an action is transferred from an agent to a patient (Hopper and Thompson 1980). At the clausal level, there is a correspondent mapping between grammatical relations and grammatical roles and these roles and relations are subject to sequential rules such that the agent is preceded by the verb and subject is before the verb. Additionally, it is sometimes stated that the object is affected by the activity, and/or that transitive clauses can be transformed into a passive clause. On the contrary, intransitive clause lacks an object. Therefore, no activity is transferred.

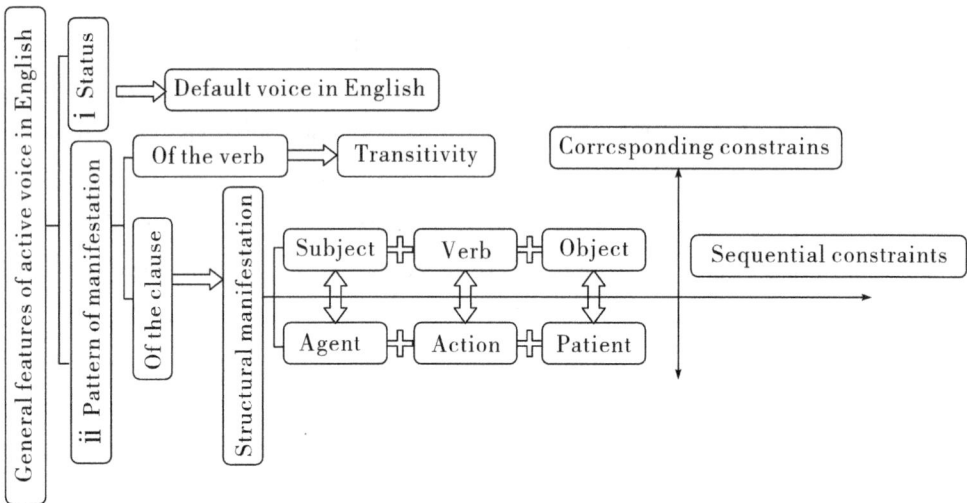

Figure 25　A General Approach to the Features of Active Voice in English

It is frequently seen that many pedagogical grammar books organize sentence types according to their function, such as: declarative, interrogative, imperative and exclamatory; affirmation, such as affirmative versus negative; complexity, such as simple or complex; voice, such as active voice versus passive; and transitivity, such as transitive versus intransitive. One question worthy of our attention is that if clauses are of diverse types with unlimited variety, then what is the prototypical sentence? Supposing all the sentences form a category, are there basic level sentences? As suggested by the literature, what many grammarians (Slobin and Bever 1983; Corrigan 1986, 1991; Givón 1993a) have consistently stated is that the simple, active, affirmative, transitive, declarative sentence is canonical. Ross (1987) argues that a prototypical sentence has the form "Agent subject+verb of action+patient (Direct) Object".

1.1.2　Cognitive Grammar Approach

Following the above line of thinking, it is natural to assume that the prototype of active construction is what Ross (1987) had presented. However, in terms of voice, the concepts of agent, verb, and patient are very vague if we take the diversity and complexity of active constructions in context into consideration. In contrast to other schools of grammar, cognitive grammarians claim that grammar is simply the structuring and symbolization of semantic content rather than an autonomous formal system.

They hold that grammatical structures are inherently symbolic units that consist of semantic and phonological structures. As a valid grammatical construct, active construction has conceptual import. There are simple symbolic units such as morpheme [READ] that can be combined with other morphemes such as [ER] or [ING] to form complex symbolic units such as [READER] or [READING]. Naturally, active constructions are complex symbolic units which can be broken down into several parts. There are two factors that need to be taken into account concerning active construction: the number of component units and the relationship between these units.

According to cognitive grammar, the things or entities that populate our physical and mental world reside in connection and relationship rather than in isolation. Though they are conceived as discrete objects, each of which occupies a distinct location at a given moment, these connections and relationships are not conceptually independent, but presuppose the participant roles.

On the other hand, these relationships can be stable or in a state of change. Whether persistent or changing, a relationship tracked through time is termed a *process*. According to Langacker (2008b: 354-355), a verb specifies a type of *process* or it is used to designate any expression that profiles a *process*, be it lexical verbs or a complex verb. It is generally claimed that a noun heads a nominal and a verb heads a clause, which typically incorporates nominals representing participants in the profiled relationship. A full clause or finite clause is said to single out an instance of the process type and specifies its status vis-à-vis the speech event and the interlocutors. Thus, clauses are our basic vehicle for talking about the world and relating occurrences to our own circumstances (Langacker 2008: 354). Primarily, a discourse is said to be composed of a series of clauses rather than nominals whose referent can be elicited while describing their participation in relationships, which naturally presuppose participant roles as we put it earlier.

Therefore, it is generally accepted that nominals are systematically included in clauses. In terms of clausal organization, three necessary dimensions are involved: (i) the role of nominal referents with respect to the profiled process, (ii) the existence of basic clause types, and (iii) how clauses function in discourse.

1.1.2.1   In Terms of Interactions between Role Archetypes

It is generally claimed by cognitive grammarians that clause structure is grounded in basic human experience, which is represented by certain archetypal conceptions that function as the prototypes for clausal elements and serve as a major factor in determining clausal structural arrangements. It is said that our cognitive models are based on these archetypal conceptions.

One archetype is the organization of scenes into global settings that are typically represented by things like rooms, buildings and geographical regions, and any number of smaller, more mobile participants that are typically represented as being people or discrete physical objects. Each participant is said to interact with other participants and occupies a distinct location while the location is regarded as part of the setting and executes the function of housing participants. The interaction is said to involve the conception of participants moving through space during a specific time and exerting impacts on each other through forceful physical contact.

Different participants or objects play different roles in the interaction. Some are the energy-initiators which supply the necessary energy through their own internal resources. Some serve as the energy transmitter or absorber. This essential archetype is defined as the billiard-ball model by Langacker, which attaches great importance to the notion of interaction between discrete objects or participants. An additional archetypal conception that attaches to the billiard-ball model is that of an action chain, as shown in Figure 26, in which a series of forceful interactions occur during a certain conceived time (T1 to T2, T2 to T3). Each involves the transmission of energy (double arrow) from one participant to another. It pertains to the conception of participants interacting energetically in a force-dynamic event (Talmy 1988). Therefore, the active construction naturally involves the conception of actions and events. There are various kinds of archetypal roles connected with actions and events.

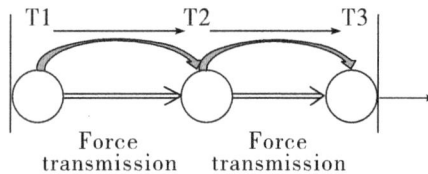

Figure 26 Action Chain and Force Transmission

For event participants, cognitive grammarians differentiate a couple of more specific roles for them which are similar to traditional semantic roles but still differ in one way or another. According to cognitive grammar, an agent often serves as an energy source and initial participant in an action chain in that it refers to an individual or an entity that volitionally starts and carries out an action, and tends to exert some effect on other entities. On the other hand, patient is said to be completely different from the agent. It is often designated as energy sink and serves as the final participant in an action chain in that it is often inanimate and nonvolitional, undergoing an internal change of state as the result of being affected by the external force coming from the agent.

In addition to these two major event roles, there are also some other roles worth mentioning here. An instrument, which is typically represented by an inanimate object, refers to something physically manipulated or employed by an agent. In terms of the status of the instrument, in its typical role it cannot independently function as the source of energy, but serves as an intermediary in the transfer of force from the agent to the patient. An experience is defined as a mental activity which is evolved by metaphor mapping from the concrete physical domain to the abstract intellectual, perceptual, or emotive domain. Therefore, an experiencer, which is typically represented by a human, is commonly assumed to be sentient and capable of having a mental experience. In contrast, a mover is anything that moves. It is measured by whether there are positional changes in contrast to its external surroundings. Therefore, an inanimate object is the typical representative of the mover. Lastly, the zero is used to refer to participants whose role is conceptually minimal and nondistinctive. It is the neutral or baseline role of participants that merely exist, occupy some location, or exhibit a static property (Langacker 2008: 356).

As we mentioned in Chapter III, the stage model is another cognitive model worth our attention, it denotes an archetype conception that relates to how we understand the outside world. It suggests that the way we observe the world is just like watching a play. Within the reach of our eyesight or maximal field of view, a limited area is selected as the general locus of attention, which is analogous to onstage region. Within the locus of our attention, we also have our focal attention, which means we focus specifically on certain elements. It naturally divides our viewing into three levels among which the maximal field of view, the onstage region and the focus of attention echo to the cognitive terms maximal scope, immediate scope, and profile, respectively.

By combining the various archetypal conceptions mentioned above, Langacker arrives at a more complex conceptualization depicting the normal observation of a prototypical action as shown in Figure 27. It is defined as the canonical event model which provides a schematic model for discussing clause structure. The stage model activates the conception of a viewer (V) from offstage, observing an event, which is the focus of attention within the immediate scope from a vantage point external to its setting. All of this unfolds within the maximal scope.

Based on the billiard-ball model, prototypical action is seen as an action chain involving two discrete objects, which represented as circles, moving about and interacting energetically through physical contact in a force-dynamic event. The two discrete objects correspond to the two archetypical participant roles which instantiate the demarcated opposite role archetypes—agent and patient. The double arrow shown in Figure 27 is used to portray the transmission of the energy. The unidirectionality of the double arrow is a criterion to differentiate the agent and patient in that the patient is the one undergoing the internal change as a result of the force exerted by the agent. A squiggly line is adopted to show the resulting change of state of the patient.

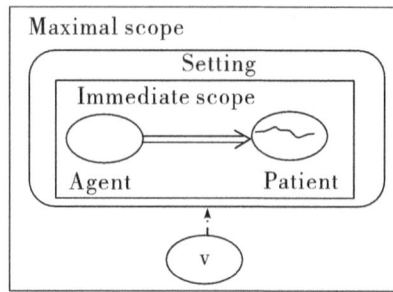

Figure 27   The Canonical Event Model (Langacker 1991: 211)

Matching these conceptual event structures with linguistic structures through coding, we can arrive at the conclusion that a transitive clause with two focused participants can serve as the prototype of the active construction. A prototypical verb is one that instantiates a good agent-patient interaction with the agent serving as the prototype for clause subjects while the patient served for the objects. The adverbial in a clause is commonly used to represent the setting. The prepositional phrases can be used to express location and non-focus participants such as instruments. The prototypical viewer in the offstage position is usually represented by third-person participants in that they typify the general case in contrast to the first-and-second person. It is also widely accepted that a human is the typical agent since a human has high volitionality and agentivity while an inanimate object is the typical patient since it has high affectedness. In addition, a prototypical clause is typically affirmative and declarative in form in contrast to other types of clauses.

1.1.2.2   In Terms of Composite Verbs

In addition to the above factors, we also have to think about the transitivity of the verb. Since finite clauses profile the process of an event, they involve a time span. It is natural that the process which the typical transitive clause describes is expected to finish within a bounded period. Therefore, a perfect verb (dynamic verb) rather than a stative verb is the prototype of a high transitivity verb.

Stative verbs in English describe situations without inherent ends, for example the verbs *to resemble, believe,* and *know* cannot be the typical transitive verbs. Only dynamic verbs correspond to Vendler's (1967: 106) three types: activity verbs, accomplishment verbs and achievement verbs.

Accomplishment verbs have both duration and telicity. Achievement verbs have no duration but do have telicity, and require a completive interpretation (in spite of indefinite objects) as they focus almost entirely on the completion of some activity. Activity verbs tend to have duration but no telicity. In terms of force and energy transmission and affectedness of the patient, it seems that the achievement verbs such as *break, kill, and damage* are the best candidates, in contrast to the accomplishment verbs such as *give, learn* and *persuade*, or activity verbs such as *kick, swim and drink*. This is equal to Tsunado's (1985) type one verb, where he claims that the verbs such as *kill, break, kick, eat, hit*, and *shoot* can manifest a direct effect on patient. However, the verbs kill and break are defined as resultant verb that have high transitivity while the rest are clarified as non-resultant verbs whose transitivity is slightly decreased. Based on the above analyses, let us flesh out the prototypical active model by taking the Canonical Event Model as the base.

As can be seen from Figure 28, in order to get the prototypical model of the active category, we take the entire active construction at the clausal level as our maximal scope. Despite the diversity and complexity of the active category, we limit our focus to the simple, affirmative and declarative active sentences and form our setting for it is more salient in our cognition. These sentences also show various features. However, we believe that these sentences describe the physical and concrete things as more salient than the abstract, psychological, and emotional domains as put by Langacker. We thus put the active sentence that describes things in the physical domain as the immediate scope. The viewer is observed from the vantage point of describing the general case. Therefore, the third person should be regarded as the default choice for the agent.

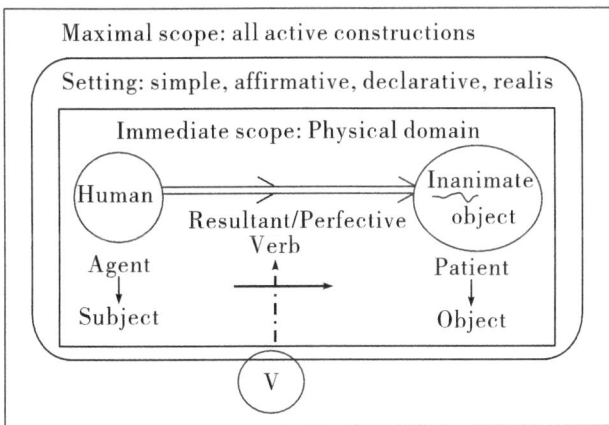

Figure 28   The Canonical Event Model of the Active Constructions

1.2   Characterization of the Active Prototype

Based on above analysis, we can summarize the semantic and syntactic characterization of the active category as follows. (i) A prototypical active construction profiles an action chain that involves two demarcated different participants: agent and patient. The former acts volitionally and serves as the head of the force or energy, and is thus fully responsible for the action chain. The latter functions as the tail of the energy and undergoes a change of state due to the action exerted by the agent, which is perceptible to an on-looking observer. (ii) In terms of the syntactic features of the prototype, the agent is coded as the subject of the clause which profiles the action chain while the patient is coded as the object of the clause. Morphosyntactically speaking, the verb is unmarked and denotes a resultant condition, which shows how the patient is influenced by the action of the agent. In addition, the verb should be in past tense to show the interaction process is over. (iii) With regard to the pragmatic features, it can be deduced that the agent, coded as the subject of the prototypical active construction, is always in the topical position of the sentence. And in most cases, there is a tacit agenthood promotion in the active constructions.

2 Active Non-prototypes and Continuous Characterization

According to prototype theory, the active prototype is the most typical member of the active category. It thus possesses most of the typical features of the category. However, due to the fact that the membership is nonbinary, different instantiations of the active category may share some of the features with the prototype rather than all the features. In what follows, our special focus will be on the deviation from the prototype in the active construction domain. Our discussion mainly falls into two aspects: one concerns active constructions that depart from the prototypical event model of the active chain and force transmission pattern and the other copes with coding differences occurring under the same circumstances with the different subjective construal. In contrast to the event prototype of active construction, divergences from the prototype can be observed in the following dimensions:

2.1 Deviation of the Role Archetype and Composite Verb in the Physical Domain

According to Langacker (2008), the most essential aspectual distinction for English verbs is between perfective and imperfective processes. Perfect verbs are often regarded as the resultant verb with causative meaning, which are the ideal verbs to depict the canonical event model of active construction. However, the resultant verb can also profile non-prototypical events where the agent and patient deviate from their archetypical role models.

As we stated above, the prototypical event usually involves an animate, human with high volitionality and agentivity as the subject. The object typically takes inanimate, nonhuman patient with internal changes. Both the agent and patient are concrete things in the physical domain. However, other members of the active category do not always conform to the typical features completely even in the physical domain. Sometimes deviation from the prototype happens to the agent or the patient respectively or synchronously.

2.1.1 Deviations of the Agent with Resultant Verbs

To put our discussion on concrete footing, let us look at some examples below. Observe and consider the following sentences.

(1) a. Floyd broke the glass.

(Langacker 1991b: 216)

    b. Leona opened the door.

(Langacker 2000: 32)

    c. The robbers ransacked the village.

(2) a. The cat broke the vase.

    b. A swarm of locusts destroyed the crop.

    c. The cormorants swallowed the small fish.

(3) a. The landslides destroyed the building.

    b. The tornado damaged the cabin.

    c. The fire burned the forest.

(4) a. A stone broke his glasses.

(Quirk et al. 1985: 743)

    b. The torch melted the ice.

(Langacker 1999: 37)

    c. The key opened the safe.

As shown in Table 4, the sentences in (1) are typical examples of active construction, which can be regarded as prototypes.

Table 4   Deviations of the Agent with Resultant Verbs

	Human	Animate	Volitional	agentive	examples
Prototypical agent	+	+	+	+	1 (1a), (1b), (1c)
Non-prototype (1)	-	+	+	+	2 (2a), (2b), (2c)
Non-prototype (2)	-	-	-	+	3 (3a), (3b), (3c)
Non-prototype (3)	-	-	-	-	4 (4a), (4b), (4c)

In contrast to (1), examples in (2), (3) and (4) seem to have similar syntactic representations and denote similar action chains, but the agents involved in the sentences show different degrees of deviation. In (2), the subjects of the three sentences—*the cat, a swarm of locusts, the cormorants*— are animate agents with volitionality but are non-human. In (3), the subjects of three sentences— *the landslides, the tornado, the fire*—play the role of external causers, which are inanimate, non-human agents without consciousness, so they have thus no volitionality as agents. In (4), the subjects of three sentences— *a stone, the torch, the key*—are archetypes of the instruments that refer to the entity that the agent uses to initiate an action or instigate a process. It seems there is a metonymical mapping occurring between the instrument and the real agent. There is one point worth mentioning here: these agents with resultant verbs display high transitivity and it is easy to transform into their corresponding passive constructions.

2.1.2 Deviations of the Patient with Resultant Verbs

Taking a look at examples from (2) to (4), we can see that though deviations of agent demonstrate in various ways, the patients that instantiate through different direct objects are typical prototypes that show the features of being inanimate, undergoing internal changes, and being affected. However, the direct objects do not always confine their roles to the typical patient. The deviation of the patient is one obvious feature that we cannot ignore. To have a clear picture of it, let us take a look at the following examples.

(5) a. The murderer killed the mayor.

    b. Detectives arrested the suspect after a five-day undercover operation. (BNC)

    c. The newcomer defeated the champion.

In (5), all of the sentences have the prototypical agent as the subject. The patients—*the mayor, the suspect, and the champion*—have undergone internal changes due to the force exerted by the agent (*the murderer, detectives*, and *the newcomer*). The action chain is complete except that the patients are all human, which deviate slightly from the prototype, but they are still the members close to the prototype, show high transitivity, and can be passivized easily.

(6) a. He drank half of a cup of coffee.

    b. The gardener trimmed one branch of the tree.

    c. A stranger patted my mother's back.

    d. My brother combed his hair before leaving.

In (6), all of the sentences show the complete action chain and there is physical contact between the agent and patient. The agents serve normal, prototypical roles since they are all human. It seems that the patients accord to prototypical roles well but deviations also occur if we take a close look at them. In (6)a the object—*half of a cup of coffee*—is an inanimate, concrete object and can function as a good patient, but in terms of the feature of internal change, it only experiences a half change rather than a full change. (6)b has a parallel structure with (6)a, for both of the patients in the sentence underwent partial internal changes. Slightly department from the prototype occurring to the patients make them less typical.

Here the verbs in the sentences show high transitivity and it is easy to transfer the sentences into the passive. Sentence (6)c and (6)d seem to have a similar structure. In fact, they differ in the archetypal roles of the participants. For the former, the subject may act as the agent who initiates a physical action to influence the patient by patting. For the latter, the patient is one part of the agent, the subject hence operates the hybrid role of the agent, instrument and experiencer. Despite the divergence from the prototype, the action chain is complete and there is successful physical contact and force transmission between the agent and patient. Both (6)c and (6)d show a high degree of transitivity.

(7) a. They move the car towards the hill. (BNC)
   b. African tribal leaders carry these carved wands as a symbol of authority... (BNC)

As can be seen in (7), the action chain can be easily observed in (7)a and (7)b and there is obvious physical contact between the agent—*they*, *African tribal leaders*—and the patient— *the car*, *these carved wands*. However, in terms of the internal changes, the patients only undergo location changes. It is preferable to take *the car* and *these carved wands* as the movers rather than patients.

(8) a. Jacob pinched his little brother playfully.
   b. William injured his rival.
   c. Lewis knocked his opponent down on the ground.

In (8), the subjects in the three sentences have typical agents that can initiate an action and physical contacts occur and a complete action chain can be sketched out. In terms the objects, it seems that it is not workable to define their archetypal role as the patients. In (8)a, the effect of the profile action exerted on *his litter brother* is more a type of sensory and emotional experience rather than an internal physical change. Hence, it is plausible to regard the object as an experiencer. In contrast, the object in (8)b can operate in double roles: one is as the patient and the other as experiencer, while in (8)c, the object—*his opponent*—can be construed as an experiencer and mover.

(9) a. They climbed the mountain.
   b. Police surrounded the building.

In (9), for the objects—*the mountain*, *the building*—the effect of the profiled action doesn't seem to cause a physical change. They are more like a locative object, as put by Quirk et al. (1985), with such verbs as *walk*, *swim*, *pass*, *jump*, *turn*, *leave*, *reach*, *surround*, *cross*, and *climb*. Superficially, the locative objects seem to be adverbials with an omitted preposition. However, in the majority of cases, their status as object can be verified by their subject role in the corresponding passive. For example, "*The building was surrounded by the police.*"

(10) a. Daniel dug the ground.

   b. Daniel dug a hole.

(11) a. Baird broke the television.

   b. Baird invented television.

Taking a look at the examples in (10) and (11), the objects in (10)a and (11)a are the typical affected patients that undergo internal changes due to the action and force exerted by the agents *Daniel and Baird*. But things are different in (10)b and (11)b. Instead of being affected, *the hole and television* serve the role of result object where the deviation happens when it is compared with the typical patient—affected object. There seems to exist an action chain, but the force transmission in (10)b and (11)b is not as clear as that of (10)a and (11)a. Despite this, they both have force transmission and interactive asymmetry takes place between the agent and patient.

(12) a. The client paid the lawyer.

   b. The manager served the customer.

We have noticed that in (5)a to (5)c, the human functions as the affected object. In (12), the objects, both *the lawyer* and *the customer* are human, but their roles are more like a recipient of the action, which slightly deviates from the prototype, but there is clear evidence of force transmission and high transitivity of the verbs.

(13) a. Wilson walked the dog last night.

   b. Bolt ran 100 meters in ten seconds.

In (13), *the dog* and *100 meters* are not affected objects. They did not undergo any physical action from the prototypical agents *Wilson* and *Bolt*. They deviate from the prototype to a large degree. An action chain is not revealed in these two sentences and neither of them have a passive form. They are one of the most marginal members of active construction though they seem to display syntactic representation that is similar to the prototype.

(14) a. He breathed his last breath.

   b. He died a miserable death.

In (14), the objects—*his last breath and a miserable death*—act the role of portraying the process or the event denoted by the verb. They are cognate objects whose function is only to repeat the action of the verb so they are not the participants of the event and greatly deviate from the prototype. Hence, they are also marginal members of the active category.

2.1.3   Deviations of Both the Agent and the Patient with Resultant Verbs

We have discussed the deviation of agent and patient in the active constructions in the last few paragraphs respectively. Sometimes the extensions occur to both the agent and patient in English. Let us take a look at the following examples:

(15) a. A red car hit a pedestrian right in front of me.

   b. A great feather in the red hat tickled Mary.

   c. The horse passed the bridge.

   d. My tent sleeps four people.

(Quirk et al. 1985: 747)

   e. Jane divorced her husband.

   f. The magazine sold 600,000 copies last week. (BNC)

As can be seen, the subject of the (15)a is non-human, inanimate object and the object of the sentence is a human who has physical contact with the agent. In terms of the action chain, it is complete and force transmission can be clearly seen. The verb has a high degree of transitivity can be easily passivized. But in terms of semantic roles, both the agent and patient are atypical prototypes of the active construction. We can arrive at a conclusion that deviation happens to both agent and patient in (15)a.

As for (15)b, the subject—*a great feather*—plays the role of the instrument which exerts some action on the object—*Mary*—who plays the role of experiencer rather than the patient since Mary doesn't seem to undergo any internal physical changes. In terms of an action chain, it is workable, but both of the arguments in the sentences deviate from prototypical role though the verb is perfective and can be easily transformed into its passive form.

In (15)c, the subject—*horse*—is animate but it cannot initiate a volitional action since it is not human. The object—the bridge—serves the role of location or setting rather than participant since it is not affected by the action of the horse. One thing is worth our attention, in that the action chain is broken actually since both the subject and object deviate from the prototype even though the verb is a perfective. Hence this sentence is one of the marginal examples of the active category.

Taking a look at (15)d, the subject is actually a location that cannot serve as a force or energy source to exert some physical influence on the object *four people*. No action chain can be bridged from the subject to the object since there is no transmission of energy. Hence this example is also a marginal member of the active construction. In addition, the verb *sleep* shows a low degree of transitivity and cannot be passivized easily. The verb *sleep* is in the present form rather in the form of past tense, which make it more marginal in contrast to the prototype.

With regard to (15)e, the verb *divorce* is a perfective verb which can be used to profile a complete process. If we take a close look at the two arguments, their position can be changed without a change of meaning. As we put above, in the prototypical active construction, the agent always takes the leading position for it serves as the energy source and initiates the asymmetrical interaction with the patient. But in this sentence, the two participants have an equal status, their interaction is symmetrical. Both the participants deviate greatly from the prototype and the verb does not have a passive form. Thus, it is marginal in the active category.

In (15)f, the subject—*the magazine*—is not the real agent. The person who sells the magazine is actually the real agent. So, *the magazine* is not the energy source, the objects—*600,000 copies*—are not affected and cannot operate as the tail of the energy, and therefore, an action chain does not exist. In addition, this sentence cannot be transformed into the passive, so it is also a marginal example of deviation of the archetypal role in the physical domain of resultant verbs.

2.1.4   Deviation of Imperfective Verbs

By contrast, in the physical domain, there are also some verbs denoting the imperfect process. According to Langacker (2008: 147), schematically, a verb is defined as a relationship scanned sequentially in its evolution through time. Imperfective verbs reflect the conceptual characterization of being not specifically bounded in time. They are represented by the verbs such as *contain, reside, like, know, love, detest, appreciate*, etc. You may notice that among these verbs, some belong to the category of verbs that describe concrete things in physical world. While others describe psychological or mental activities. In this section, we only choose those verbs that can be used to describe concrete states or things.

(16) a. Martin owns a big company.

　　b. Fellini's new film stars Brygida Rudzka.

(Langacker 1991b: 233)

　　c. This little ball of gold weighs a quarter of an ounce.

　　d. Marsha resembles Hilda.

(Langacker 1991b: 222)

In (16), the verbs in each sentence—*own, star, weigh, resemble*—in each sentence are stative, imperfective verbs. (16)a describes a stative possessive relationship between the subject and the object. The state of the two participants does not change with the passing of time. *Martin* is the agent, who exerts some influence on a *big company*, and though the object is not affected by the agent, it is rather controlled by the agent actually. The asymmetry of interaction between the subject and object indicates that there exists an energy transmission despite a slight departure from the prototype. The sentence thus possesses a comparatively higher degree of transitivity and can be passivized easily.

(16)b depicts a stative condition. Taking a look at the subject *the film*, we can tell that it is not a real participant of the action but functions as the setting of the whole sentence. No action chain exists in this sentence since only one participant is involved in the event, let alone an energy transmission. In cognitive grammar, participants in events unrelated to the energy flow are called absolute participants. *Brygida Rudzka* can be construed as an absolute participant. Both the subject and object deviate from their prototypical roles in active construction. Therefore, no passive form is available for this sentence and it is a marginal member of the active category.

With regard to (16)c, it describes the permanent characteristic of an object, this feature cannot be deprived from the object with time passing by. The subject is an inanimate object which cannot initiate an action, and the object is a quantifier. Neither of them can be participants in an action chain. No force or energy is transmitted. *This little ball of gold* functions as an absolute participant. Semantically speaking, it greatly deviates from the active prototype.

In terms of (16)d, the verb *resemble* portrays the state of being that *Marsha* and *Hilda* are similar to each other. Since this example displays a stative situation, the notion of interaction doesn't seem to be feasible. In addition, while the relationship of similarity between *Marsha* and *Hilda* are symmetrical and reciprocal with regard to its intrinsic content, a discussion of asymmetrical interactions seems to digress from the topic.

According to Langacker (1991b), it is logical to conclude that there are symmetrical relationships between the two participants, but in terms of cognition, people tends to take the subject as a reference point to judge the second participant. Under this analysis, this sentence is regarded as one of the limited cases with respect to subject asymmetry. However, we must notice that these two participants are both absolute participants. They deviate greatly from the prototype and have no passivized correspondence.

2.2   Deviations of the Role Archetype and Composite Verb in the Abstract Domain

As we have shown above, active constructions show diversity and complexity in many aspects. One aspect worth our attention is that not every process profiled by an active clause displays concrete and physical things or things that can be easily touched or involves a force dynamic interaction. There are active constructions that describe psychological, mental, or social interactions between abstract participants, which can be construed as a metaphorical extension of the active construction.

(17) a. Ted hated pets.

    b. The pupils love their teacher. (BNC)

    c. The Panda likes bamboo leaves and bamboo shoots.

(18) a. I really admire your enthusiasm. (BNC)

    b. Tom respected our professor's opinion on most subjects.

    c. Some team members regret their decision.

(19) a. The airline regrets any inconvenience.

    b. The country resents those defectors.

    c. The committee respects different proposals.

Consider the examples in (17) first. The verbs *like*, *love*, and *hate* used here all express emotional changes in the mind. Different from verbs in the physical domain, these verbs profile psychological processes rather than physical processes. Defined as the subject experiencer verb by Pesetsky (1995), the clauses taking these verbs tend to depict an emotional energy transmission between the two participants. In (17)a and (17)b, the subjects—*Ted* and *the pupils*—are human, animate, both able to act as agents that instigate an activity and fulfill the prototypical archetype role. The objects in (17)a and (17)b are animate but both of them slightly divagate from the prototype patient. The subject volitionally transmits the emotion in the mind to the object metaphorically through mental contact. The objects thus are under the subject's emotional control, but they do not experience internal changes. In contrast to (17)a and (17)b, the subject of (17)c is a bit deflected from the prototype while the object also slightly veers away from prototypical role archetype, for it is an abstract concept rather a concrete thing. One of the essential features worth our attention is that all the three sentences denote an emotion transmission between a concrete human or object.

When it comes to the examples in (18), all the subjects seem to work well as the prototypical agent role, but the objects are abstract things that do not undergo internal changes but are under the control of the subjects. The verbs in these sentences are also subject experiencer verbs portraying an emotional energy transmission between the two participants.

In (19), each sentence uses the emotional verb that profile an asymmetrical interaction of emotion transmission. Being different from the examples in (17) and (18), the subjects in the sentences of (19) are non-human and inanimate. There is metonymical extension involved in each sentence, they use the institution, the organization, or an area of land to designate the people who belongs to them, which greatly deviates from the prototypical agent role. As the patient, the object of (19)a and (19)c are abstract concepts while the object of (19)b is human. All the objects are under the control of the subjects though they do not undergo any internal changes. As can be seen, although the degree of deviation increases from (17) to (19), they are all still marginal members in contrast to the prototypical active construction since the verbs expressing emotion indicate a stative process rather than a perfective condition.

In addition to emotional verbs, those perception verbs can also denote a psychological transmission of energy between two participants, as in the sentences of (20) and (21), illustrating two types of usages of perception verbs in the clauses.

(20) a. The little girl smelt the flower in the garden.

b. Fifty thousand people saw the match. (BNC)

c. I noticed a rip in the fabric.

(21) a. He can smell the trouble long before it gets serious. (BNC)

b. This stadium has seen many thrilling football games. (BNC)

c. Recent years have witnessed a growing social mobility. (BNC)

In (20), perception verbs are exemplified by the verbs smell, see, and notice. The subjects—*The little girl, fifty thousand people*, and *I*—are humans who can initiate a mental action consciously or unconsciously, and which can be construed as prototypical agents. The objects—*the flower, the match*, and *a rip in the fabric*—are concrete things that can be touched or get involve in. Thus, they can function as the prototype of the patient. The verbs differ from the prototype and the examples in (20) make the sentences slightly deviate from the prototype.

Indeed, there is mental contact between the subjects and objects, but the former can be volitional or non-volitional. The latter receives the mental force from the former, the interaction asymmetry is clear shown between the agent and patient, but the patients seem not to experience any internal changes. However, in contrast to sentences in (21), the examples in (20) are closer to the prototype.

Let us turn to the examples in (21). As can be seen, the perception verbs are instantiated by the verbs *smell, see* and *witness*. The subject of (21)a is a prototypical human agent which can function as the force or energy source while the object is an abstract concept—*the trouble*—that cannot be illustrated by the concrete image or be smelled or touched in a real sense. The olfactory feeling in the real things is mapped to the abstract things through metaphor. The mental transmission of energy or force occurs since we assume that there is mental contact between the subject and object. With regard to (21)b, it is obvious that the subject—

this stadium—cannot be an agent that initiates a visual activity but the locational setting that people use metonymically to transfer their mental energy to external things. In conceiving the world, people maximize the locational setting and make it a trajector of the clause. As we observe, only one participant gets involved in this sentence, that is, *many thrilling football games*, though it is under the control of the visional scale, no internal changes happen and no mental contact is involved. Thus, example (21)b can be assumed as one of the most marginal cases of the active construction in that the sentence has no passive transformation and shows the features of intransitive clause. Sentence (21)c possesses shared features with (21)b in that the subject—*recent years*—is also the temporal setting of the event that the clause depicts rather than a participant. People intentionally magnify the time of the event in their cognition but it cannot serve as the subject to influence the object *a growing social mobility*. As only one participant gets involved in the event, the object in (21)c is an abstract concept in contrast to that of in (21)b, and (21)c therefore shows a high degree of divergence in contrast to the prototype. It is even more marginal in the active category than that of (21)b.

What we discuss above is concerning emotional and perceptional verb in the psychological domain. There is still one type of verb that is worth our attention. Those verbs usually pertain to our ideation and intellectual activity in the psychological domain, as seen in the sentences of (22).

(22) a. Emily understood the instructions.

    b. She remembered her childhood.

(Langacker 1991b: 221)

    c. I have carefully considered your offer.

(Langacker 1991b: 221).

Consider the case in (22), where the subjects in these sentences are human, animate, and seem to be able to initiate volitional action. In fact, as put by Langacker, the subjects in these examples play the role of experiencers who involve themselves in some type of mental activity.

On the other hand, the experiencer in these sentences may be externally induced or under volitional control. It seems that the notion of an action chain does not apply to the cases in (22), but there is a shared feature between the role of the experiencer subject and that of the prototypical agent in a canonical event; that is, asymmetrical interaction seems to exist in both cases. What makes the experiencer subject different is that it interacts with the patient through a mental contract which can be reckoned to be the metaphorical mapping from the source domain—the physical domain—to the target domain—the psychological domain. It is important to note that the difference between these two sorts of asymmetric interactions cannot be neglected even though there are apparently shared features.

It is suggested by Langacker (1991) that we are groundless to presume any kind of transfer from the experiencer to the other participant. Thus the role of the second participant, the objects in (22)a to (22)c—*the instructions*, *her childhood*, *and your offer*—neither can be an energy source nor the energy sink. In fact, they are nonenergetic, and serve the role of absolute participant. The interactions in (22) can therefore be construed as the mental contact that the experiencer establishes with the object of perception or conception. In these sentences, the experiencers have strong volitional consciousness to transfer this perception energy to the object of the perception verb and take the object under their control. Though the object may not undergo any internal changes, it can be seen that the ideation or intellectual verbs show high degree of transitivity. They still play the role of a marginal member of the active category.

Having suggested the complexity and diversity of active construction resides in the transmission of energy beyond the physical domain, we are in the position to extend the conception metaphorically to the social domain. The sentences in (23) might be taken as the simple instantiation of social energy transfer while the examples in (24) might be understood as the extension of the notion of force dynamics from the physical domain to social domains in more complex sentences. It is natural to map the force of physical domain to social domains because it is obvious that people vary in their social status and social behavior and these variations make those people who have high social status exert some force to others during social interaction and communication.

(23) a. The police interrogated the offenders.

b. His remarks pressed David Cameron.

c. You must obey the captain's commands.

(24) a. They forced him to resign.

b. Irving persuaded me to clean the garage.

c. I urge you to give up that crazy idea.

(Langacker 1991b: 220)

As illustrated in (23), the subject of (23)a is a human who can exert some social power over the patient, *the offenders*. Though the patient is not the typical prototype of the canonical event, it can be influenced by the force of the subject or under the complete control of the subject. The force is not concrete but the social power understood by resorting to the source domain of the physical force. Despite the deviation from the prototype of active construction, it can function as a typical example of the social energy transmission in the social domain which other members in the social domain can take as reference points.

As for (23)b, the subject *his remarks* is inanimate but it can serve as the energy source of social power and transfers abstract force to the patient *David Cameron*. An interaction asymmetry occurs and the patient is under the control of the agent. Though there are no internal changes caused to the patient, it has been influenced by the subject to some extent. Still, (23)b shows a certain degree of departure from the prototype. With respect to (23)c, the agent and the patient seem to exchange their role archetypes. It appears that the object is more powerful than the subject in the sentence. We are quite sure that an asymmetry of social interactions occurs between the two participants. The first participant seems to be in the inferior position while the second participant looks to be more powerful in making the first participant obey it. This sentence breaches the principle of unidirectionality of energy transmission in the canonical event, it is far away from the prototype of active construction, and hence it can be seen as one of the most marginal member of the active construction as well as a peripheral member of active construction in the social domain.

Those listed in (24) exhibit the familiar energy transmission between the subject and object. The verbs such as *force*, *persuade*, and *urge* profile processes that need the participant with high agentivity. All the subjects in (24) are agents with high volitionality who can exert some influence on the objects such as him, me and you. What makes the sentence more complicated is that all the objects need to participant in the action through the influence of the agent. The asymmetry interaction does occur and the action chain is completed by social contact. Though complicated, each sentence in (24) can be easily transferred into a passive form, which provides evidence that the energy transmission occurs in the social domain.

2.3 Cognitive Construal of Continuous Deviations of Non-Prototypes

Having discussed the prototype of active constructions and their extensions by mainly resorting to how force dynamics applies to the action chain between the two participants, the second question posed here can be restated as follows: that is, how can we justify the deviations within the active category? According to Bolinger (1977), meaning is created by the speakers through their construal. That is to say, the speaker is considered to act as a *cognizing subject* as well as *speaking subject* before uttering a sentence. Further supported by (Langacker 1987a, 1991a, 1991b, 1999, 2008, 2013), construal involves our ability to conceive and portray the same situation in alternate ways. To be concrete, in viewing a scene, what we actually see depends on how closely we examine it, what we choose to look at, which elements we pay most attention to, and where we view it from (Langacker 2013: 55).

The choice of voice is said to involve different models of construal as put by cognitive grammarians. Within the category of active construction, the construal model can be used to interpret the reasons for diversion and variations in viewing the same event. The interpretation of the typical characterization of active construction relies not only on the semantics of objective events but also resorts to the speaker's construal of the situation and event. As we discussed in Chapter Ⅲ, construal is instantiated in several different dimensions. Here we choose three key dimensions to illustrate the conception in the active category, that is, specificity, prominence, and perspective.

2.3.1   Specificity and Active Construction

One dimension involved in the concept of construal goes to the degree of precision and perceived concreteness and detailedness at which a scene or a situation is characterized, i.e. specificity. On the one hand, the participants of active construction, or, we can say the nominal, can be characterized with degree of explicitness and meticulousness, as exemplified in (25).

(25) a. A man killed a porcupine.
b. A strong man killed a ferocious porcupine covered with sharp quills.

(Adapted from Langacker 2013: 56)

In (25), the verb *kill* is a perfective verb taking two nominal arguments. Both subjects in (25)a and (25)b can act as the prototypical agent that initiates an action and both objects in the two sentences are affected by the force exerted by the agent. The specificity of nominal arguments seems to have less influence on the transmission of energy and the action chain works well in both sentences. The difference between the two sentences lies in the specificity of the two participants. In (25)a, the nominal argument is in general sense while in (25)b it is in concrete and specific sense. (25)b entails (25)a rather than vice versa. In depicting the event, (25)b gives a fine-graded portrayal while (25)a give a coarse-graded snapshot. (25)b is closer to the prototype of the active construction while the (25)b is a bit less so in that it has to more information to process.

On the other hand, variations of verbs in active constructions reveal a hierarchy of specificity, as in the sentences of (26).

(26) a. Someone did something.
b. Someone fastened something.
c. Jimmy locked the door.

As can be seen in (26), in viewing the same scene, it can be encoded linguistically in different ways. The specificity increases from (26)a to (26)c in that (26)c denotes a complete action chain and has a prototypical agent and patient while in (26)a and (26)b, *someone* and *something* indicate the general things rather than specific entities. In addition, the verbs in each sentence show different degrees of specificity. *Locking* entails the action of *fastening* and *doing* rather than vice versa. It can be seen that the specificity of the verb selection also exerts some influence on the status of the clause in the active category in that the verbs with a more specific meaning can be more accurately identified than verbs with a general or abstract meaning.

2.3.2　Salience or Prominence and Active Construction

The next dimension which entails in the concept of construal is concerning salience or prominence. A natural question to ask at this point is how we can connect the concept prominence to active construction. The notion residing in this concept is that numerous types of asymmetries are displayed in various language structures, with active construction being no exception. These asymmetries in cognition naturally make anything selected salient when compared with what is unselected. Focusing therefore accords with this notion to a great extent. The concept of prominence is too vague to explain the encoding of language, hence its many subconcepts, (base and profile, scope, foreground and background, landmark and trajectory) are employed here for a more detailed explanation, as introduced in Chapter III. An important point to note in this regard is that the prototype tends to be more prominent than its various extensions within a category. Langacker (1987a, 1991a, 1991b, 2008b, 2013) presents a variety of concepts to explain his notions of salience and prominence. Taking a closer look at these concepts, we can see there are a lot of overlaps. For example, base, background and ground seem to have similar values. Profile, foreground and figure also appear to possess the same value.

In this section, the focus is on three particular sorts of prominence used in discussing the active construction: (ⅰ) profiling; (ⅱ) figure, ground and scope; and (ⅲ) trajector and landmark alignment. Though not equal in value, they are akin to one another inasmuch as each has a bearing on the act of focusing the attention, which is not only validated on semantic grounds but is also verified to be significant in grammatical descriptions. To better understand the internal relationship between prototype and non-prototype, let us look at these three sorts of prominence in turn.

2.3.2.1　Profile and Active Construction

First, let us see how profile and base work in the active construction. Consider some deviations of non-prototypes in the following examples.

(27) a. Charlie broke the vase (with the hammer).

　　 b. The hammer (easily) broke the vase.

　　 c. The vase (easily) broke.

(28) a. Charlie hit the vase (with the hammer).

    b. The hammer hit the vase.

    c. Charlie hit the hammer against the vase.

Following the above line of analysis, we can say (27a) profiles a complete action chain with the instrument added as the intermediary in which *Charlie*, the agent, is coded as the subject and *the vase*, the patient, is coded as an object that experiences some internal change due to the force volitionally exerted by the human, *Charlie*. As Figure 29 shows, the three participants in (27b) are all present in the event, and it exemplifies a complete model of the interaction between the agent, the patient and the instrument and corresponding relationship between the subject and object, as in (i) and (ii) in Figure 29. In contrast to (27a), (27b) profile an action chain that is not self-contained, where the agent is absent, as in (iii).

Alternately, (27c) illustrates a construction where the instrument functions as the subject and patient as the object, as sketched in (iv) in Figure 29. Only two participants are present. The interaction is available, but one of the important participants is missing. With regard to (27c), the sentence shows significant deviation from (27a). Both the agent and instrument are missing in the action chain. Only the patient is left and acts as the subject of the clause. Comparing examples in (27) with those in (28), we can see that the verb *break* is replaced

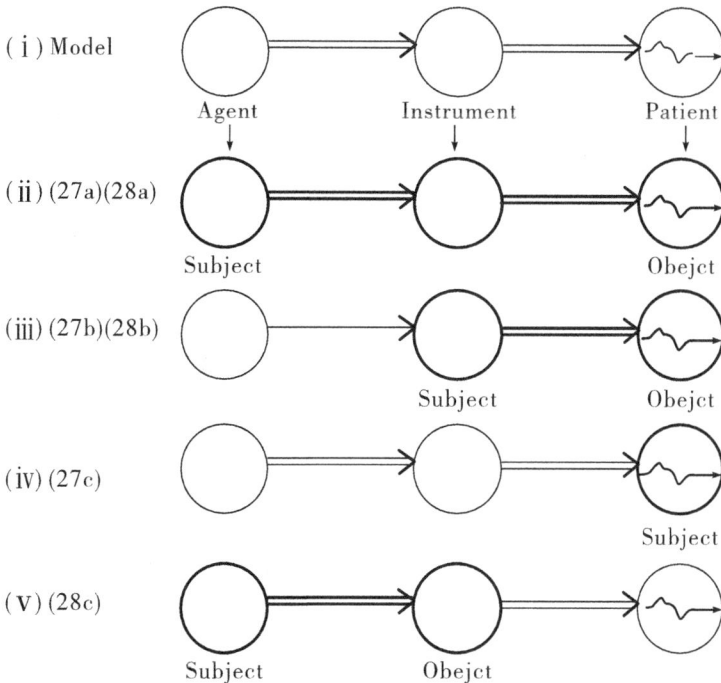

Figure 29   The Interaction of Profile and Action

by the verb *hit*. The former is a typical resultant verb while the latter is an activity verb. (28a) and (28b) seem to have parallel structures in contrast to (27a) and (27b), thus they can be represented by roughly the same action chain, as in (ii) and (iii). By contrast, (28c) designates a different structure in which the instrument (*the hammer*) functions as the object. The prepositional phrase denotes the resulting contact with *the vase*, as shown in (28c).

Based on above analysis, we can arrive at the conclusion that there are various deviations in the active category in addition to the prototypical active construction. Obviously, there is no one-to-one correspondence between the subject and any single role archetype such as the agent, the direct object or the patient in the active category. As we can see from the above examples, either the agent, the instrument, or the patient can be chosen as the subject.

2.3.2.2 Figure, Ground, and Scope in Active Construction

As put by Langacker (2008: 58), many kinds of asymmetries lend themselves to a metaphorical description as foreground vs. background. It is justifiable to employ the notion of background and foreground in any case where one conception precedes, and in some way facilitates the emergence of another. A manifestation in perception is the phenomenon known as figure vs. ground where figure precedes ground in the salient position while ground acts as a background that is indispensable. It is generally said that figure and ground segregation are reflected at different levels of language expression.

As put by Talmy (2000a: 289), figure and ground are necessary components of an event of motion. This argument lends support to the action chain model in English active construction. In addition, the conception of figure and ground is said to be applicable to the analysis of English single sentences in which the subject is in the most salient position and can so be construed as the figure, and the object is an important component that is secondary to the subject. The other elements can be rendered as setting. Being the unmarked case, the prototype of active construction seems to fit comfortable under this rubric. To set our discussion on a concrete footing, let us take a look at the following examples:

(29) a. The twenty-first century saw many changes.

    b. People saw many changes in the twenty-first century.

(30) a. Olivia crossed the bridge.

    b. Olivia crossed over the bridge.

(31) a. The Government provided houses for the squatters.

    b. The Government housed the squatters.

(Taylor 2003: 237)

(32) a. Line A intersects line B.
     b. Line B intersects line A.

(Langacker 1991b: 222)

Examples (29) to (32) illustrate the segregation of figure and ground by drawing the focus to the different components of the sentences. Though there are deviations from the prototype of active construction to varying extents, these sentences shed light on how the notion of figure and ground are revealed in active constructions.

Consider the sentences in (29) first. We have discussed similar sentence types in terms of action chain above. From the dimension of figure and ground, we can tell that the differences between (29)a and (29)b lie in the fact that they have different subjects. In view the same scene, the subject of (29)b is a human experiencer of the event, one who acts as the figure that is put in the prominent position. The object *many changes* functions as the ground. *In the twenty-first century* is the temporal setting that is put in the least important position. By contrast, the setting is put in the subject position in (29)a for an expressed purpose, and it functions as the figure while the role of the object is same as that in (29)b. (29)b is a normal construal of the scene and is closer to the prototype of the active construction where two participants are involved in the events while (29)a is said to be an unconventional construal, in which only one participant is entailed, and is thus a bit farther away from the prototype.

In view of (30), it is obvious that both sentences take the same subject and that the role of the subjects as figure is unquestionable. The difference between (30)a and (30)b resides in the choice of ground. In (30)a, the object *the bridge is* taken as the ground and there are two participants involved in the event. By contrast, in (30)b, the position of *the bridge* is weakened as it does not serve as the ground anymore, instead, it becomes the locational setting of the event. It is natural to conclude that (30)a exemplifies a common construal while (30)b an atypical one. The selection of the ground in the active sentences provides further evidence of how the focusing of the attention can influence our language expression.

When it comes to (31), the two sentences are apparently examples of non-prototypical active constructions. (31)b seems to be closer to the prototype, for it involves two participants. For (31)a, the structure is more complicated in that three participants are involved, that is, the agent, the patient, and the benefactor. The difference between the two sentences rests in the selected of the verb. In (31)a, the verb *provide* profiles a process. By contrast, in (32)b, the original noun *house* in (31)a is verbalized, while the benefactor *the squatters* comes to function as the patient. For these two sentences, the choice of the subject as the figure is identical and the action chain is obviously intact. But for the ground, in (31)b, the object *the squatters* is selected, while in (31)a the object *houses* is selected and *the squatters* figures as the settings. This seems to also lend support to how figure and ground segregation can exert some influence on the selection of the object in active construction. One thing needs to be noted: the structure of (31)b is less productive, and it may have many restrictions but we will not go into the details here.

By comparison, the sentences in (32) reveal a different picture of the structure since they depict static situations. As we discussed above, it seems that there is no asymmetrical interaction between the two participants in each sentence if we view the event objectively, since the relationship of intersection is symmetrical in terms of its intrinsic content. In addition, both the participants are inanimate objects denoting an abstract concept by acting as absolute participants. In spite of the above analyses, it is obvious that the two participants in each sentence are not semantically equivalent. There exists within these constructions the subjective asymmetry in the depiction of the participants as described by Langacker (1991b).

Consider (32)a, *line A* acts as the figure or a standard of comparison with regard to which *line B* is assessed. Here, *line B* is the ground that is put in the less important position. On the contrary, in (32)b, these roles are reversed, where line B serves as the figure but line A the ground. By using nearly identical items, these sentences prove that the pattern of construal does not solely depend on the inherent content or the objective features of the event, but, rather, sometimes subjectivity itself plays an important role in conceptualization and cognition. The point further echoes the arguments of cognitive linguistics; that is, sentences are not autonomous. The experience of being human plays some parts in it.

Having discussed figure and ground segregation in the domain of focus, let us move to another notion: scope, a concept that can be used to exemplify how the act of focusing works in active construction. As we discussed in Chapter III, there are two types of scope, one is maximal scope, which is concerned with the full extent of its coverage, and the other is immediate scope, which highlights the portion directly relevant for a particular purpose. Let us see how these concepts work in active construction, as in (32) and (33).

(33) a. Greg hit Sheila's back with his fist.

    b. Greg hit Sheila's back.

    c. Greg hit Sheila on the back.

    d. Greg's fist hit Sheila's back.

(Adapted from Langacker 1991b: 219)

(34) a. Margaret cut Bill's arm with her dagger.

    b. Margaret cut Bill's arm.

    c. Margaret cut Bill on the arm.

    d. Margaret's dagger cut Bill's arm.

(Adapted from Levin 1993: 7)

As the examples in (33) illustrate, the four sentences seem to depict the same event, but the subject and object show different levels of prominence with regard to the scope they take as the reference point. It can be easily figured out that (33)a indicates a complete action chain, with the agent, patient both involved, and the instrument functions as the intermediary. The subjects of (33)a to (33)c act as the figure of each sentence. The construal of the object is similar in (33)a and (33)b in that they both take the object as the ground by taking the immediate scope; that is Shelia's back is foregrounded against *Shelia's* whole body, which functions as the maximal scope and is taken as the background. On the contrary, (33)c takes *Sheila* as the immediate scope while *the back* is construed as settings. For (33)d, the expression is used in a specific condition in which one part of body is put in the prominent position, where *Greg* can be taken as the maximal scope, and *his fist* the immediate scope. In terms of the archetypical role, *Greg's fist* functions as the agent as well as the instrument, and, therefore, it seems that the instrument is profiled in this sentence.

Taking a look at the examples in (34), it appears that the sentence structures are similar to that of those in (33). (34)a designates a complete action chain with the object directed at the immediate scope of Bill's body. Though not complete, sentence (34)b can also exemplify a typical active construction with its object directed the same target as (34)a. The difference between (34)c and the two preceding examples rest in the scope of the object as ground. Here *Bill* is foregrounded as the immediate scope while *Bill's arm* acts as the settings. In (34)d, the subject that serves as the figure selects only the instrument that is held by *Margaret* as the immediate scope, while taking the image of Margaret with a dagger as the maximal scope. It needs to be noted that there are some differences between (33)d and (34)d in that the former takes only part of body as the instrument which functions as the figure and immediate scope while the latter choses an external instrument as the immediate scope.

2.3.2.3   Landmark/Trajector Alignment and Active Construction

The next dimension relating to prominence is the concept of landmark-trajector alignment. As put by Langacker (1991b), within a verb's processual profile, the most prominent element is called the trajector and that this may be either a setting or a participant. Accordingly, a nominal that elaborates a clause-level trajector is the subject. A landmark which indicates a thing or a relationship, refers to the prominent element secondary to the trajector. The direct object usually elaborates a primary landmark and usually lies downstream form the trajector. Let us see how these two concepts work in the active construction.

(35) a. Emma [tr] bought a dress [lm].

b. The money [tr] bought a dress [lm].

(36) a. The little girl likes that toy.

b. The toy pleases the little girl.

(37) a. He tied his shoe.

b. He tied his shoelaces.

c. He tied a bow with his shoelaces.

(Langacker1991a: 355)

As can be seen above, the sentences in (35)a can be interpreted as the typical example of an active construction where the subject Emma functions as the agent and acts as the most prominent participant. Hence it is selected as the trajector. The patient, *a dress*, that is less salient than the agent, can be construed as the landmark. In describing the same event, sentence (35)b takes the instrument as the subject, which denotes a difference in the selection of the trajectory, while taking the same landmark. The sentences in (36) show a different picture. It is clear that a different selection of verbs leads to the reversal of the trajector and landmark. However, only (36)a is a representation of a normal construal in which a human is the experiencer of the event. (36)b is unconventional in that it puts the inanimate stimulus in the subject position.

As for the sentences in (37), they each select the same trajector. The difference between the three examples resides in the choice of different landmarks. In (37)a the object *his shoe* brings into focus those relations involving *the shoe* as a whole whereas in (37)b, the object his shoelaces focuses on the relationship relating to the shoelaces in particular. In (37)c, the shoelaces function as the instrument. Instead, the bow is taken as the landmark. These examples provide support for the conclusion that a landmark varies when people focus on different parts of an event.

2.3.3　Perspective and Active Construction

Based on the above analysis, we can see that the dimension of prominence is useful in elucidating different iterations of active constructions. There is still one dimension worth our attention, that is, perspective. It may involve the concept of vantage point and mental scanning as we pointed out in chapter III. It has to be pointed out that the concept of prominence is closely related to the concept of perspective. Usually, the object in the most salient position is where we start our observation. Therefore, sometimes we can use the same type sentence to prove the application of prominence and perspective in that there are always some overlaps. To strengthen our understating, let us take a look at how it works in active construction by discussing the following examples.

(38) a. The fifth floor contains a library.

   b. A library occupies the fifth floor.

(Langacker 1991b: 222)

(39) a. She hammered the nail in the wood gradually.

   b. The hammer fixed the nail into the wood.

(40) a. A number of people saw the accident.

   b. The accident was seen (by a number of people)

(Quirk et al. 1985: 58)

Evidently, the sentences in (38) to (40) provide evidence as to how the dimension of prominence works. In the meantime, they can shed light on how the dimension of perspective works. As can be seen in (38), both examples are in active form. They choose a different perspective while observing the same scene. For (38)a, they view the scene by considering the relationship of part-and-whole, where the subject *the fifth floor* is considered to be the whole while the object *a library* is one component of the whole. By contrast, the same scene is viewed from the spatial fullness where the subject *a library* is construed to flesh out the space of the object *the fifth floor*. It can be seen that different ways of encoding the language can be attributed to the conceptualizers' perspective while mental scanning. Though the two sentences seem to describe the same scene, the differences in scanning the scene lead to the different linguistic encoding.

In (39), (39)a reflects a typical active construction where the scene is scanned mentally from the perspective of speaker. The speaker puts focus on how the event undergoes a process through a progressive process of time. By contrast, (39)b is not a conventional construal of the scene and is a bit far away from the prototypical active construction. It denotes a stative picture of the event where neither a dynamic process nor an external causer is involved in this sentence. (39)a is said to represent dynamic mental scanning while (39)b the stative mental scanning.

With regard to (40), the difference between (40)a and (40)b rests in the perspective of the different participants of the event. (40)a is a normal, unmarked construal of the event from the perspective of the agent, so active is the natural choice of voice, whereas (40)b is a marked coding from the perspective of the patient, hence passive is the natural choice of voice. Since the focus is put on the active construction in this section, we do not go into detail about the voice differences here. These two sentences just lend support to how perspective difference can lead to voice difference in canonical simple sentences.

3   The Active Schema Based on Prototype and Its Extensions

Having discussing the prototypical model of the canonical active construction, we make comparison and contrast between the prototype and non-prototype to evaluate the diversity and complexity of the sentence construction in the category of active sentences, where action chain and force dynamic models are applied to judge deviations in the active construction. In addition, we explain the differences of these active constructions by using the theory of construal where normal construal and unconventional construal are assessed three-dimensionally; that is, through specificity, prominence, and perspective. With a firm foundation of general information, now it is high time to build the schema of the active voice at the clausal level.

As mentioned earlier, cognitive grammarians claim that grammar is symbolic in nature. To be concrete, grammar and lexicon form a continuum residing exclusively in assemblies of symbolic structures. It is clear that active construction is not a single symbolic unit but a complex symbolic unit that involve the process of composition and integration.

According to Langacker (2008b: 161), a symbolic structure (Σ) consists in the pairing of a semantic structure (S) and a phonological structure (P), as in Figure 30 (a). As illustrated in (b), a more elaborate symbolic structures can be formed by combining one symbolic structure with another to form a symbolic assembly, a process which is illustrated as [Σ1] + [Σ2] = [Σ3]. More complicated symbolic structures can be formed by combining [Σ3] with another symbolic structures as shown in (c) and illustrated as [Σ3] + [Σ4] = [Σ5].

Following the above analysis, it is obvious that active construction is a complex symbolic structure that consists of several components. In addition, as we said earlier, a schema is more abstract than a prototype concerning categorization. Through schematization, a commonality inherent in the grammatical structure and multiple experiences are supposed to be extracted. Then let us see how to generate the schema of the active construction by combining the semantic structure and the phonological structure together.

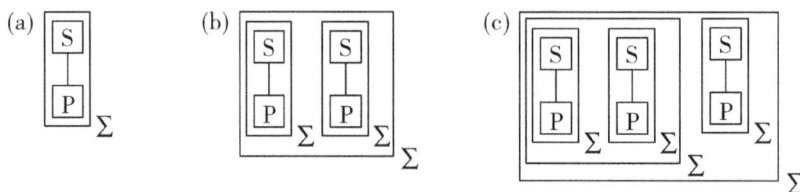

Figure 30   The Formation of Symbolic Structures (Langacker 2008b)

Based on the above analysis, we arrive at the conclusion that active construction is a symbolic assembly that consist of three simple symbolic units [as shown in Figure 31(b)],

Σ1, Σ2, and Σ3, respectively, each of which designates a combination of semantic and the phonological structure [as shown in Figure 31(a)] . To make it concrete, the schema of active construction can be sketched as in Figure 31(c). As can be seen, the basic schema of the actives consists of the two nominal participants and a verb that takes the default form (or unmarked) and profiles a process. There is an interaction between the two participants.

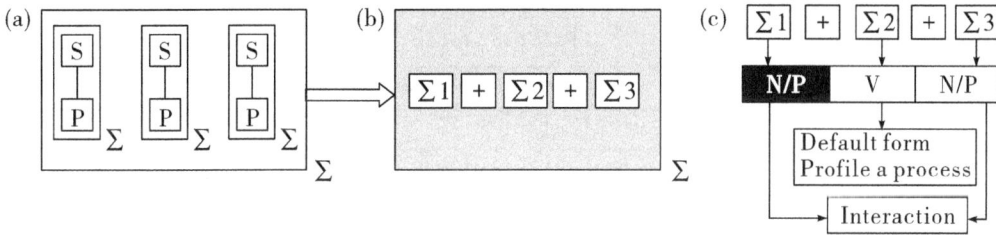

Figure 31   The Schema of the Active Constructions

4   Proposed Sketch of the Active Cognitive Model

Since the schema of active construction is abstract and the prototype of the active construction can only serve as an idealized cognitive model of the active construction, our understanding of active construction seems to still show in a broken way. To bridge the gap between general understanding and real conceptualization, we generate the complete mind-map we should have as an advanced learner of English.

As can be seen from Figure 32, the active is not a simple and clear grammatical category that can be accessed effortlessly. It is complex and varies in diverse ways. The prototypical effect can be clearly seen in the category. To get a typical prototype of an active construction, we have to go through some procedures.

First, we eliminate interrogative, negative, and imperative sentences and select a declarative, affirmative and realis sentence as the basic level representation. Next, we extract a simple sentence from among complex sentences and compound sentences. The individual components of the sentences are analyzed to reach the respective features of the subject, verb and object and their corresponding role archetypes. We find that the subject and object are not confined to one role but, on the contrary, show various deviations. The concrete perfective verb in the physical domain can serve as the prototypical verb while the verb in the physical domain and social domain can also illustrate the active voice in an abstract way. The prototype can be regarded as the idealized cognitive model of the active which shows discrete features of the active while the non-prototypical instantiations flesh out the active category and display the continuous feature among the members of the active category. The schema of the active voice offers an abstract picture of the active category, but it is not enough to direct real practice in grammar. Therefore, a cognitive model can be conductive in one way or another.

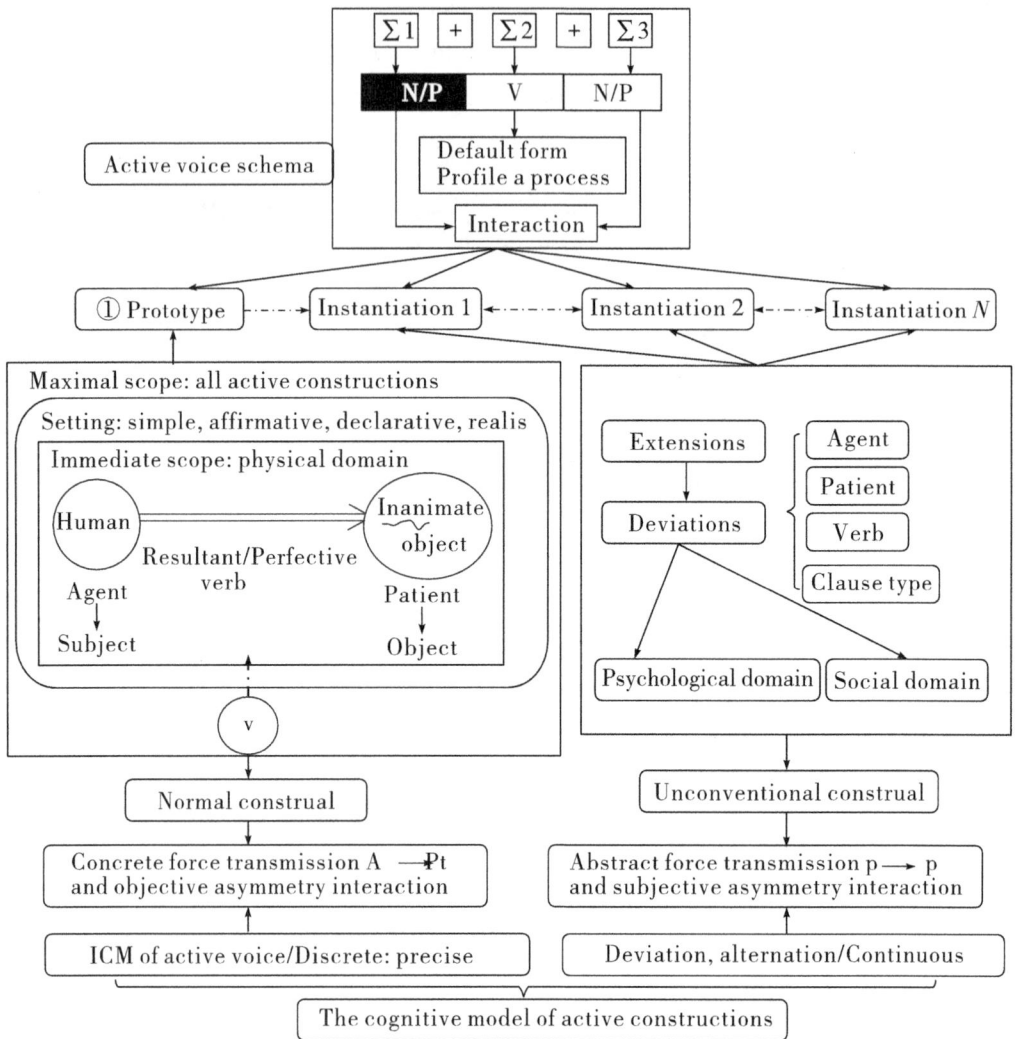

Figure 32 The Cognitive Model of the Active Constructions

5 Summary

To sum up, in this chapter, efforts have been made to investigate the prototype and non-prototype in the active category at the clausal level. On the one hand, we see that the active category is far more complicated than most grammar books have presented. The traditional definition of the active is far from being satisfactory.

As a category, the members within the active show great variation, though they share some features with the prototype, the qualities of the membership as an active   construction are still fuzzy. Only the prototype can typify very feature of the active, while those non-prototypes tend to display continuous feature rather than discrete features of the category. It provides further evidence of the notion that variations in language data do not always fall neatly into a simple grammatical system. Precision and fuzziness are not binary, there are always middle spaces between them. On the other hand, it is argued that the active is most essential member of the voice category in English. It always serves as the default and unmarked member of the voice category in English. In the following chapters, the active voice is taken as a reference point for other voice types to adjust their focus of attention and perspective. Comparisons and contrasts are made between the active voice and other voice types to show the continuous features of the voice category.

VI

The Fuzzy Features Shown in the Categorization of Passive Constructions and Their Cognitive Model

In this chapter, we endeavor to solve the following issues: (i) to conduct an overview of the passive voice category and determine the prototype by resorting to the traditional grammar and pedagogical grammar; (ii) to characterize the semantic, syntactic and pragmatic features of the prototypical passive by resorting to the patterns of the force dynamic model and the construal model of active construction, especially the models of action chain and canonical events; (iii) to discuss the non-prototype members of the passive voice and to show the deviations of membership and overlaps with active voice; (iv) to generalize a schema of passive voice construction and (v) to sketch a cognitive model of passive construction.

1   The Passive Prototype and Its Discrete Characterization

To better understand and account for the prototype of passive construction, it is instructive to view it against the background of the comprehensive passive system in English. Following the prototype theory, it is natural to observe that the category of passive voice consists of several members that are represented by the prototype and organized by family resemblance.

1.1   Personal Passive and Impersonal Passive

According to the previous discussion, passive constructions in English fall into two distinct groups. One is the personal passive which is identified as the conventional pattern of passive construction applying to transitive verbs. The other is the impersonal passive, which is defined as an informal and unconventional model of passive construction accessible to an intransitive use of the verb in the passive voice. In English, the former is universally used while the latter confines its uses only to verbs of perception, such as *think*, *say*, *know*, *presume*, *believe*, *report*, *consider* and *hope*. In addition, the two types of voice construction have structural differences. In (1)a and (1)b are typical active and passive constructions respectively. In (2)a is a complex active construction that has two passive transformations; (2)b is a normal one where the verb is often followed by a to-infinitive form while (2)c is the impersonal passive where it is used as the subject.

(1) a. The workers build houses.

   b. Houses are built by the workers.

(2) a. People say that girls are afraid of spiders.

   b. Girls are said to be afraid of spiders. (Personal passive)

   c. It is said that girls are afraid of Spiders. (Impersonal passive)

Obviously, the personal passive is the default passive construction in many grammar books and in the research. To determine the prototype of the passive, it is instructive to resort to the research of traditional and pedagogical grammar on the personal passive system. Though their notion of the passive is incompatible with the concept we maintain in this study, the research tends to address the most essential part of the passive in English and undoubtedly render assistance to our present discussion.

1.2   In Terms of Formal Features

Given that, let us first see how those grammarians define the passive voice in advance. According to Jespersen (1933: 85), the English passive is formed with an auxiliary, generally *be* (but often also *get* or *become*) and a past participle. As discussed by Svartvik (1966: 4), the term passive is used for all sentences which have verb combinations of be (or auxiliaries commutable with *be*) and a past participle. Another definition comes from Quirk et al. (1985: 159), who hold that a *true* passive clause is one whose VP contains a combination of be or get and a past participle. Though applying the label "passive" only to clauses or sentences whose main verb is a passive past participle fails to account for the whole picture of the passive category, it sheds light on a general understanding of basic passive form that helps to facilitate our ideation of a passive prototype.

In addition to the definition, let us take a look at the general classification of passive construction presented by some pedagogical grammar books.

Biber et al. (1999) categorizes the passive not only according to whether the agent is expressed or not, but also based on the construction where it occurs. The former one, in which the agent is expressed in a by phrase, is called a long passive and the opposite is called a short passive. The latter one can be classified as passive in finite construction, as in (3)a, and passive in non-finite construction, as in (3)b.

(3) a. Andy may be adopted or something like that.

    b. Let us look at an example given by Ballieul et al.

(Biber et al.1999: 936)

Parrott (2000) claims that there are two distinct types of passive construction: standard constructions and causative constructions. He holds that much attention should be paid to the standard passive in which object, two-object, and object-complement verbs can be used, as in (4)a. The causative passive, in which we use only object verbs, can be introduced when learners are already confident in using standard passive constructions, as exemplified in (4)b.

(4) a. Our car was/got broken into.

    b. We have had/got our car repaired.

Barry (2002) categorizes the passive according to whether the subject of the corresponding active clause is expressed or not. This point is illustrated in (5).

(5) a. The child was bitten by the dog.

    b. Her car was wrecked in the accident.

(Barry 2002: 139)

(5a) is defined as a full passive in which the subject of the corresponding active clause is expressed as the object of the preposition *by* while (5)b may be called a truncated passive because the subject of the corresponding active clause is left unexpressed.

Larsen-Freeman and Mariann (2016) classify the passive according to the use of various auxiliary verbs in their grammar book for English language teachers. In addition to the prototypical auxiliary verb *be* in Be-passives, *get* and *have* are also mentioned in the causative passive constructions. Let us consider the following sentences:

(6) a. Paul McCartney was knighted by the queen.

    b. Did Bruno get arrested? No, he didn't even get caught.

    c. Mary had her purse snatched.

(Larsen-Freeman & Mariann 2016: 352-355)

(6a) is a default passive with the helping auxiliary verb *be* serving as a prototype. In (6)b, *get* is an alternative to *be* though it is not an auxiliary at all by most syntactic criteria. *Have* is also a possible candidate for a passive auxiliary as is shown in (6)c, where *have* is experiential rather than causative.

A look at the traditional categorization of passives reveals that a lot of grammarians (Sweet 1892; Jespersen1933; Svartvik 1966; Visser 1973) may regard "Be (get)+V-en" as the only passive form in English. Though their notion of passive is problematic in some way, it is unquestionable that the Be+V-en construction is the prototype of the passive category.

On the other hand, a small minority of grammarians (Parrott 2000, Larsen-Freeman & Mariann 2016) count Get+(NP)+V-en and Have+NP+V-en as passive constructions though "get" and "have" are not necessarily real auxiliary verbs in that they represent the conceptual fuzziness between the causative and passive voices. However, one thing needs to be noted here is that for the sake of our argument that every category should be considered according to the discrete features it possesses, and so we put the causative passive aside for later discussion.

Following the overwhelming majority of grammarians' views, however, it seems natural for us to tacitly assume that the [Be+V-en] construction is the prototype of the passive category as it exemplifies the most frequently used member and the best and clearest example of the passive category. However, the [Be+V-en] construction is not self-supporting in being a completely unproblematic prototype due to its variations in forms.

As we discussed earlier, there are different degrees of passivization within the subcategory of the [Be+V-en] construction. Both Quirk et al. (1985) and Palmer (1987) have provided some evidence for it. Since we have examined the deviations of the [Be+V-en] construction in Chapter IV, we only recapitulate the five examples of it here.

(7) a. The violin was made by my father.

b. This difficulty can be avoided in several ways.

(Quirk et al. 1985: 167)

(8) a. He was embarrassed by her actions.

b. The problem is very complicated.

c. They were married for many years.

(Palmer 1987: 86-88)

Following Quirk et al. (1985), (7)a and (7)b are true passives in that they have a direct active-passive correlation. The difference between the two is that the former has an expressed personal agent, but the latter does not. Thus, (7)a can be defined as an agentful passive, whereas (7)b can be identified as an agentless passive.

As maintained by Palmer (1987), in sentences like those in (8), it seems that (8)a has a corresponding active sentence yet it manifests adjectival features; hence it is a semi-passive in nature. (8)b is regarded as a pseudo-passive in that the *V-en, complicated*, is wholly adjectival. (8)c stands for the statal passive in that the *V-en, married*, also has some adjectival functions and indicates the state of the event.

Considering Quirk et al.'s (1985) and Palmer's (1987) classifications, we can assume that the agentful true passive should serve as the prototype of the [Be+V-en] construction category as well as the prototype of the entire passive category.

1.3   In Terms of Role Archetypes and Composite Verbs

Having settled the issue of selecting a prototype of the passive, the focus should be shifted to generate the characteristics of the passive in contrast to the default voice. When we come to analyze the components of every single agentful true passive, further evidence shows that the internal structure of the agentful true passive is as complicated as the internal structure of active constructions. Therefore, to generate the features of the typical features of an agentful true passive, it is necessary to make a contrast to the prototypical active construction and to see what changes occur while transforming to a passive construction from an active construction. Just like the active prototype, we put our attention on the most basic level of passive sentences, namely, the affirmative, declarative and realis simple sentences. Consider the following examples:

(9) a. Lora broke the plate.

   b. The plate was broken by Lora.

(10) a. Terry ate the apple.

   b. The apple was eaten by Terry.

As can be seen above, (9)a and (10)a are prototypical active constructions where the agents are a third-person human who can initiate a volitional action. The objects are inanimate concrete things which interact with the agent and experience some internal change. The verbs *break* and *eat* are concrete perfective verbs that profile typical action processes. In contrast, (9b) and (10)b are true agentful passive constructions that function as corresponding counterparts of (9)a and (10)a. Having active correspondence hence can be taken as one essential feature of a prototypical passive.

In terms of form, the original patient in the (a) sentences is promoted to the subject position. The default verb form is transferred to the *V-en* past participle and the agent is demoted to be oblique object of the preposition *by*. Having the auxiliary *be*, the *V-en* past participle (verbal), and the phrase [By+Agent NP] are three other essential properties of the agentful true passive.

The above essential features seem to fit comfortably to the characterization of the prototype of the passive clauses. However, Langacker (1991b: 127) explains the rough synonymy, while sentence pairs such as (9)a and (10)b have the same composite structure, these are arrived at by different compositional paths.

In addition to this, Langacker (1991b:127) claims that three grammatical morphemes—*V-en (perfect participle)*, *the passive be* and *By-phrases*—are meaningful and figure actively into the semantic structure of passive expressions, contributing to their semantic distinctness from the corresponding actives. These three morphemes show variations in different contexts. To arrive at the prototype, it is essential to evaluate the very nature of these morphemes in passive constructions. Let us look at how these morphemes behave in the clauses in turn. In Langacker's (1991) opinion, there are three variations of the perfect participle, as exemplified in (11).

(11) a. Janice is gone. (Langacker 1991b: 129)

   b. The cathedral is totally destroyed.

(Langacker 1991b: 130)

   c. The infield was covered with a tarp (in five minutes).

(Langacker (1991b: 132)

   d. The infield was covered with a tarp (all morning).

(Langacker (1991b:132)

The sentences (11)a to (11)c instantiate three variations of *V-en* respectively. Identified as [$PERF_1$], (11)a demonstrates the perfective participle that is purely aspectual in nature. To be exact, the V-en *gone* manifests the final state in the process where the single participant is taken as the base on which only the final state is profiled, though its trajector experiences some changes. The profile indicates that [$PERF_1$] is a type of adjective that reveals a stative relation rather than the verb. Alternatively, in (11)b, the V-en *destroyed* is defined as [$PERF_2$] that elicits the conception of a change of state or location. It is said that [$PERF_2$] is more complicated than [$PERF_1$] due to the fact that its base incorporates a two-participant process and whose trajector exerts a force that incurs the change in its landmark. Both the [$PERF_1$] and [$PERF_2$] profile only the final state resulting from the change and take the participant that experience changes as the trajector. What make them different from each other is that [$PERF_1$] is applied to intransitive verbs that denote a stative relation while [$PERF_2$] fits apparently to transitive verbs.

By contrast, (11)c elucidates [$PERF_3$] that manifests the feature of *V-en* in a passive construction. Contrast can be made between (11)c and (11)d, which is another example of [$PERF_2$]. As can be seen, the *V-en* in both the two sentences combines with transitive stems and occur in constructions with *be*. The time scale is added to differentiate between the two. Apparently, (11)d only designates the resultant state whereas (11)c is processual in a passive form in that it conveys all the states within a process as it unfolds.

The next morpheme we address here is *the passive be*. It goes without saying that the form *be* is omnipresent in English grammar. Just like the perfect participle, it has many variations, some of which are exemplified below. Langacker (2004) lays emphasis on two variants of *be* and instantiates them as be_1 *and* be_2.

(12) a. Diana is attractive.

   b. The windshield is cracked. ([PERF$_1$])

(Langacker 2004: 202)

   c. This car is undoubtedly stolen. ([PERF$_2$])

(Langacker 2004: 202)

   d. We were attacked by bandits ([PERF$_3$])

(Langacker (1991b: 135)

(12)a is a typical example of *be* used in the basic or standard way, that is, be_1. Be_1 tends to combine with atemporal structures such as adjectives, prepositional phrases, and predicate nominatives, and provides them with the temporal extension and sequential scanning needed. As can be seen, *attractive* in (12)a is a stative relation whereas *be attractive* functions as an imperfective process eligible for heading a finite clause. Be_1 is also said to derive imperfective processes from the stative expressions formed by PERF$_1$ and PERF$_2$, as illustrated by *be cracked* and *be stolen* in (12)b and (12)c, respectively. By contrast, *be* in (12)d typifies another variant be_2, which combines particularly with a passive participle, namely [PERF$_3$]. Its functions are to reimpose sequential scanning, thus deriving a processual expression that can serve as a passive clausal head (Langacker 2004: 206).

The next concept worth our attention is the *By-phrase*. It is evident that English passives frequently lack a *By-phrase*, so it is argued that *By-phrases* are not an intrinsic part of the English passive construction but it is meaningful. Consider sentences in (13):

(13) a. The willow tree is by the river.

   b. That sculpture is by Zúñiga.

   c. Bragging by officers will not be tolerated.

(Langacker 1991b: 139)

   d. The bread was made by his mother.

The *By-phrase* in (13)a indicates a stative relation in the spatial domain, which has concrete meaning and can be defined as byP_1 whereas in (13)b it designates the dynamic relationship between the process and resultant state, that is, the execution of an act, and can be identified as byP_2. In (13)c, *By-phase*, called byP_3 profiles the relationship between a reified activity and actor that is considered as being the source of that activity. As for the *By-phrase* in (13)d, it is the passive byP_4. Since it combines with the [$PERF_3$], it designates a stative relation with a specified landmark and a schematic trajector characterized as a complex atemporal relation (Langacker 1991b: 142).

Based on above analysis, we can make a preliminary judgement that the basic structure of the passive should be as follows:

Patient +Be_2+ $PERF_3$+By_4+ Agent

This rough judgement seems to take us one step closer to the prototype of passive construction. But if we take the variation of role archetype and verbs of the finite clause into account, we still need to narrow down the concepts of the patient, the verb, and the agent. In other words, we have to make the concept more concrete.

As we discussed above, the prototypical agent in the active voice should be highly affecting, whereas the prototypical patient highly affected. It is better for the verbs to denote a concrete action with perfective properties. These features can make the sentence have high transitivity thus be more salient in demonstrating the active function. This notion meets with Tsunoda's (1994) viewpoint. Sometimes affectedness is viewed as a prerequisite for the passivization of active clauses. Likewise, the prototypical role archetype of the patient and agent in the passive should have the similar features. The affectedness often indicates that the patient undergoes a change of state or is influenced by the force or energy transmitted from the agent. Accordingly, concrete, inanimate objects are easily affected, and, therefore, can serve easily as the subject of the passive construction. Agents which can instigate a volitional action are human. The perfective resultant verbs indicating a concrete action rather than a psychological or social activity should be taken as the prototype.

There actually is no derivational relationship between active clauses and passive clauses. As we mentioned earlier, construal offers alternatives for people to view the world by selecting different focus and specific perspectives. The interlocutors are able to profile different portions of the same action chain and produce diverse expressions. In Langacker's view, the passive construction is developed by observing the event from the angle of the patient. Based on these essential features, we attempt to analyse how these changes can be explained from two cognitive perspectives, namely the force-dynamic model and the construal model.

With regard to the force-dynamic model, let us first resort to the action chain and canonical event model to see how they affect the construction. As sketched in Figure 33, the subjects of (9a) and (10a) act as the head of force or energy while the object functions as the tail of the force that undergoes some internal change due to the asymmetry interaction between the agent and the patient. By contrast, the choice of subject, as in (9b) and (10b), runs directly counter to the pattern observed in the canonical event in the corresponding passive sentences, as illustrated in Figure 33. The tail of a profiled action chain is elevated to the status of trajector rather than the head. The action chain is completed and directs from the agent to the patient. It is viewer's perspective that is changed.

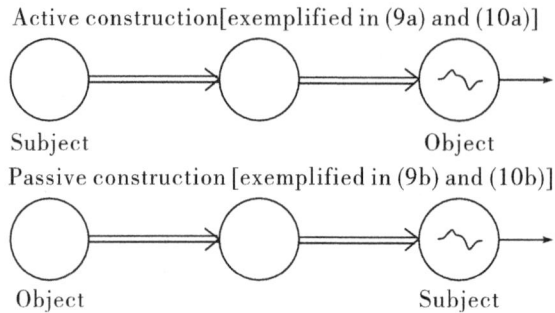

Figure 33   The Contrast Between Active and Passive in Terms of Action Chain

Following above line of thinking, we can adjust and flesh out the prototypical passive model by taking the canonical event model and active event model as the base. As can be seen in Figure 34, as in the active canonical event model, we take all the passive constructions at the clausal level as our maximal scope so as to get the prototypical model of the passive. First, we narrow our focus on the simple, affirmative and declarative personal passive sentences and form our setting for it is more salient in our cognition. These sentences also show various features, one of which is to denote the process in the physical domain as well as the abstract domain such as psychological, or social processes. As mentioned earlier, a concrete action in the physical domain is more salient and therefore it is natural to take it as the immediate scope.

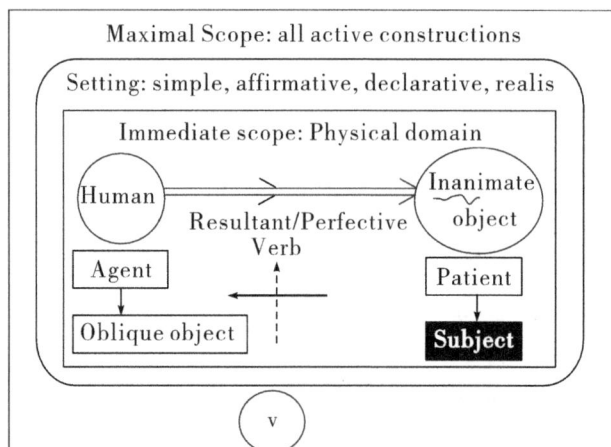

Figure 34   The Canonical Event Model of the Passive Constructions

The difference between an active event model and a passive event model is that the latter promotes the patient into the subject position and weakens the position of agent by putting it after the preposition *by*. Thus, the agent serves as the complement of *by*. Though the passive tends to be patient-focused, the causal force interactions remain as it is. However, the original transitive event is transferred into an autonomous event when the agent is removed from the focal prominent. The verb loses its ability to take a direct object, hence passivization is regarded as the process of detransitivization, as put in Givón (1994). In addition, the third person viewer changes vantage point from agent-orientation to patient-orientation.

1.4   Characterization of the Passive Prototype

In line with the above discussion, we can characterize the typical features of a passive prototype as follows:

(1) Semantic features.

a. A Prototypical passive construction profiles an action chain that involves two different participants: the agent and the patient. The patient, or terminus, is construed as the trajector while the head of action chain, the agent, is interpreted as the landmark, a role either left implicit or identified periphrastically, even though it lies upstream.

b. The viewer is observing the event from the perspective of patient and leaves the agent in the defocused position.

(2) Syntactic properties.

a. The patient is coded as the marked subject of the clause, which profiles the action chain while the agent is coded as the object of preposition in the oblique phrase.

b. The verb is morphosyntactically marked according to how a language speaker's construal denotes the action.

c. The morpheme Be_2 combining with $PERF_3$ form a verb phrase that codes the punctual, telic action, taking realis forms, and functioning as a passive clause head.

(3) Pragmatic Properties.

The typical passive tends to defocus the agent. It is always used when the receiver of the action is crucial, or when the agent is unknown or irrelevant. In addition, it is applied to indicate a softer, less authoritative tone by which the agent's responsibility can be diminished. In addition, it is used to express a professional, neutral, or objective tone that commonly occurs in scientific reports and instructions.

2   Passive Non-prototypes and Continuous Characterization

In contrast to the active construction, the extension of a prototype in the passive category seems to be trickier. There are five factors contributing to this trickiness. (i) As in the active construction, deviations in patient, agent and composite verb of the passive construction are one hundred percent certain. (ii) Not all Be+V-en passive constructions stay consistent with the prototype. (iii) The Get-passive is thought to be the second important passive in English, which diverges from the prototype syntactically as well as pragmatically. (iv) The prepositional passive is another non-prototype that needs to be taken seriously. (v) There are some overlapping areas between the active category and the passive category, where notional passives are another concern.

2.1 Deviation of the Role Archetype and Composite Verb in the Physical and Abstract Domains of the Be+V-en True Passive

Taking the above characteristics of prototype as the yardstick, we can deduce that (9b) and (10b) can be regarded as the prototype of the passive construction in that their subject acts as the patient that shows high affectedness while the agent that shows the high agentivity is demoted and serves as the object of oblique. In addition, the verbs denote perfective concrete action in the physical domain rather than an abstract notion. As we know, in the active construction, deviations from the prototype are shown in various ways since the subject, the object and the composite verb do not always stay consistent with the prototypical role archetype model or the verb type. In the same vein, the patients in the passive construction always display different degree of affectedness, the agents vary from human, to animal, and even to abstract concepts. And the composite verb selection ranges from concrete action verbs to the abstract verbs. Consider the following examples:

(14) a. This scarf was knitted by my grandmother.

b. The deer was chased by a bear.

c. The general was admired by the soldiers. (BNC)

d. This conclusion is hardly justified by the results.

(Quirk et al. 1985: 167)

Under our assumption, (14)a typifies the prototype of a passive in that the subject serves as the patient, which is an inanimate concrete thing that is highly affected, and the oblique object is a human who can initiate a highly volitional action. In addition, the verb *knit* is perfective and resultant, denoting a concrete action. By contrast, *chase* in (14)a also designates a concrete action but both the patient and the agent slightly diverge from the prototype. Contrastively, the verbs in (14)c and (14)d suggest an abstract notion where *admire* is a psychological verb expressing an emotional state, while *justify* is a verb for ideation performing a social function. The degree of deviation for the two sentences varies in that both the patient and agent in (14)c are human while both the patient and agent in (14)d are abstract notions. Hence, (14)d is more marginal than (14)c. The caveat is that these deviations in (14)b to (15)d often go unheeded in contrast to the other members within the category of Be+V-en structures due to the complexity of passive construction.

2.2   Deviations in the Be+V-en Passive Construction

In this section, our discussion falls into two parts. One is the gradient feature of the passivization. The other is the schema of Be+V-en passive.

2.2.1   Gradient Feature

As we mentioned earlier, within the Be+V-en passive category there are four other constructions which share similar syntactic features with the prototype while varying greatly semantically in their degrees of passivization, as shown in (15).

(15) a. The thieves were caught. (Agentless passive)

   b. He was very elated by his success. (Semi-passive)

   c. The room is very crowded. (Pseudo-passive)

   d. They are already divorced. (Statal passive)

(Palmer 1987: 78-89)

As the examples in (15) illustrate, there are combinations of Be+V-en that are definitely not true passives. This dovetails with the concept of passive gradience that suggests the existence of fuzzy category boundaries. (15)a instantiates a typical agentless passive in which the agent is omitted. Even so, the agentless passive is still much closer to the prototype since nearly 80% of English agentless passives involve a presupposed agent, as claimed by Givón (1979: 63). It is clear that (15)a has a corresponding active counterpart and *V-en* is definitely verbal. As for (15)b, it seems easy to transform it into an active construction: e.g. *His success elated him*, but the *V-en elated* appears to have adjectival features. It can represent the semi-passive whereas the *V-en* is somewhere in-between the verbal and adjectival. Concerning (15)c and (15)d, they diverge greatly from the prototype semantically. The former typifies the pseudo-passives in that the V-en *crowded* is adjectival for certain. One piece of supporting evidence it that the V-en *crowded* can be modified by intensifier *very*. The latter is a typical example of statal passives in that the adjectival feature of the *V-en divorced* can be affirmed by the modifier *already* which normally requires the perfect. As sketched in Figure 35 the gradience of passives shows the hierarchy inside the Be+V-en passive construction, that is, true passives (agentful and agentless)> semi-passive> psesudo-passives and statal passives, when taking the verbal feature as the sole standard. This evidence provides further support to the fuzzy feature within the passive category.

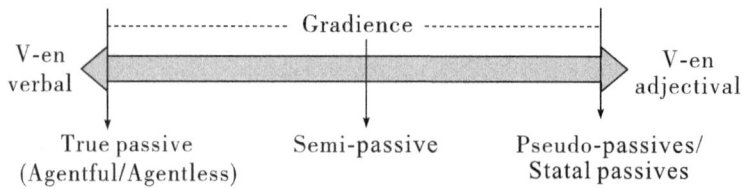

Figure 35 Gradient Feature of the Be+V-en Construction

2.2.2 The Schema of Be+V-en Passive

What calls for our special attention is that semantic deviation in the structure *Be+V-en* is not the only example of variation in the passive construction. The Get-passive construction is considered to be the second important passive construction that cannot be neglected. Due to differences in structure, it is better for us to sketch the schema of the Be+V-en first and then contrast it with the Get-passive.

As sketched in Figure 36, it is clear that the Be+V-en Passive construction is a symbolic assembly that consists of three complex symbolic units, Σ1, Σ2, and Σ3, respectively, signifying the complex of semantic structure and phonological structure. Like the active schema, there are two nominal participants: N/P1 and N/P2. Contrary to the active schema, the position of N/P1 and N/P2 is reversed and N/P combines with the *by* preposition and can be omitted in most cases. In addition, the Be+V-en replaces the default verb in the active and designates an atemporal relation. This V-en form exhibits the gradience feature ranged from verbal to adjectival.

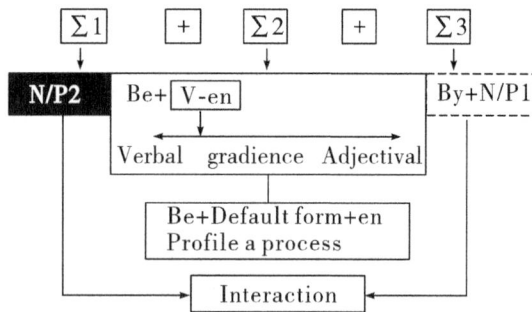

Figure 36 The Schema of the Be+V-en Passive Construction

2.3 Syntactic Deviation in Passive Construction

In this section, our discussion consists of two parts. For one, the syntactic deviation shown in Get+V-en construction is addressed. For another, the syntactic deviation exhibited in the prepositional passive is designated.

2.3.1 Get +V-en Construction

It is generally agreed that the Be-passive is the most established passive form of widespread use whereas the Get-passive, is a more recent innovation, appearing in written English at the end of 18th Century or earlier (Givón 1993), an up and coming candidate for a passive that is seen to have increased remarkably in frequency in written English in recent decades. Two natural questions come up here: (ⅰ) What are the similarities and differences between Be-passive and Get-passive? (ⅱ) Why has usage of the Get-passive become more common?

2.3.1.1   Difference between Get Passive and Be-Passive

To have a better understanding, let us go to the concrete examples. Consider sentences in (16):

(16) a. The child was killed (by a car).

b. The child got killed (by a car).

(Palmer 1987: 89)

Observing the two sentences in (16), it seems the Get-passive is very similar in its components with Be-passive. In contrast to the corresponding active—*A car killed the child*, both patients in (16)a and (16)b are put in the grammatical subjecthood and the demoted agents are optional, either omitted or appearing as the oblique object headed by the preposition *by*. For the verb *kill*, it is morphologically marked by the same perfect-participle form *killed*. These ostensible similarities seem to deceive most of us into believing they have the almost the same usage. In fact, they are very different from one another in many respects. Many contemporary grammarians (Quirk et al. 1985; Givón 1993; Collins 1996; Parrott 2000; Huddleston and Pullum 2002; Cowan 2008) have involved themselves in differentiating Be-passives from Get-passivse, and some common properties of the Get-passive are evolved by making comparisons with Be-passives. The main differences between the two types of passive are shown in the following aspects:

1. Morphosyntactic Differences: *Be* Versus *Get*, Auxiliary versus Non-Auxiliary.

It is easy to tell that having auxiliary is one of the most obvious properties of the Be-passive. As put by Quirk et al. (1985), the only matched contender for *be* is *get*. Though *get* seems to be an auxiliary, syntactically speaking, it shows great divergence when compared to *be* auxiliary (Haegeman 1985). Then, a natural question to ask here is that what properties does *get* have. Contrast the following sentence pairs:

(17) a. Was the child killed by a car?

b. *Got the child killed by a car?

c. Did the child get killed by a car?

The sentence labeled (17)a is a *yes/no* question that results from the application of a subject auxiliary inversion to a declarative passive sentence. However, the ungrammaticity of (17)b seems to designate that get is not auxiliary in a real sense since it cannot have a subject-auxiliary inversion in a yes/no question.

> (18) a. The child was not/wasn't killed (by a car).
> b. *The child got not/gotn't killed (by a car).
> c. The child didn't get killed by a car.

> (19) a. The child was not killed by a car, was he/she?
> b. *The child got killed by a car, gotn't he/she?
> c. The child didn't get killed by a car, did he/she?

> (20) a. The child was killed by the car, and the adult was __ too.
> b. *The child got killed by a car, and the adult got __ too.
> c. The child got killed by a car, and the adult did __ too.

As the sentences in (18) illustrate, the auxiliary *be* can form a negative construction by combining with not directly or showing in the form of abbreviation as in (18)a, whereas *get* does not have this property as in (18)b. Moreover, the auxiliary *be* itself or with negation not can be used to form tag-questions after the declarative sentence as in (19)a whereas *got* does not have this property as in (19)b. In addition, in some compound sentences, we tend to keep the auxiliary as it is, omitting the verb to avoid repetition, as in (20)a. However, *get* fails to pass this test too since the VP followed by *get* cannot be elided as shown in (20)b. It seems that we would struggle to identify *get* as auxiliary. However, if we observe from a different angle, it seems natural to take *get* as a lexical verb. In this way, we introduce the *do* auxiliary in all the ill-formed (b) sentences from (17) to (20), and we get the correct sentence form as shown in (17)c to (20)c.

All the evidence suggests that *get* is not an auxiliary verb but a lexical verb in terms of its syntactic features. Here it is instructive to take Gronemeyer's view since he gives us a reasonable compromise. It is suggested that *get* is only 'semi-grammaticalized' word that lies in between lexical verbs and genuine auxiliaries in that it is far more syntactic than most lexical verbs, both in meaning and distribution, while less grammatical than functional verbs (Gronemeyer 1999: 2).

2. Semantic and Pragmatic Properties.

a. In most cases Get-passives are found with dynamic verbs with causative meaning "denoting a resultative state."

As discussed above, being a half lexical verb, *get* is much more common regarded as a resulting copula that indicates a dynamic process in which an object reaches a specified state or condition differing from the initial state. This feature makes *get* hard to combine with perceptive or psychological verbs that describe a stative condition or durative process. Consider the following example:

(21) a. The captain was liked by the crew.

    b.* The captain got liked by the crew.

(22) a. The women haven't been seen or heard from in two weeks. (COCA)

    b. *The women haven't got seen or heard from in two weeks.

(23) a. Obviously, the manager is feared by most of the staff.

    b. *Obviously, the manager gets feared by most of the staff.

(Huddleston and Pullum 2002: 1442)

As can be seen, a verb of a process of affection such as *like* in (21), verbs of mental processes of perception such as *hear* or *see* in (22), and a verb of a process of emotion such as *fear* in (23) are incompatible with the Get-passive in that they can hardly denote an action like dynamic verbs. By contrast, the *be* auxiliary in a Be-passive is more tolerant of verb types other than dynamic verbs as shown in (21)a to (23)a.

In line with above analysis, it is said that the Get-passive tends to carry dynamic verbs while denoting the meaning of "reaching a resultative state". Then we can deduce that there exists a causative relation that elicits a resultative state. It seems that resultative feature is essential for the Get-passive, just as put by Vanrespaille (1991: 97), who claims that resultativeness is present in virtually every instance of the get +V-en constructions. In addition, Downing (1996:185) argues that causative element is equally fundamental.

(24) a. He got hurt on the pitch.

    b. He was hurt on the pitch.

(Adapted from Downing 1996: 184)

As can be seen in above examples, (24)a denotes a resultative state where X causes him to be hurt whereas (24)b indicates a relational state where X hurt him or he is in a hurting condition.

In contrast with the features of causative meaning and action-denotation, the resultative constraint seems to be more essential in the Get-passive, as exemplified in (25) and (26).

(25) a.*The newspaper got read by the journalist.

    b. The newspaper was read by the journalist.

(26) a. The robber got caught in one hour.

b.*The robber got caught for one hour.

In (25), the verb *read* is a dynamic verb for sure, but we cannot say that *the journalist* caused the newspaper to be read, as in (24)a, in that no resulting state from the action is shown. Being resultative means being telic, which is why the durative preposition in (25)b it is awkward whereas in (26)a is natural.

b. In terms of agentivity, the Be-passive is agent-oriented whereas the Get-passive is subject-oriented.

As we discussed above, agentivity, involving the agentive role and the matter of control or intent in a situation, is a core feature of transitivity. It is generally claimed by many grammarians (Givón 1993; Collins 1996; Parrott 2000; Huddleston and Pullum 2002) that agentivity plays a significant part in differentiating the Be-passive and the Get-passive. In the Be-passive, as we know, though it is demoted to a peripheral position or even omitted in most cases, the agent is vested with purpose and control over the event. In contrast, in the Get-passive it is the promoted patient that retains agentive control. To better understand this feature, let us take a look at the examples in the following sentences.

(27) a. John was shot by Mary deliberately.

b. John got shot by Mary deliberately.

(Givón 1993: 67).

As can be seen, adding the purpose adverb *deliberately* in the two types of passive can help us strengthen the understanding. (27)a can be interpreted as *Mary* acts deliberately. (27)b can be understood as *John* acts deliberately. On the other hand, the Get-passive in (27)b implies that the subject *John* involves himself in the event and is assumed to take responsibility in some cases, as in (28).

(28) a. *Mary decided to be arrested (by the police).

b. Mary decided to get arrested (by the police).

(29) a. She was found crying in the room.

b. *She got found crying in the room.

Here we can see that the ungrammaticality of (28)a is due to the misinterpretation of the agentive role in the sentence. *To be arrested* implies that *Mary's* being arrested is the result of a decision induced by the agent (the police) that carries out the action of arresting, so it is illogical for *Mary* to make the decision.

Unlike the Be-passive, the Get-passive signals the intent or control of the surface subject *she*, in the case of (29)b. However, *crying in the room* has the connotation of no such intent or control in the part of surface subject, so a contradiction occurs in terms of meaning.

Following the above line of analysis, we can arrive at the conclusion that subject of the Get-passive is a causal factor in promoting the event, and the intent, control, and responsibility of and for the action are vested in them. Then it is natural to deduce that, in most cases, contrary to the Be-passive as in (30)a, the human subject is more preferable for the Get-passive, as in (30)b.

(30) a. A house can be built of stone, brick or clay.

b. *A house can get built of stone, brick or clay.

(Givón 1993b: 68)

c. Get-passives are characteristically used in clauses involving adversity or benefit.

As we discussed above, Get-passives tend to be subject-oriented. The subject-oriented preference usually involves the favorability of the process for the subject-referent. That is to say, the Get-passive is often employed to reflect the attitude of the speaker towards the event described in the clause (Hatcher1949; Chappel 1980; Quirk et al.1985; Downing 1996). In Hatcher's view, the favorability for the subject can reflect two types of event description: fortunate consequences or unfortunate consequences. Chappell (1980) develops Hatcher's view and classifies Get-passive into two types: adversative and beneficial, as in the following expressions.

(31) a. Kim got sacked.

b. My watch got stolen.

(Huddleston and Pullum 2002:1442)

(32) a. Kim got promoted.

b. My letter got published.

(Huddleston and Pullum 2002:1442)

(33) a. Fred got examined by a specialist.

b. The mail gets delivered every day.

(Cowan 2008: 405)

In terms of favorability for the subject-referent and speakers' attitude, the Get-passive in (31)

141

is used to talk about events that influence the subject in an adverse way. That is, the event of sacking and stealing is inherently unfortunate or unfavorable to the ones (*Kim and the owner of the watch*) who undergo it. On the contrary, the events in (32), promotion and publication, are comparatively beneficial to the ones (*Kim and the writer of the letter*) who experience the process. However, for the expressions in (33), neither adversity nor the benefit is implicated for the subject-referent in the examples in that it is natural for the speaker to have the neutral attitude toward the event. Just as was investigated by Collins, it is shown that, of the 291 central get-passives collected in the corpus, 196 (67.4 percent) conveyed an adversative implicature, 68 (23.4 percent) conveyed a beneficial implicature, and the remaining 27 (9.3 percent) were neutral (Collins 1996: 52).

    d. The Get-passive tends to be avoided in formal style.

The pragmatic discussion of the Get-passive has never stopped. Quirk et al. (1985) claim that the Get-passive is avoided in formal style, and even in informal English it is far less frequent than the Be-passive. A lot of research has been done by means of the corpus. It suggests that usage of the Get-passive has increased in a steady manner from 1990 to present whereas the frequency of the Be-passive is gradually decreasing. A survey of the literature (Collins 1996, Carter and McCarthy 1999, Huddleston and Pullum 2002) reveals that the Get-passive is subject to stylistic and regional variation in contemporary English and there is a tendency for the Get-passive to rise in spoken or informal registers in both American and British English in recent decades.

2.3.1.2   Classification of Get+V-en Construction and Selection of the Prototype

What calls for our special attention here is that the internal structure of the Get+V-en construction doesn't seem to be so clear. Taking a look at Get-passives, we can see that the Get-passive exemplifies itself by taking the configuration Nominal Phrase+Get+V-en. But if we take this form as the only yardstick to gauge the get passive, we will get into trouble in that there are not only the typical Get-passive of the definite core status in this category but also some periphery members whose status are marginal though they can satisfy this formal requirement.

The notion of fuzziness in the category surely provides some evidence for this feature. That means that we have to differentiate the Get-passive from other Get+V-en constructions. As claimed by Quirk et al. (1985), just like the Be-passive, there are also passive gradients in Get+V-en construction. They hold that Get+V-en construction mainly falls into two groups: one is the passive sentence, as in (34)a, which can be construed as a typical Get-passive. The other is a copular sentence, as in (34)b, which can be taken as pseudo-passive, for it could not be expanded by an agent.

(34) a. This story eventually got translated into English.

b. I have to get dressed before eight o'clock.

Based on Quirk et al.'s (1985) discussions, Collins (1996) maintains that Get-passives form a sort of *fuzzy set* by conducting a more detailed survey on the classification of Get+V-en construction. To be exact, the prototypical Get-passive is for sure at the core of the set, but beyond it, there are other members having gradually fewer properties in common with the prototype and merging gradually with other constructions at the boundary. Under Collins's (1996) assumption, there are five types of Get-passives featuring the gradient from the prototype to the marginal members. To get a better understanding, let us resort to sentences as follows:

(35) a. Mary got asked to work overtime by her manager.

b. Chandler got bitten by the peacock at the zoo.

(36) a. The living room window got broken.

b. Davis got punished for his ill conduct.

(37) a. The beetle children got bored with peering into the distance. (BNC)

b. We always got excited over the journey.

(38) a. He got dressed quickly and let himself out of the house. (COCA)

b. They get washed whenever I can be bothered...(COCA)

(39) a. The couple got married in 2007 after dating for two years. (COCA)

b. They got engaged.

(40) a. His explanation is getting complicated.

(Cowan 2008: 405)

b. We're not going to get fossilized...(COCA)

(41) a. I have to get accustomed to the climate here.

b. Your brain will get used to this way of thinking.

As Collins (1996) demonstrates, a couple of factors are of critical importance whenwe rank the examples within Get-passive: (i) availability of an agent-phrase, (ii) the semantic properties of the agent, (iii) the stative/dynamic meaning of the lexical verb, and (iv) their potential relatedness to a propositionally equivalent active clause.

Considering these factors, the sentences in (35) are naturally categorized as central Get-passives in that presence of the agent enables them to easily satisfy the criteria of having a propositionally equivalent active clause. In addition, the lexical verbs in the sentences are clearly dynamic verbs. One thing needs to be noted here, that is, the rank of (35)a and (35)b are slightly different despite the fact that they both fulfill the requirements of a central Get-passive in that the notion of agentivity and volitionality fit more comfortably and adequately for a *human* than for a *peacock*. In contrast, sentences in (36) do not have overt agents. As a result, the subject of the active counterpart is undetermined. Accordingly, they rank lower in priority regarding the availability of the agent, but we can still take them as central Get-passives even though they are agentless. For one thing, we can infer or retrieve their agents pragmatically to some extent. For another, both Get-passive and Be-passive have been found to occur more frequently without an overt agent (Svartvik 1966), partially due to the agent being unknown or not worthy of mention.

In Collins's (1996) view, the examples in (37) can be classified as psychological Get-passives. This subclass seems to cater to the notion of a semi-passive when we discuss the Be+V-en construction. It is easy to see that the lexical verbs bored and excited display a mixture of verbal and adjectival properties. On the one hand, it seems that we can arrive at their active analogues easily (e.g. *Peering into the distance bored the beetle child*; *The journey always excited us*.) On the other hand, they can be modified by very or rather to show their gradable adjectival features (e.g. *very bored/ excited; rather bored/excited*). In addition, it is easy to see that in both (a) and (b) the agent phrases are introduced by *with* and *over* respectively rather than *by*. The reason for this is that the psychological processes are initiated by agent-phrases denoting various mental phenomena rather than the concrete physical existence.

The sentences in (38) and (39) can be classified as *reflexive* get-passives and *reciprocal* Get-passives respectively. As can be seen, from these examples, the reflexive meaning and reciprocal meaning are inherent, without any overt reflexive or reciprocal syntactic manifestations. They are semantically different from their intransitive counterparts, such as *he dressed, they washed, the couple married*, and *they engaged* or transitive constructions with overt reflexive or reciprocal features such as, *he dressed himself, they washed themselves, the couple got themselves married*, and *they got themselves engaged*.

Quirk et al. (1985: 161) accept that that there is an affinity between such sentences and central passives, though they repudiate the membership of these examples as Get-passive because it is argued that they cannot be expanded by an agent and the participial is stative in sense.

On the one hand, the lexical verbs, *washed, dressed, married*, and *engaged* have the features of being verbs for they undergo a process of *washing, dressing, marrying* and *engaging*. Huddleston (1984: 445) notes that, a *reflexive* Get-passive and a *reciprocal* Get-passive will be excluded if we add an agent. This feature echoes to one of the significant features of a central Get-passive, that is, subject favorability for the subject-referent and the speakers' initiative and responsibility. One feature is that participials such as *dressed, washed, married,* and *engaged* are not gradable. For example, you cannot say, *very dressed, or*quite married. Also, it seems impossible to coordinate them with a central adjective (e.g. They *got washed and ready*.) However, it seems that the status of *reflexive* Get-passive and *reciprocal* Get-passive is ambivalent due to its vagueness in predicting the adjectival or verbal features. But here we also believe that they belong to the semi Get-passive since their participle is somewhere at the boundary of verbal and adjectival.

As for the sentences in (40), it is clear that they are adjectival Get-passives. *Get* here can be replaced by *become* and it is a copular for sure. *Complicated* in (40)a is stative and gradable and *fossilized* in (40)b indicates a result of state from a process where no agent can exert any influence on it. Neither sentences has an active counterpart and so they can be construed as the second most marginal member of the class. It fits comfortably under the rubric of pseudo-passive in that it only possesses the superficial form rather than the actual passive features.

As shown in (41), the expressions *get accustomed to and get used to* seem to be the Get-passive superficially, but these are only formulaic expressions evolving historically and turning into a conventional collocation in language where the relationship of *get* and *V-en* is not easy to designate. Hence, it is regarded as the most marginal member of the Get-passive.

In line with the above analysis, we can arrive at the conclusion that fuzzy features can be clearly seen in the subcategory of Get-passive. There is a gradience or continuum from the central passive to adjectival formulaic passive as Figure 37 shows. Though their similar superficial forms oblige us to consider them as the passive, their status varies. The central Get-passive shows discrete features within the subcategory Get-passive and can be regarded as the prototype. When it is compared with the Be-passive, it loses its prototype position and shows continuous features with agentful true passive within Be-passive category beyond the domain. The word *get* is gradually changing from a lexical verb to a copular gradually.

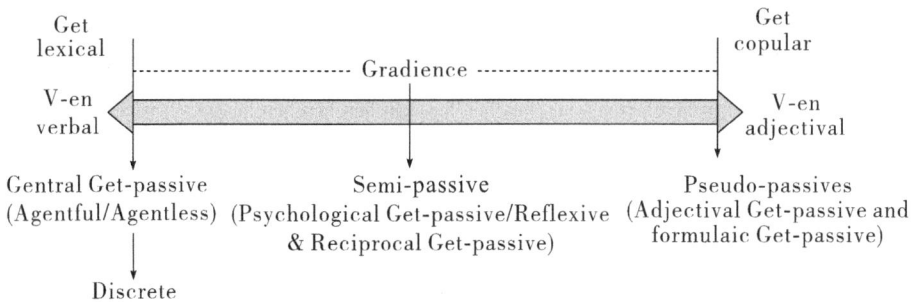

Figure 37   Gradient Features of the Get+V-en Constructions

Based on the discussion of the general features and classification of Get-passive above, let us see how the schema of Get-passive is different from that of be-passive as follows:

As can be seen in Figure 38, except for the syntactic deviation from Be-passive, Get-passive has more restrictions semantically and syntactically. However, it is the expedient alternative for adjusting our communicative strategy in our daily communication. In terms of action chain, there is an interaction between the agent and patient, but this interaction is dim due to the fact that the focus of the action is always on the subject's affectedness rather than agent's intentionality. Therefore, the agent in the Get-passive is more demoted in contrast to the Be-passive, whereas the patient is more elevated. In addition, the continuous features are clearly shown in the category of Get-passive. The prototype central Get-passive denotes an action with causative meaning with its focus on the result of the predicate and how its subject is affected adversely or beneficially as result of the action. For the non-prototypes, the action is gradually turning into the resultative state and even formulized as idiomatic expression in English.

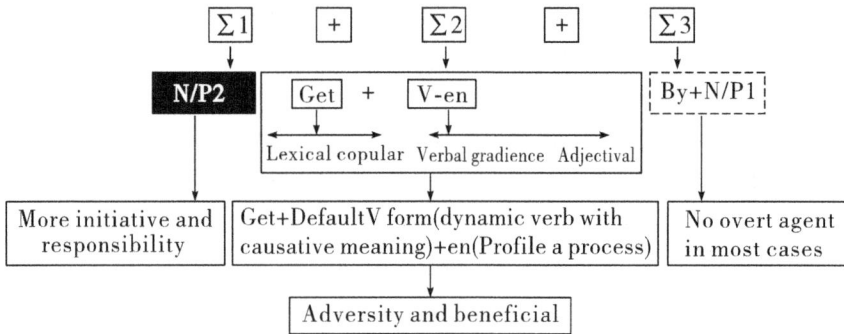

Figure 38   The Schema of the Get+V-en Constructions

2.3.2   Prepositional Passive

The sentences discussed in active construction in the last chapter all had objects. In most cases, it is the object of verb that is promoted to the subject position with passivization, as illustrated in (42)a where *the town hall* functions as the direct object in the monotransitive clause and appears as the subject in the passive construction. (43)a is a ditransitive clause where both a direct object (*this necklace*) and an indirect object (*me*) are included. (43)b promotes the indirect object to the topic position whereas in (43)c the direct object is the focus, but it is accepted in limited scope.

(42) a. The fire damaged the town hall.

   b. The town hall was damaged by the fire.

(43) a. My mother gave me this necklace.

b. I was given this necklace by my mother.

c. This necklace was given me by my mother.

Despite the variations, the above examples clearly imply that passivization is highly related to the transitivity of the verb. It seems that only those transitive verbs or verbs that have objects are possible candidates for the passive.

However, the occurrence of a prepositional passive in English, as exemplified in (44)b, seems to be an occasion of surprise for most EFL learners. Intransitive verbs aren't expected to have objects, so how can these verbs be used transitively by combining them with prepositions?

(44) a. People laughed at Allen for his remarks.

b. Allen was laughed at for his remarks by the people.

It is such an unorthodox structure but it is comparatively common usage in English by the native speakers. Some grammarians (Svartvik 1966; Couper-Kuhlen 1979; Siewierska 1984; Quirk et al. 1985; Huddleston and Pullum 2002; Truswell 2008; Findlay 2016) have involved themselves in the discussion of the prepositional passive, but their views vary to some extent. Despite the variation, it is widely accepted that the existence of prepositional passive arises from the common allowance for prepositional stranding in English, that is, an NP is allowed to move out of a PP, leaving the preposition behind.

In terms of defining prepositional passives, Scheurweghs (1959: 16) points out that some verbs are used with a preposition followed by a noun that serves as the object. They behave much like a transitive verb with its direct object, where the prepositional object can become the subject of a verb in the passive to which the preposition remains attached.

With regards to its status in the passive category, traditional grammarians such as Svartvik (1966) and Siewierska (1984) hold that passives like the one in (44)b are pseudo passives because they are not based on transitive verbs. Quirk et al. (1985) only mention that prepositional verbs occur in the passive as voice constraints without classifying them as the subclass of the passive at all.

However, for Couper-Kuhlen (1979), Huddleston and Pullum (2002), and Findlay (2016), the prepositional passive is regarded as a separate subclass of the passive construction. As far as its syntactic features are concerned, it deviates from the prototype of the passive to some extent. In this study, we believe it is one of the subcategories of the passive that is worth special attention. In light of this, it is still intriguing to investigate what a prepositional passive is and how many properties they have. To facilitate our understanding of the properties of the prepositional passive, let us look at some of the following examples:

(45) a. The committee didn't face up to these problems.

b. These problems weren't faced up to (by the committee).

(Huddleston and Pullum 2002: 1433)

(46) a. Queen Victoria has slept in this bed.

b. This bed has been slept in (by Queen Victoria).

(Adapted from Wanner 2009: 68)

As can be seen in the sentences in (45)b and (46)b, like the prototype passive, prepositional passives have the same auxiliary choice *be* and the same morphological configuration concerning the verb, *the past participle*. Moreover, they both have an implicit argument reading, and a *by-phrase* could be added or omitted.

One of the typical features of prepositional passive is that the subject of the passive corresponds to the prepositional object in the active rather than the verbal object. As put by Alsina (2009: 45), this is the only conspicuous feature that differentiates prepositional passive from canonical passives.

The second feature of prepositional passives is that they have restrictions which rule out many possible candidates. That is, not all *V+PP* sequences are eligible for usage in prepositional passives. As put by Huddleston and Pullum (2002), whether a specified preposition can be stranded in a prepositional passive is not something that can be predicted by a general rule. First, phrasal verbs need to be distinguished from prepositional verb. As in (47), *bring up* is a phrasal verb where *up* functions as a particle rather than a *preposition*, which is why they can follow their NP complement even if the NP is instantiated as a pronoun as in (47b). On the contrary, *approve of* in (48)b is a prepositional verb. That is why they cannot follow the pronoun it. It is said that the NP after the particle moves ahead to get case but it seems strange for an NP after preposition to move ahead in that the preposition can assign case to it.

(47) a. Rose brought up three children.

b. Rose brought them up.

(48) a. They approve of my idea.

b. *They approve it of.

Next, roughly speaking, (45)b and (46)b represent two different types of prepositional passive. In type one, the prepositional phrase *face up to* in (45)b is shown in the construction of *verb + preposition + preposition*, they cannot be analyzed *as complex verbs* but can only be regarded as *verbal idioms*. This feature will eliminate those transitive prepositional verbs in that they are not eligible for the prepositional passive as shown in (49). In addition, only the abstract, figurative subject seems to be acceptable by the prepositional passive rather than the concrete subject which has a literal meaning. As illustrated in (50), the abstract *result* is eligible while the concrete *stadium* fails to satisfy the felicitous requirement.

(49) a. I convinced him of my innocence.

   b.* My innocence was convinced him of.

(50) a. The expected result was eventually arrived at.

   b. *The splendid stadium was eventually arrived at.

(Quirk et al. 1985: 163)

In type two, the prepositional phrase in (46)b designates different features, as the locative preposition *in* is not specified by the verb. As claimed by Huddleston and Pullum (2002), semantic constrains only allow type two to be felicitous on the condition that the VP indicates either a significant property or a change in a significant property of the subject-referent.

(51) a. We slept beside the river.

   b. *The river was slept beside.

Comparing (46)b and (51)b, we can see that *the bed*, where someone slept in it is more affected than *the river* where someone only slept beside it. That is to say, a *bed* looks different if someone slept in it, but *the river* is not affected if someone just slept beside it. The unacceptability or inaccessibility of (51)b indicates that sleeping beside is not a significant property that can cause the river to change in some way. In Langacker's (1982:60) view, the rubric *passive* is applied to a wide variety of constructions which, in one way or another, enhance the prominence of a landmark. As can be seen from (45)b and (46)b, both *these problems* and *this bed* are prominent elements in the salient subject position while the agent is taken as the background.

In addition, it is said that there is a tendency that verb plus preposition are usually positioned adjacent to one another in the passive, but not in the active, as exemplified in (52). That means the verb and preposition are supposed to be adjoining, but this adjacency is only a common practice, and counterexample is not difficult to find.

(52) a. We rely increasingly on David.

    b. * David is relied increasingly on.

(Findlay 2016: 3)

To sum up, prepositional passives resembles the prototype passive in many aspects, but syntactically and semantically they still deviate from the prototype to some extent. Since it is easy to get the active from a prepositional passive, we assume that its status is better than a pseudo-passive even though the verb is intransitive. Based on above analysis, let us sketch the schema of the prepositional passive.

As sketched in Figure 39, it is clear that the prepositional passive construction is a symbolic assembly that consists of three complex symbolic units Σ1, Σ2, and Σ3, respectively. As in the Be-passive schema, there are two nominal participants: N/P1 and N/P2. But the N/P1 has more constraints; that is, it is more preferable to the abstract, metaphorical entities that are more affected by the agent that is overt or covert. It is evident that there is an asymmetrical interaction between the N/P1 and N/P2, otherwise the subject-referent would not be affected by the agent. In terms of the verb and preposition, they combine together and function as an organic whole. They tend to behave like a verbal idiom or indicate locative meaning. The verb is intransitive and shown in *V-en* form like the prototype, and it is adjacent to the preposition in most cases.

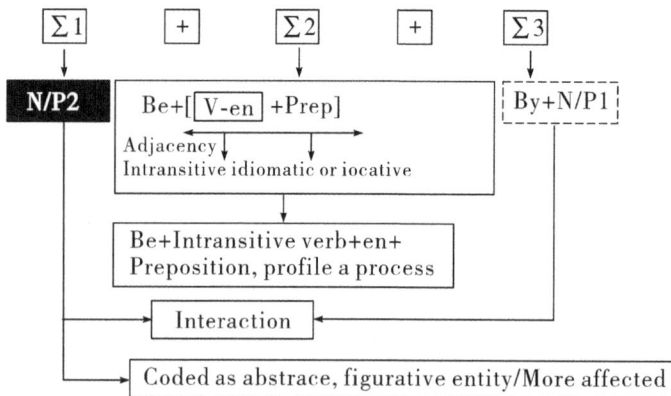

Figure 39   The Schema of the Prepositional Passive Constructions

2.4 Continuous Features at the Boundary of Active and Passive

So far, we have examined the Be-passive, Get-passive, and prepositional passive which manifest syntactic default forms and deviations ranging from discrete prototypical passive to continuous non-prototypical passives, where the fuzzy feature is evident within the passive category. However, the passive implicature of English sentences has never confined to formal representation. The notional passive or semantic passive is easy to see in context.

Taking the continuous feature of category into account, we see that many expressions that have passive implications actually do not have passive syntactic configuration at all. In other words, there are cases of passivization which have a passive-like interpretation in terms of meaning but do not seem to share syntactic features with their canonical counterparts. Instead, they borrow forms from the other subcategory to produce notional passives that conform only to the semantic principles. If we take be/get+past participle as the only yardstick for a passive, we may only see the partial discrete features of language, and leave many expressions at the boundary of the category unexplained or untouched. Therefore, it is reasonable to argue that there are overlaps between active and passive due to the fuzziness at the boundary.

Against this background, let us now look more closely at some examples that the traditional definition of a passive seems to fail to account for but still have been argued to represent non-canonical passives in English. It is generally claimed that there are four constructions worth our attention in that they are active in form but passive in meaning, as illustrated in (53).

(53) a. My momentum is building and I'm excited about...(COCA)

　　 b. The pen writes smoothly.

　　 c. Some bulbs need replacing and you may want to re-wire the house eventually. (COCA)

　　 d. A " normal" stock-flow ratio is not directly observable. (COCA)

As can be observed, both (53)a and (53)b are unaccusative constructions that denote passive interpretation. The difference is that the former is an unaccusative progressive construction, and the latter is an unaccusative middle construction, both of which deviate greatly in form in contrast to the canonical passive. Since we will deal with middle voice in the next chapter, we will not examine the middle construction here. In the case of (53)c and (53)b, both are compatible with modality and convey passive meaning. In this study, (53)c is defined as a [V1+V2ing] construction and (53)d is defined as a Be+V-able construction. As can be seen, the forms replacing in (53)c and observable in (53)d are not passive past participles but they are semantically and syntactically analogous to passive past participles. In what follows, we attempt to examine and characterize the above three constructions and designate their shared properties with the prototypical passive and their idiosyncrasies.

2.4.1　Unaccusative in Progressive [Be +V(Intr)+ing]

It is evident in English that some verbs occurring chiefly in the present progressive can denote a passive meaning. In contrast to the prototype passive, this construction has many constraints.

First, the number of verbs which apply to this structure is very small. Only the verbs *print*, *cook*, *build*, *bind*, and *owe* are commonly used and these verbs shows ambivalent features; that is, an intransitive verb in this unaccusative construction can be transitive in other contexts. In most cases, the actor is not overtly expressed. In addition, a verb used in this way can also be made passive, as exemplified in (54)b and (55)b.

Second, instead of having the form of *be+past participle*, this structure is confined to the progressive aspect and instantiated as *be+present participle*. The unaccusative progressive is said to be eventive, that is, it can indicate a particular time reference regardless of its tense. It is assumed that there are external causes initiating the action, but this construction suppresses these causes and makes the event happen spontaneously on its own. Making a comparison between (56)a and (56)b, we can tell that an unaccusative progressive construction denotes a generic and habitual meaning while the active with a personal pronoun does not show this feature.

(54) a. The dictionary is printing.

b. The dictionary is being printed.

(55) a. The apartment is building.

b. The apartment is being built.

(56) a. The lunch is cooking.

b. We cooked dinner last night.

From the perspective of an action chain, there seems to be only one participant available. It is coded as the subject. There seems to be a transfer of energy from the implied agent to the salient patient in the subject position, but it is the patient that is put in the subject position and serves as the trajector. This patient-oriented feature coincides with the prototype in the way of construal. Its limited productivity in English and constraints in practical use naturally make it a marginal member of the passive.

Thus far, we have argued that the unaccusative progressive construction, though without overt formal features of the prototype passive, still views the event from the patient perspective. It stands at the boundary of passive and active and witnesses the multiplex, unbounded, homogeneous and indeterminate features of the grammatical voice category.

Having considered the shared properties and idiosyncrasies of unaccusative progressive, let us now generalize our discussion and sketch its schema.

As can be seen in Figure 40, there is one nominal participant (N/P2) that had more control over the event in the schema where the N/P1 is completely eliminated due to the construction suppression. The only participant, though implying an assumed interaction with an external cause, designates the spontaneous action by itself. The *V-en* is replaced by *V-ing* present participle where possible *V* are of very limited choice. In addition, the composite verb profiles an implied process and the *Be+V-ing* always denotes a generic and habitual meaning.

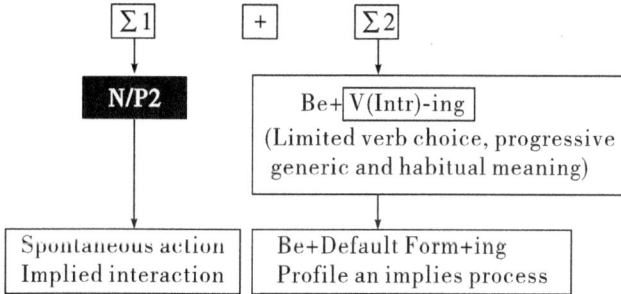

Figure 40   The Schema of the Unaccusative Progressive Constructions

2.4.2   Be+V-able Construction

It is believed that one of the uses of the passive across languages is to create potentiality (Shibatani 1985; Rona 1998). Unlike some other languages, the English passive cannot inherently fabricate potentiality. It seems that only by resorting to the modal auxiliary can or the verbal phrase *be able to* can do so. Conversely, *Be+adjective* with suffix-*able* construction is often used to denote potentiality but without clear passive marking.

Before we look into this construction, let us first take a close look at the suffix-*able*. Qurik et al. (1985) identify two types of deverbal suffixes that are related to verbal voice, both of which are applied to form adjectives from verbs. One is suffix-*ive* which is associated with the active. The other is suffix-*able* which is connected with the passive, referring to *of the kind that can be V-ed*. However, as shown in the corpora, suffix-*able* has several variants. To see the nature of the passive-able, consider the sentences in (57-61).

It should be noted that suffix-able may be attached to both nouns and verbs. But the adjectives that derive from nouns (defined as -*able*$_1$ from now on), such as, *knowledgeable*, *pleasurable*, as shown in (57)a and (57)b, should be eliminated from consideration for this construction in that they do not convey any passive meaning. In addition, there are two other suffixes,-*ible*, and -*uble*, and, though they occasionally have passive implication, as shown in (57)c and (57)d, they also need to be excluded. There are two reasons: for one, the suffixes -*ible*, and -*uble* are not productive. For another, they are both found in loan words, and their verbal counterparts are hard to identify based on the configuration of the adjective itself.

A close look at *V-able* formation reveals that even the *V-able* does not confine its usage only to the passive. There are two variants of *V-able*. Consider the sentences in (58): *neither changeable* nor *suitable* can convey a passive meaning. The former means being apt to transform while the latter refers something which is fitting. We define *V-able* without a passive meaning as *-able₂*. Next, let us take a look at the *-able₃*, the deverbal suffix that denotes passive, as exemplified in (58-61). These sentences all manifest a kind of potentiality, but there are slight differences among them. *Understandable and disputable* in (59) manifest something which can be understood or disputed. *Laughable* and *readable* in (60) mean that something is worthy of being laughed or read. *Admirable and desirable* in (61) refer to the quality of being deserve of admiration or something merits being desired. Conversely, *payable* in (62)a means that something must be paid or required to be paid and *finable* in (62)b means something which must be fined.

(57) a. The average Englishman is tremendously <u>knowledgeable</u> about his own concerns...
(wordhippo.com[①])

b. ...Once you get into it, the experience is very <u>pleasurable</u>. (BNC)

c. The tumor is often <u>visible</u> with basic radiological techniques...
(wordhippo.com)

d. Most metal sulfates are <u>soluble</u> in water...(wordhippo.com)

(58) a. ... the inadequate moisture levels are also highly <u>changeable</u>...(COCA)

b. The versatile Easi-Stow is <u>suitable</u> for a wide variety of yachts. (COCA)

(59) a. Evans' caution, however, is <u>understandable</u>. (COCA)

b. ...such questions of statutory construction are inherently <u>disputable</u>.
(wordhippo.com)

(60) a. My needlework was <u>laughable</u>. (COCA)

b. ...Such files are not <u>readable</u>...(BNC)

(61) a. Being anti-racist is <u>admirable</u>...(wordhippo.com)

b. Prior experience is <u>desirable</u> but not essential. (BNC)

(62) a. The rent is <u>payable</u> in advance. (wordhippo.com)

b. The offence is <u>fineable</u>.

In light of the above analysis, we can reach the conclusion that *-able₃* is a suitable candidate for the passive. Now let us compare *-able₃* with the *V-en* in the prototype passive. A review

①   It is an online Thesaurus and word tools (https://www.wordhippo.com/).

of the literature reveals that only sporadic research discusses the *-able* in passive use. We assume that there is general consensus among scholars that voice is the function of verb, and *V-en* is a verbal form whereas *-able*$_3$ is more adjective-forming suffix. It is no denying that *-able*$_3$ is more adjectival in that it shows many properties of adjective, as in (63). (i) It can be modified by very to show its gradability, as in (63)a. (ii) It can be used as the attributive adjective to modify noun phrases, as in (63)b. (iii) It is able to coordinate with common adjectives as in (63)c. (iv) It serves as predicative adjective followed the copular *look* or *seem*, as in (63)d. (v) It cannot take an NP as its complement, as in (63)e.

(63) a. Windows, for example, are very breakable.

b. He is a respectable professor.

c. As a film, *Cinderella Man* is terribly weak, thoroughly sentimental and predictable. (wordhippo.com)

d. The beer looks drinkable./A cool breeze seems bearable.

e. *He was wearable a brown uniform.

Despite the fact that the *V-able* (or *-able*$_3$) is more adjectival, it still remains questionable to say-*able*$_3$ has nothing to do with voice. The reason is that the boundary between the verb and adjective is graded, fuzzy rather than being clear-cut, as does the *V-en*. In fact, *V-en* itself is half verbal and half adjectival. Though superficially-*able*$_3$ is more adjectival, it shows certain commonality with the-*V-en* in several aspects:

First, in term of the selection of the verb in *-able*$_3$ and *V-en*, as put by Puckica (2009), they both choose transitive verb stems, but exclude intransitive verbs, such as *happen*, *occur*, *remain*, etc. Or the verb that is transitive syntactically, but does not have passive counterpart, such as *have*, *resemble*, etc. However, the verb slot in *-able*$_3$ is comparatively more constrained than that of *V-en*, but it is still productive for it is commonly seen in the discourse.

Second, semantically speaking, both *-able*$_3$ and *V-en* characterize relations with a second participant, usually the patient in the corresponding active construction, as in (63) and (64). Both *the solicitor* and *these qualities* function as the object in active construction and it is promoted in the subject position in both the *Be+V-able* construction and the prototype passive. As for the subject, it is fairly evident that this construction is predominantly inanimate-oriented (Toyata 2008) in that a human subject tends to signal the active reading, an inanimate subject the passive reading (Strang 1970: 135).

In addition, we notice that, syntactically, the agent can be covertly or overtly shown by the oblique phrase in the prototype passive. For the Be+V-able construction, though frequently it does not have an overt agent, an agent can still be found in the examples, as illustrated in both (64) and (65). They both take an oblique phrase (*by the solicitor and by the colonial potters* respectively) to denote the agent. It is noteworthy that the agent in the Be+V-able construction is primarily a general agent rather than a specific one (Quirk et al.1985; Puckica 2009).

(64) a. Law Society are lower than those in the bill, only the lower sum is recoverable by the solicitor. (BNC)

b. The lower sum can be recovered by the solicitor.

c. The solicitor can recover the lower sum.

(65) a. …These qualities were apparently not achievable by colonial potters.

b. These qualities cannot be achieved by colonial patters.

c. The colonial potters cannot achieve these qualities.

In a nutshell, the shared semantic and morphosyntactic features enable the -able$_3$ and *V-en* to have a closer affinity with each other within the English participle system than basic adjectives. That is why the Be+V-able construction can be a comparable alternation of passive construction in English, though its status is marginal.

Moreover, the nature of the verb *be* in this structure should be scrutinized. Ostensibly it appears that *be* is an auxiliary, but this is not the case. In fact, it is a main verb with copular function, which is different from the passive-forming *be*.

In light of this examination and characterization of the components of Be+V-able construction, let us consider the how we sketch the schema of this structure.

As Figure 41 illustrates, *Be+V-able* exemplifies the comparable passive construction that conveys potentiality without resorting to the modal verb. It is clear that nominal participant two is put in the subject and taken as the primary core participant that is instantiated by inanimate entities in most cases. As for the individual component, *be* is the main verb rather than the auxiliary. *V-able* has many variants but only -*able*$_3$ applied to this construction within which V should be a transitive verb. As for the nominal participant one, it is omitted in most cases but even the implicit agent can indicate that there is an asymmetry interaction between the two participants. In terms of construal, the N/P2 serves as the trajector that is foregrounded. There is an implied abstract action chain showing the transmission of energy or force from N/P1 to N/P2. It is shown in active form but denotes a passive meaning, so it can be regarded as the marginal member in both the subcategories. In addition, it exemplifies the fuzzy feature at the boundary of the category.

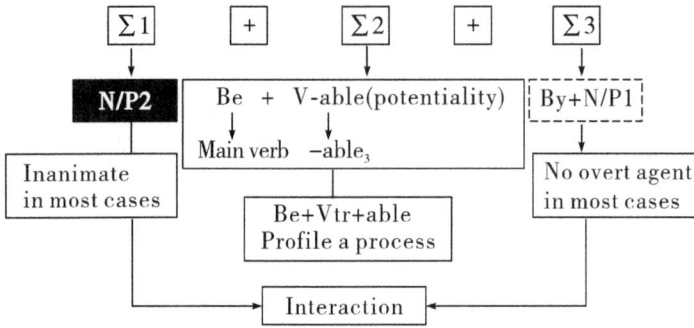

Figure 41   The Schema of the Be+V-able Passive Constructions

2.4.3   [V1+V2-ing] Construction

A tacit assumption made in the last part is that Be+V-able construction, as a comparable passive, can express a potentiality that is closely related to the modality. With respect to modality, there is another comparable passive construction in English which can express necessity or obligation; that is, the [V1+V2-ing] construction. To see the general properties of this construction, observe the following examples:

(66) a. Two light bulbs <u>need replacing</u> on the same day. (BNC)

　　b. The lorry got there on Monday morning, <u>wants unloading</u>… (BNC)

　　c. A transfer normally <u>requires signing</u> only by the seller.

　　d. The school's efforts to overcome the problem <u>deserves emphasizing</u>. (BNC)

　　e. The housewife geographer implied that she was not serious and did not <u>merit funding</u>.(COCA)

　　f. The great champagnes <u>repay keeping</u> for years and years. (BNC)

In (66)a to (66)f, the subjects of the passive construction are instantiated by NPs such as *two light bulbs, the lorry, a transfer, the school's efforts, she* and *the great champagnes*. *V1* is instantiated by verbs such as *need, want, require, deserve, merit,* and *repay*. *V2* is realized by verbs such as *replace, unload, sign, emphasize, fund* and *keep*. We can arrive at a conclusion that *subject NP, V1* and *V2-ing* are essential parts of the [V1+V2-ing] passive construction. From now on, we will name the Subject NP and the complement NP of *By-phrase* as NP2 and NP1, respectively. A close examination of (66)c suggests that a *By-phrase* can be added as one of the optional elements and it will be defined as *By+NP1 agent*. Based on this analysis, we can generalize the complete form of [V1+V2-ing] Passive Construction as follows: [V1+V2-ing] Construction=NP2+V1+ [V2-ING+( ) (*By* NP1 agent)]

Let us recap the main points here. First, the matrix clause (V1) is complemented by a subordinate-ing clause as is shown between the square brackets. For example, in (66)d, matrix

V1 is deserve, and it is complemented by *emphasizing* which is regarded as a subordinate clause.

Second, in this construction, what is in the parentheses (.) are optional parts that may be omitted in actual use. To be exact, the *V-ing* form that heads the subordinate clause may be complemented by an agent *By-phrase* (*By NP1 agent*), as in (66c). But the *By NP1* agent is an essential feature in most cases just as in (66a), (66b), (66d), and (66f), where *By NP1* agent is not expressed.

After examining the general properties of the [V1+V2-ing] construction, the typical features of the [V1+V2-ing] construction are supposed to be generalized in contrast to the prototype.

First, in terms of the feature having a be auxiliary, [V1+V2-ing] construction does not have a *be* auxiliary. Instead, it has *V1*. *V1* fills the matrix verb slot in the [V1+V2-ing] construction. It is not stable but only has a few variations. In addition, only those verbs whose semantic/ lexical characteristics involve endurance and necessity survived in this construction (Toyota 2008: 207), as illustrated in (66)a-f. Possible candidates for the *V1* slot are discussed in the academic research. Visser (1963–1973) for example, lists about twenty such verbs. These verbs include only *need, require, want, merit, bear,* and *deserve,* which appeared as early as 1400, and they can still be considered active and productive in present day English. In order to get the hierarchy of use frequency, let us resort to some other research works. Cowan (2008) only lists three verbs: *need, require,* and *want.* Puckica (2009) cites six verbs: *need, want, require, deserve, merit,* and *repay.* The first three are of higher frequency while the remaining three are comparatively of lower frequency. As can be seen in (66), we have given every verb in Puckica's list an instantiated example.

Second, with regard to *V-en,* the [V1+V2-ing] construction does not have a *V-en* past participle. Instead it has the *V-ing* form. Two issues will be involved in dealing with *V-ing.* First, is *V-ing* a gerund or participle? Second, what are the possible candidates for *V2*?

It is interesting to note that the *V-ing* form in English commonly has two interpretations: one is as a gerund, and the other is as a participle. It is generally understood that a gerund is a word formed from a verb and used as a noun having an ending of *-ing,* while the participle is a word form that is also formed from a verb and used as an adjective and ended with *-ing* or *-ed.* According to Huddleston and Pullum (2002), many grammarians have now abandoned this traditional distinction and recognize a single *gerund-participle* form. On the contrary, some grammarians (Abney1987; Taylor 2000) argue that the distinction between the *-ing* participles and *-ing* gerund and the distinction between accusative gerunds and possessive gerund are of equal importance. However, the main point worth discussing here is that whether *V-ing* form in [V1+V2-ing] construction is noun-like or verb-like. In order to have a clear train of thought, let us look at some examples:

    (67) a. The used clothes needed sorting and repackaging by my nurse.

        b. The right rear fender need replacing [regularly/*regular].

        c. The right rear fender need (*the) replacing.

In (67), the V-ing form is realized by *sorting* and *repackaging*, *redecorating* and *replacing*. A close observation reveals that *V-ing* form is more verb-like in three aspects: (i) it can have its complement, as in (67)a, where the prepositional phrase *by my nurse follows V-ing*. (ii) It can be modified by an adverb but not adjective as in (67)b, where *replacing* can be modified by *regularly* but not *regular*. (iii) It cannot be modified by an article for it is more verb-like as in (67)c, where *replacing* cannot be modified by *the*.

The next question deserving our attention is what verbs can be put in the slot of V2 compared with standard active-*ing* clauses. Some examples will be presented here to facilitate our reasoning.

    (68) a. John likes reading.

        b. *John likes to be read.

        c. John likes to read.

    (69) a. This computer needs fixing.

        b. This computer needs to be fixed.

        c* This computer needs to fix.

    (70) a. The accident happened.

        b.*The accident is happened.

        c.*This accident doesn't need happening.

    (71) a. They recommended a nice house.

        b. A nice house is recommended.

        c. A nice house deserves recommending.

    (72) a. They have a nice house

        b *A nice house is had.

        c. *A nice house deserves having.

As we can see, (68)a is a standard active-*ing* clause, and its meaning cannot be paraphrased as (68)b but it is close to (68)c. (69)a is a typical example of [V1+V2-ing] construction. It is commonly acknowledged that it can be paraphrased as (69)b but not (69)c. Therefore, one of the vital features of the [V1+V2-ing] construction is that it can be transformed from *V1+V2-ing* to *V1+ to be+V2-en*, which means the V2-ing requires the verb in a simple V-ing form but not in *Being V-en*.

Let us further our analysis by looking at the sentences in (70): *happen* is an intransitive verb in active form, so it can neither have its corresponding true passive form like (70)b nor have a [V1+V2-ing] passive form as in (70)c. Observing all the sentences in (71), we find that the transitive verb *recommend* indicates its active use in (71)a, true passive use in (71)b, and [V1+V2-ing] passive use in (71)c. In contrast, *have* in (72) is also a transitive verb and it has its active form as in (72)a but fails to appear both in a true passive form as in (72)b, as well as a [V1+V2-ing] construction, as in (72)c. According to Quirk et al. (1985: 162), there are greater restrictions on verbs occurring in the passive than on verbs occurring in the active. In addition to copular and intransitive verbs, as the verb *happen in* (70)b and (70)c, which having no object cannot take the passive, some transitive verbs do not occur in at least some senses in the passive, as the verb *have* in (72)b and (72)c. The analysis along this line suggests that the verbs that can fill the V2 slot of the [V1+V2-ing] construction are the same as those that can be used in the Be+V-en true passive construction. Both intransitive verbs and verbs which are syntactically but not semantically transitive are excluded.

Speaking of taking By+Agent NP, it can be one of the shared features both possessed by the prototype passive and [V1+V2-ing] construction. As shown in (73)a and (74)a, both constructions include By+Agent NP. Though sometimes it can be omitted as in (73)b and (74)b, the omission does not affect its passive meaning,

(73) a. These women don't need rescuing by someone else.

b. These women don't need rescuing.

(74) a. This issue is addressed by the government.

b. This issue is addressed.

Next, concerning having active counterpart, it seems that it doesn't work well for the [V1+V2-ing] construction. As can be seen, Sentence (75)a is a typical [V1+V2-ing] construction instantiated by *V1* verbs. It seems that they have the same meaning as the passive illustrated in (75)b. However, when we try to convert all the (a) sentences into their active, some problems occur. We have two versions of active counterparts (75)c and (75)d. As for the former, *V1* is inserted in the sentences in dealing with the active. In terms of the latter we try to only focus on the *V2*. No matter what we try, the meanings in the active are distorted to some extent with regard to the passive meaning.

(75) a. This article needs checking by the editor.

    b. The article needs to be checked by the editor.

    c. The editor needs to check the article.

    d. The editor checks the article.

As put by Tamba (2018: 264), in passives, the object is promoted to the subject whereas the subject is demoted through suppression or deletion. In discussion of the subject in the [V1+V2-ing] passive construction, we need to take the *NP2* into consideration. To facilitate our understanding, let us examine some arguments about it.

One of the typical descriptions of the subject in a [V1+V2-ing] construction can be found in Biber et al's (1999) work. They claim that there are small numbers of verbs that express required action, making the *-ing*-clause an action that needs to be done. These verbs control the *-ing*-clause in a passive sense, so that clause subject corresponds to the implied object of the *-ing*-clause. For better understanding, let us look at some examples below.

(76) a. The roses in your garden want watering.

    b. The chimney will need cleaning before a fire can be safely lit. (COCA)

As we can observe, *the roses* and *the chimney* represent the subject of the matrix clause in (76)a and (76)b, respectively and they do not correspond to the implied object of the *-ing* clause *watering* and *cleaning*. These two examples lend support to Biber et al's argument.

Another significant description of the subject in the [V1+V2-ing] passive construction comes from Puckica (2009), who argues that what could be the subject of a Be-passive sentence involving a given transitive verb could be the (main or subordinate) subject of a V-ing passive sentence involving the same verb (as *V2*). One thing that needs to be pointed out here is that the Be-passive only indicates a prototype passive construction in this study. In order to further our understanding, let us look at some examples below:

(77) a. The man respects her.

    b. She is respected by the man.

    c. She need respecting.

(78) a. Mary [taught Tom a lesson].

    b. Tom was [taught _ a lesson].

    c. Tom needs [teaching _ a lesson].

In (77)a, the transitive verb *respect* is shown in active form and is followed by the object her. In (77)b and (77)c, the object her changes into nominative form and is promoted to the subject position. It seems that *she* fits the two passive constructions well. The sentences in (78) are different from the sentences in (77). In (78)a *teach* is a transitive verb that can take two objects: *Tom* and a *lesson*. In the prototype passive the indirect object *Tom* is promoted to the subject position as in (78)b, which is also applicable to the [V1+V2-ing] passive construction, as in (78)c.

Another possible explanation comes from Palmer (1965), who argues that the *V2-ing* clause in the [V1+V2-ing] construction is subject-less and in fact it is a typical non-finite clause. But we argue that if we combine Biber et al's (1999) argument and Puckica's (2009) argument together, it is better to facilitate our understanding of subject in [V1+V2-ing] construction.

Having examined the general properties and partial properties of every component, now let us generalize all the features of the [V1+V2-ing] construction in a sketched schema.

Figure 42 illustrates the general schema of the [V1+V2-ing] construction. As can be seen, it is more complicated than other passive constructions. First, this construction has this form: N/P2+V1+V2-ing+(By+N/P1). Here the participant *2* in the matrix subject position has interaction with participant *1* (if it is overt) and is in a coreferential relation with V2-ing.

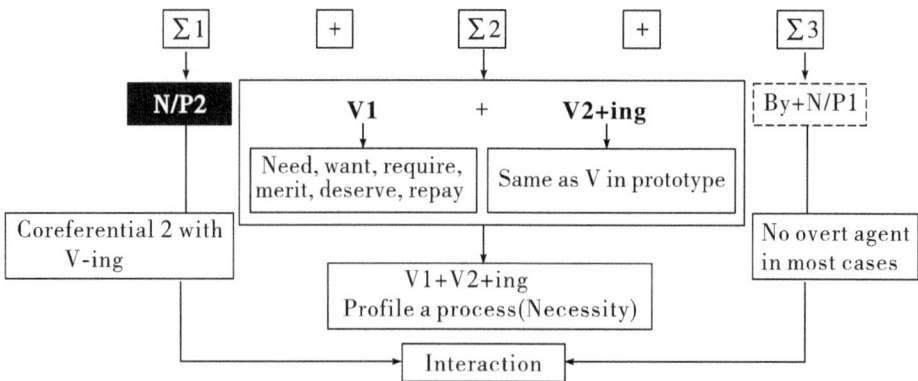

Figure 42   The Schema of the [V1+V2-ing] Constructions

This construction seems to be active in form but passive in meaning. Though it does not have a normal active counterpart, the N/P2 is just like a patient put in the salient position. For the *V1*, only six candidates (*need, want, deserve, require, merit*, and *repay*) are of frequent use, and indicate necessity and obligation. *V2-ing* is more verbal-like, among which the suitable candidates are the same as the *V* in the prototype. The oblique phrases are omitted in most cases, but they do get involved in the action chain. Given the above properties, it is natural to assume that the [V1+V2-ing] construction is a marginal member of the passive. Meanwhile, it has something to do with the active. Moreover, it lends support to the fuzzy feature at the boundary of the subcategory on the one hand, and the continuous feature of grammatical categories on the other hand.

3   Proposed Sketch of the Passive Cognitive Model

Unlike active construction, the deviations of non-prototypes are mainly from role archetypes. Here in the passive, there are many variations in form, which result in many subtypes or subcategories. These subcategories are of various statuses within the passive category and connect with the active category in various ways. Plus there are subtypes within each subcategory showing in a hierarchical model. Before we look into the cognitive model of the passive voice in English, let us first recategorize the passive system in English in terms of prototypicality based on the above analysis.

As can be seen, Figure 43 illustrates the categorization of the English passive system in a fine-graded way. We saw some research ascribes the impersonal passive to a separate voice in voice category across languages in literature. However, in English, it is adequate to put the personal passive and impersonal passive within the passive voice category because personal passive always receives a good amount of attention from researchers. Likewise, the personal passive is our first concern in this study.

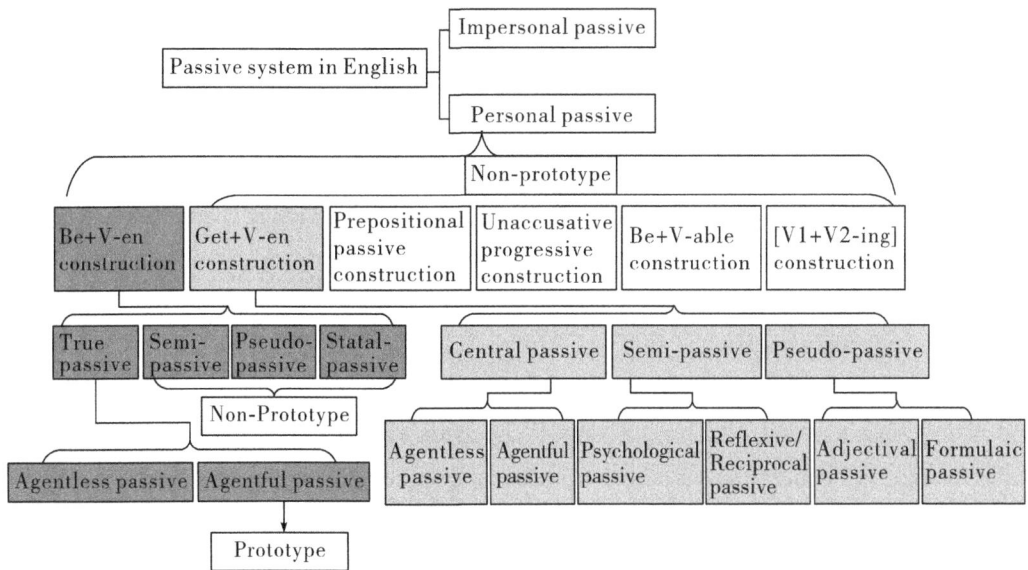

Figure 43   Categorization of Passive System in English in Terms of Prototypicality

Within the personal passive category, it can be assumed that the Be+V-en construction is the tacit formula of passive in English syntactically, but it is worth noting that this construction falls into four subcategories that form a voice continuum in which only the true agentful passive can serve as the prototype of both the Be+V-en construction category and the passive category.

The Get-V-en construction is widely accepted to be only secondary to the Be+V-en construction, but to most EFL learners' surprise, its internal structure is more complicated than the tacit construction. To grasp the essentials of the Get-V-en construction, it is necessary to observe the data closely and grasp the continuous features ranging from central to semi-, and pseudo- forms. And it is worthwhile to even go a step further to differentiate its variations by probing into agentful and agentless Get-passive, the psychological Get-passive, the reflexive and reciprocal Get-passive, the adjectival Get-passive, and the formulaic Get-passive. Despite many similarities between the prototype and the central agentful Get-passive that can be regarded as the prototype of the Get+V-en construction category, deviations are also evident.

Another construction that really grabs our attention is the prepositional passive construction. The peculiarity of this construction is the intransitivity of the verb. It actually provides further evidence for the existence of a transitivity-intransitivity continuum in the grammatical domain. In addition, it poses a challenge to the definition of the passive voice in traditional pedagogical grammar books. Syntactically, the unaccusative progressive construction, the Be+V-able construction and the [V1+V2-ing] construction diverge greatly in form from the prototype.

As Figure 44 shows, the cognitive model of passive voice consists of two parts: one is the normal construal that directs at the prototype which designates the discrete features of passive voice. The other is the unconventional construal that targets at the various instantiations of the passive constructions, which demonstrate the continuous features within the subcategory and at the boundary of the subcategory. It is clear that we select the agentful true passive as the prototype, but the agentful true passive still shows divergence in selection of agent, patient, composite verbs and various types of sentences in contrast to their active counterparts. Because of the diverse subcategories of the passive category, we identify the component variation within the prototype as internal deviations whereas the subtype variations within the passive category as external variations.

As for the prototype, we can deduce that there exists an action chain between the agent and patient, because the force transmission is the same as that of its active counterpart. The difference is that it puts the patient in the salient position (or serves as a trajector that is foregrounded) while the agent is demoted to the oblique phrase, serving as the landmark that is backgrounded. The asymmetry interaction is still evident but the perspective that the viewer observes has changed from the agent-orientation to patient-orientation.

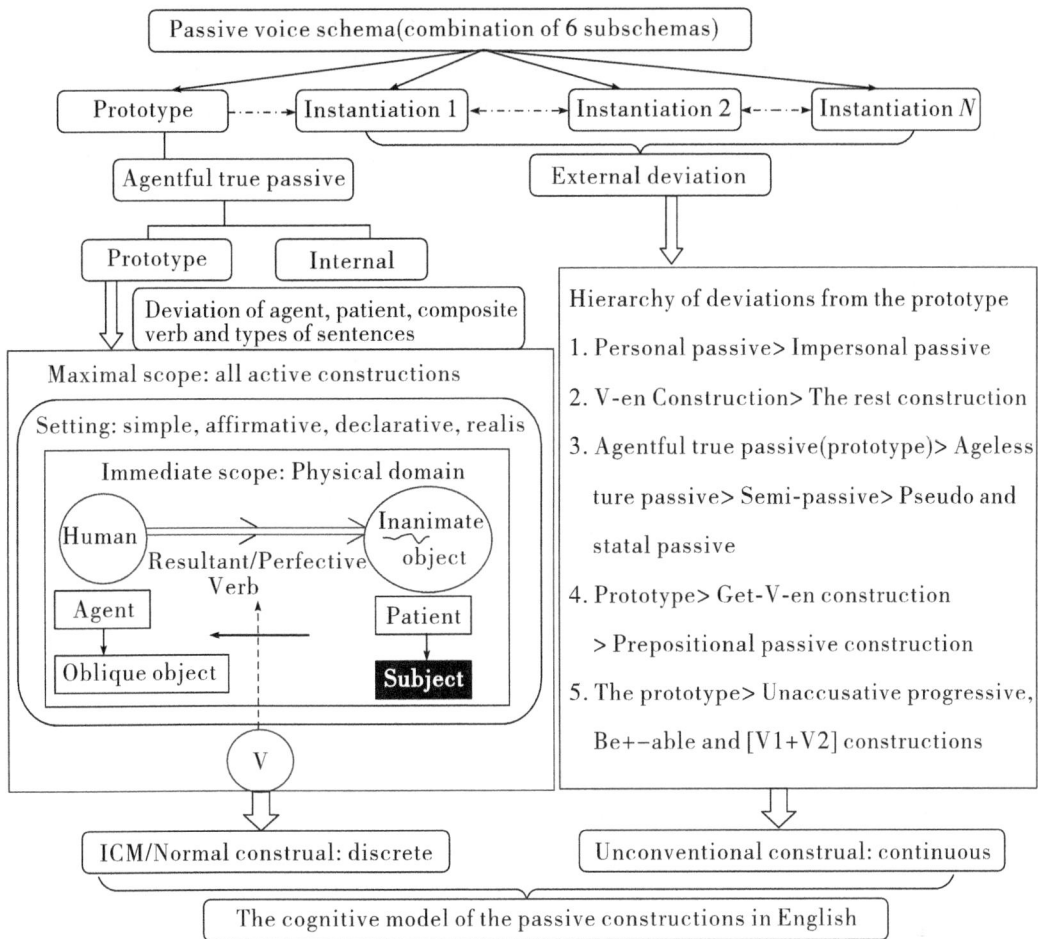

Figure 44   The Cognitive Model of the Passive Constructions

There is a hierarchy of deviations from the prototype. At the first level, personal passive is foregrounded while impersonal passive is backgrounded in term of the general types of passive.

At the second level, in terms of the degree of prominence, the V-en construction is taken as the profile while the remaining constructions serve as the base. At the third level, the agentful true passive is profiled by taking the Be+V-en construction as the immediate scope where the ageless true passive, the semi-, pseudo-, and statal passives are arranged in a hierarchy.

At fourth level, the prototype is foregrounded in contrast to the Get+V-en constructions and the prepositional passive construction that are backgrounded in terms of syntactic and semantic properties. At the fifth level the prototype in the passive category is in stark contrast with the marginal members (unaccusative progressive construction, Be+-able construction and [V1+V2] constructions) at the boundary of active and passive in terms of meaning and form. In term of passive schema, we do not summarize the general pattern of whole categories because of the complexity and diversity in the subcategories of passive voice in terms of morphosyntactic and semantic features. Thus, we prefer to use the six combined schemas to represent the whole schema of the passive category. All in all, the construal of the prototype and its deviations show both discrete and continuous features of English passive in the category and beyond the category, which provide further evidence for the fuzziness in the category of English grammatical voice.

4 Summary

In this chapter, we have looked at how the fuzzy feature is shown in the category of the passive and how the cognitive model of passive constructions are organized according to the both the prototype and its deviations. Our discussion mainly falls into three parts:

Section one has been centered on the selection of a passive prototype and the characterization of its discrete features. Considering the emphasis traditional grammar put on the most basic form of the passive, we have assumed that the Be+V-en construction represents the most basic formal configuration of the passive category. However, by observing the data, we have reached the conclusion that there are deviations not only in the prototypical agentful passive in terms of its role archetype and its composite verb but also in the external deviation within the Be+V-en construction where semi-passives, pseudo-passives and statal passives co-exist with the prototype in terms of its semantic indication. It is suggested that the prototypical passive is in most cases puts the patient in the subject position as the trajector of the event though the force transmission is identical with the active counterpart but the perspective of viewer is changed accordingly.

Section two has discussed the subtype deviations in the passive category where passive non-prototypes and their continuous features have been our focus. We began with the examination of the deviations of the role archetype and composite verbs in physical and abstract domain of passive constructions and then move to a discussion of the syntactic deviation of passive construction where Get+V-en construction and preposition passive construction are analyzed in a detailed way. And finally, we have attempted to investigate the continuous features shown on the periphery by members at the boundary of active and passive where the unaccusative progressive construction, the Be+V-able construction and the [V1+V2ing] construction have been investigated thoroughly.

Based on the discussions of section one and section two, we have generalized a cognitive model of the passive category in section three. We claim that both normal construal and unconventional construal contribute to the conceptualization of the passive voice in present day English. Though the prototype is always in the salient position and helps us understand the discreteness of the passive category, the diversity of non-prototypes is also worth our attention in that continuous features in the passive category are unavoidable and play an important part in understanding the holistic picture of the passive category as well as the whole voice category. Finally, we have concluded that there is a deviation hierarchy in the passive category where five levels have been illustrated according the general types of the passive, the degree of prominence, the selection of immediate scope and maximal scope, and the considerations of syntactic and semantic features. In addition, we have suggested that the schema of the passive consist of a combination of six schemas of the subcategories of the passive constructions.

VII

The Fuzzy Features Shown in Medial Voice Constructions and Their Cognitive Models

We have assumed that there are three major subcategories of voice in English where active and passive represent opposite poles of the voice continuum and the medial voice is in the intermediary position. In what follows, our focus is put on seven types of medial voice: middle, causative, anticausative, antipassive, reflexive, reciprocal and applicative.

Our discussion falls into three aspects for each voice type. First, we endeavor to characterize the discrete features of each voice by elucidating their role archetypes and composite verbs and how they are combined to form the sentence syntactically and semantically and how they function pragmatically in the context. Second, we attempt to address the problem of how construal plays a certain role in forming and interpreting these voices. Next, a special effort is made to observe how these voice types resemble the active voice and the passive voice in one way or another. Based on these overlaps, we intend to provide further evidence for the continuous features at the boundary of each subcategory. In addition, we lay emphasis on the schema of each type of voice and create a sketch of the formation of a cognitive model for each voice type, both of which are intended to provide some reference for facilitating our understanding of the comprehensive voice system as a whole. In this chapter, we also make further the argument that it is problematic to suppose English voice is a binary dichotomy of two voices. In order to put our argumentation on the stable footing, let us address each voice type in turn thoroughly.

1　Middle Constructions

A review of literature reveals that the middle voice has been receiving a wealth of attention from scholars and researchers in recent decades. These studies fall into two camps. For one, most traditional studies have always been pro the dichotomous view of grammatical voice in English, that is, apart from the active voice, there is only one single non-active voice, passive. For them, the term middle, being dubious and implicit, is always applied and confined to indicate the special property of certain verbs reflecting features of both active and passive voices. For another group of scholars, the middle voice has been set apart as a distinct subcategory of English voice along with active and passive in descriptive and typological studies. For them, there are two types of non-active voices: one is passive and the other is middle. It is evident that the English middle seems to be syntactically similar to the active for they share the same morphology, while, semantically speaking, they seem to be comparable to the passive.

Based on the views of these two camps, it is natural to deduce that the fuzzy features of voice are clearly shown in the middle voice. In this section, we claim that there is no denying that middle voice is an independent subcategory of grammatical voice in that it has its own discrete features. Despite this, we are not obliged to separate the middle absolutely from the other constructions for there are always overlaps, and that is where the continuous features are shown in the grammatical category. Due to these facts, we intend to begin with a discussion of the discrete feature of middle voice by resorting to its role archetypes composite verbs, and additional modifying elements. Next, the focus is placed on the continuous features that embody the boundaries between the middle voice and the two leading voice type, active and passive. Finally, we aim to work out a schema of English middle voice and sketch the corresponding cognitive model. It is worth noting that, like active and passive, the features of the middle voice mostly reside in discourse; that is, how they perform at the clausal level. That is why we will center on the clausal constructions rather than the verbs.

1.1 Discrete Features

In this section, we focus on the semantic realization of the middle construction by discussing the participants of the event, the composite verbs and additional modifying elements of the middle construction in turn. It aims to reveal the very nature of middle construction by laying emphasis on its components and relationship between the components.

1.1.1 In Terms of Role Archetype and Composite Verbs

In order to delineate the idiosyncrasies of the middle voice at clausal level, it is instructive to make a comparison between the middle construction, passive construction and active construction. To facilitate our understanding, consider the following example:

(1) a. The wall paints easily.

(Keyer and Roeper 1984: 384)

   b. The wall is painted (easily) (by them).

   c. They paint the door (easily).

(2) a. Bureaucrats bribe easily.

(Keyer and Roeper1984: 384)

    b. The Bureaucrats are bribed (easily) (by them).

    c. They bribe the bureaucrats (easily).

(3) a. *Bureaucrats bribe.

    b. *The wall paints.

(4) a. At yesterday's house party, the kitchen wall painted easily.

    b. Yesterday, the mayor bribed easily, according to the newspaper.

(Keyer and Roeper1984: 384)

(5) a.* The wall is painting easily.

    b. *Bureaucrats are bribing easily.

(Keyer and Roeper1984: 385)

(6) a. *Paint easily, wall.

    b. *Bribe easily, bureaucrats.

(7) a. It was painted easily by the wall.

    b. It was bribed easily by the Bureaucrats.

As can be seen, the sentences exemplified in the (1)a and (2)a are middle constructions. In contrast to the passive construction in (1)b and (2)b, and the active construction in (1)c and (2)c, middle constructions ostensibly only take one participant (*the door*; *Bureaucrats*) that functions as the non-agent role and occupies the subject position syntactically. The non-agent role can be further validated by the ungrammaticality of both (7)a and (7)b, where a passive is not applicable to the middle construction by demoting the subject to the oblique position as happens in the normal passive construction. Unlike the middle construction, the active construction and passive construction usually take two participants, though in the passive the agent can be omitted in most cases.

In addition, the modifying adverbial can be deleted without affecting the meaning of the sentences in the active and the passive as shown in (1)b to (1)c and (2)b to (2)c. However, in the middle construction, the adverbial is obligatory in the sentences, as shown in (3)a and (3)b, in that it plays a decisive role in differentiating between the middle construction and the anticausative or ergative constructions that we will discuss in the latter part of this chapter. In addition, as shown in (4) and (5), the middle construction seems to denote non-event reference where the simple present tense can only be compatible with them rather than other tenses such as the simple past, or the progressive aspect. In addition, unlike a prototypical active and passive, middle construction does not apply to vocative or imperative construction as in (6)a and (6)b.

Based on the above analysis, it can be concluded that the essential structure of middle construction is *Non-agent participant+Verb+Adverbial*, where *Non-agent* is coded as the subject of the sentence, and *verb+adverbial* is coded as the predicate. It may be surprising to see that there is no agent slot in this construction. Two questions arise here: Does the middle construction have the agent? And what role does the non-agent play in this construction?

Furthermore, this seemingly syntactic structure only gives a rough sketch of middle construction. With above question in mind, let us examine each component thoroughly in order to designate their concrete features.

The Arbitrary Reference of the Implied Agent and Genericity.

First, concerning the agent in the middle construction, a lot of researchers have involved themselves in the discussion. Their arguments fall into two camps. One school of thought represented by Van Oosten (1977, 1986), Hale and Keyser (1987), Ryder (1991), Fangan (1992), Kemmer (1993), and Rapoport (1999), proposes that there is no implied agent in the middle construction. They seem to equate middle construction with anticaustive construction to some extent. For example, scholars such as Ryder (1991) and Kemmer (1993), both ascribe the agentivity to the subject and claim that the subject, the non-agent, or the agentive patient is the initiator of energy. Rapoport (1999: 147) goes even further and argues that the English middle is not inherent agentive since no logical subject argument resides in this construction. By resorting to the *all by oneself test*, he suggests the sentences in (8) can provide further evidence to the agentive patient role in the middle construction where *milk chocolate* and *the glass* can initiate an action autonomously.

(8) a. Milk chocolate melts smoothly all by itself.

    b. This kind of glass breaks easily all by itself.

(Rapoport 1999: 147)

The other school of thought represented by Keyser and Roeper (1984), Fellbaum (1986), Langacker (1991a), and Stroik (1992), takes the opposite view. They maintain that two participants are involved in the English middle construction where the agent is always targeted at the general reference that is undoubtedly implied. The subject is a non-agent nor has any agentivity, for sure.

In Stroik's (1992) view, there is an empty agent (PRO) adjoining the VP in the English middle construction. It serves as the logical subject of the verb though in most cases it is covert at the syntactically level or only occasionally realized by a *for-phrase*.

Some scholars such as Halliday (1985) even contend that the inherent voice of the middle construction is nevertheless passive despite its syntactic oddity.

Langacker (1991a), contra Van Osten (1977, 1986), suggests that it is unreasonable to assume that the agent is irrelevant in middle construction, and certainly, the agent is anyway implied. We can imagine the subject *boat* in (9)b can sink by itself without human involvement in that it is an ergative construction or an anticaustive construction as in our study. However, for *the ice cream* in (9)a, it is hard to envisage *the ice cream* can remove itself from the carton with a scoop. There is agentive (in most cases, a human) intervention for sure. In addition, the property of easiness can only be attributed to the capability of an agent rather than the non-agent in the subject position.

(9) a. This ice cream scoops out quite easily.

(Langacker 1991a: 334)

    b. The boat is sinking. (Kitazume 1996: 164)

Moreover, some scholars such as Keyser and Roeper (1984), and Kitazume (1996), provide further evidence that middle constructions, as in (10)a, cannot realize themselves without external aid in the ergative construction, as in (10)b, where the event occurs in the absence of any external aid.

(10) a. *Bureaucrats bribe easily all by themselves
     b. The boat sank all by itself.

(Keyer and Roeper 1984: 405)

Looking into these two viewpoints, we allege that it seems reasonable and appropriate to assume that there is an agent participant implied in the middle construction since it differs from the anticaustive in some ways. Now that we have affirmed the implied agent in the middle construction, two questions arise: What is the status of the agent in this structure? Why are they different from agents in the passive?

Though Stroik (1992) insert oneself, for phrase or by someone to the middle construction as in (11)a, (12)a, and (13)a, the anaphor oneself, for-phrase and by someone cannot be self-supporting in all cases. The sentences in (11)b, (12)b and (13)b are counter examples.

(11) a. Letters to oneself compose quickly.

(Stroik 1992)

b. Letters to oneself usually stink.

(Ackema and Schoorlemmer 1995)

(12) a. That book read quickly for Mary.

(Stroik 1992)

b. That book is too thick for Mary.

(Ackema and Schoorlemmer 1995)

(13) a. *The car drives smoothly by Mark.

b. The car is driven smoothly by Mark.

Then we are in the dilemma, on the one hand, if we assume that there is an implied agent. On the other hand, there is no slot at the syntactic level for the agent to fill. Ackema and Schoorlemmer (1994) claim that there is demotion of the agent and a promotion of the patient in the middle construction, but these features reside in presyntactic operations. It is the arbitrary references of the agent in the middle construction that make it covert at the syntactic level. Thus, the agent of middle construction refers to people in general or anyone or anybody. This arbitrary reference of the agent seems to also provide a good interpretation for the generic reading of the construction.

As mentioned earlier, middle construction in the overwhelming majority of cases is only congenial to the present tenses. This non-eventiveness property also points to the generic features of middle construction that is widely accepted by grammarians of various schools. As put by Krifka et al. (1995), there are two basic varieties of genericity, one referring to a kind or a genus that is exemplified in noun phrases that are usually designated by means of articles, and another referring propositions shown in the sentences that report a regularity that sums up a group of particular events, as in (14). (14)a is in active voice and (14)b is in the middle voice, which satisfies the requirements of a generic reading. It should be pointed out that this generic reading echoes and coincides with the time-irrelevance features and arbitrary references of the agent in the middle construction to a large extent.

(14) a. A potato contains Vitamin C, amino acids, protein and thiamine.

b. These shirts wash easily.

(Krifka et al.1995: 3-7)

Non-agent Responsibility and Modality.

It is widely accepted that the subject of the middle construction is the non-agent. For this non-agent, there are two alternations. One is the patient, which refers to an argument, which, after undergoing an experience and an act, is changed by or is directly affected by a predicate. The other is a theme that undergoes an act without being changed. But we prefer non-agent here in that the subject is either changed or unchanged by the action. As in (15), it is easy to denote that *these oranges* in (15)a seems to be more affected than *the thesis* in (15)b where affectedness is less visible.

(15) a. These oranges peel easily.

　　 b. The thesis reads smoothly.

As we discussed earlier, for the functions of the non-agent in middle construction, those researchers who claim that there is only one participant prefer to lay a great deal of emphasis on the responsibility of the archetypal role of the non-agent. According to Van Oosten (1977, 1986), it is the non-agent that is responsible for the occurrence of the action in the middle construction. The middle verb profiles a process in which the non-agent is the initiator of the action (Kemmer 1993). He (2007) holds that the non-agent subject plays a significant part in the middle construction in contrast to the covert agent and that it is the inherent features of the non-agent that cause the event to happen. However, as we take a closer look at middle construction, it is feasible to accept that the subject itself is important in the sentences, but it is not reasonable to exaggerate the role of the non-agent since the subject itself does not have the volitiality, agentivity as that of agent in active and passive. It is tenable to say that the non-agent really exerts some influence on the occurrence of the event but that the non-agent itself cannot make the event happen autonomously. As in (16), there are, of course some external causers that make *the ball roll* or make *the pen write*, and in the majority of cases, there is an implied human agent who is responsible for the action.

(16) a.The ball rolls nicely.

　　 b.The pen writes smoothly.

However, we still value the partial responsible role of non-agent in that the adverbial elements that usually denote the outcome of an action to some extent strengthen the role of the non-agent. Consider the sentences in (17) and (18); the ungrammaticality of (17)b and (18)b reveals that the manner adverbs that direct at the agent do not fit the middle construction where easily is only postverbal and denotes the quality of any agent in general rather than the specific action of the agent as indicated by the manner adverbs such as expertly and cautiously, which usually denote a specific action of the agent rather than the quality of general actions for an arbitrary agent.

(17) a. This flashlight plugs in easily.

   b. *This flashlight plugs in expertly.

(18) a. Cotton irons easily.

   b.*Cotton irons cautiously.

(Fellbaum 1986: 27)

Moreover, this partial responsibility is said to echo the property of modality in middle construction as put by Fagan (1988, 1992). It is generally assumed that the concept of modality may involves (ⅰ) a capability that can be expressed by modal verbs such as *can or could*, (ⅱ) a probability that can be expressed by the modal verbs such as may or might, (ⅲ) an obligation expressed by modal verbs such as *must* or *should*, and (ⅳ) an inclination, as expressed by *will*, etc. As for middle construction, it is more amenable to type (ⅰ) and type (ⅱ), capability and probability. Just as put by Fagan (1988, 1992), middle construction is equivalent to the passive realized in a *can* passive, as in (19) and (20) where (a) and (b) depict generic cases of the potentiality of an event rather than the resultative state of the event.

(19) a. The piano plays beautifully.

   b. The piano can be played beautifully.

(20) a. The cartoons translate easily.

   b. The cartoons can be translated easily.

Composite Verbs.

 Having discussed the two role archetypes, agent and non-agent, now let us look into verbs in the middle construction. To facilitate our understanding, let us take a look at the following sentences:

(21) a. The novel sells well.

   b. They sell the novel well.

(22) a. The coat washes easily.

   b. They wash the coat easily.

(23) a. The chickens kill easily.

(Sachiko 1996: 161)

   b. They kill the chickens.

(24) a. This car handles smoothly.

(Fellbaum 1985: 75)

    b. They handle the car smoothly.

As can be seen from (21)-(24), the (a) sentences instantiate middle constructions where verbs *sell*, *wash*, *kill*, and *handle* are intransitive in that there is only one argument in the sentences. In contrast, the (b) sentences exemplify normal active constructions since the verbs are identical to the verbs in the (a) sentences, but they function as transitive verbs that take two arguments. From above analysis, we can assume that the verbs used to be transitive before they entered the middle construction. However, there are still some rare cases in which the verbs remain intransitive as they enter the middle construction, as illustrated in (25).

(25) a. After the heavy rain the pitch bowls almost too fast.

    b. This artificial snow does not ski badly.

    c. The new tartan track runs much faster.

(Legenhausen 1998: 56)

As can be observed, the three verbs, *bowl*, *ski* and *run* are intransitive even before they enter the middle construction. The subjects in these sentences cannot be logical objects of the verb as the sentences in (21)a-(24)a.

These inconsistencies may be the cause of these disparities between the different schools of thought. Some scholars (Keyser and Roeper 1984; Kemmer 1993) hold that verbs in the middle construction are transitive, some researchers such as (Fagan 1992; Massam 1992) maintain that they are intransitive. Judging by Hopper and Thompson's (1980) transitivity theory, it is untenable for the verbs in the middle construction to be transitive according to the ten criteria of transitivity. If we assume the verb is intransitive by inferring from superficially syntactic representations, the subjects functioning as the logical object of the verbs then become problematic. It also eliminates the possibility of an implied agent in the middle construction. In facing this problem, O'Grady's (1980) reclassification of the intransitive verb may offer some help for us. According to his analysis, there are at least three distinct types of intransitive verbs.

(26) a. Joyce laughed.

    b. *Joyce laughed Mary.

(27) a. The sun rose.

    b. *The sun rose the sky.

The sentences in (26) and (27) typify the first type of intransitive. As the examples demonstrate, verb such as *laugh*, and *rise* are pure intransitives, as shown in the (a) sentences, and which almost never occur in a transitive cognate form, as in the (b) sentences. Verbssuch as the *go*, *depart*, *slip*, *die*, *live* and *exist* satisfy the criteria of this group.

(28) a. Ashley melted the snow.

b. The snow melted.

(29) a. We changed the color.

b. The color changed   .

A close look at the sentences in (28) and (29) reveal that they are different from *type one*. These are normally construed as ergative verbs or alternating intransitives, as put by O'Grady (1980), for they normally include two participants, an agent and a patient, in the transitive constructions as illustrated by the (a) sentences. They can also be used in intransitive constructions, as in the (b) sentences, where the patient-like participant is put in the subject position and agent is not coded at all. Verbs in this group always have a causative meaning and can be instantiated by *burn*, *dry*, *move*, *cool*, *change*, *drown*, *close*, *heal*, and *spoil*.

(30) a. My fighter doesn't knock out easily.

b. *They don't cause my fighter to knock out.

(31) a. These drapes clean quickly.

b. John causes the drapes to clean.

Examples in (30)a and (31)a demonstrate a third type of intransitive that seems to resemble *type two* to some extent. They are defined as derived intransitives. What make *type three* different from *type two* is that the latter possess causative meaning whereas the former express potentially *self-originating* events (O'Grady1980: 58), which is why (30)b and (31)b are ungrammatical. It can be assumed that the derived intransitives fit comfortably under the rubric of middle construction in that they usually denote a generic meaning and need to be modified by adverbial elements of such as *easily*, *well*, etc. One thing needs to be noted is that derived intransitive verbs remain transitive in contexts other than the middle construction.

Having analyzed the composite verb by discussing its transitivity, we still feel obliged to figure out the concrete verb types that can fill in the slot. For this issue, it is instructive to resort to Vendler (1967) and Fagan's (1988, 1992) interpretations. In Vendler's (1967)'s opinion, there are two types of verbs in term of time schema: one is the process verb and the other is the non-process verbs. The former tends to be compatible with the progressive tense and consists of activity verbs such as *run, walk, swim, push*, etc. and accomplishment verbs such as *paint, make, build, read*, etc. The latter tend to be incongruent with the progressive tense and consist of achievement verbs such as *recognize, lose, find win*, etc. and state verbs such as *know, possess, want, believe*, etc. Under this understanding, we assume that only process verbs, that is, activity and accomplishment verbs can be qualified as candidates for the middle verb.

(32) a. *This peak does not reach easily.

b. *This match does not win easily.

(Fagan 1992)

The ungrammaticality of the sentences in (32) shows that the verbs *reach* and *win* are achievement verbs that do not fit middle construction. But one thing needs to be noted: we just give an explanation for the most general cases, there are always some exceptions. Just as claimed by Fagan (1992), it is feasible to say that middle verbs in most cases are process verbs but not vice versa. Just as the example shows in (33), on some occasions, non-process verbs also enter the middle construction.

(33) a. Politicians anger easily.

(Hale and Keyser 2002: 38)

b. The bass notes don't hear very clearly.

(Halliday 2005: 18)

Therefore, it is more reasonable to take a compromising view in selecting the verb type for middle construction. We may arrive at a conclusion that the verbs in the middle constructions are derived from transitive verbs, with activity verbs as the top candidates in the overwhelming majority of cases.

Based on the above analysis, we can summarize the properties of the typical middle construction as follows: (ⅰ) Syntactic speaking, there is only one participant—a non-agent (patient or theme) in the middle construction, which is coded as the subject and is partially responsible for the act of the verb. This responsibility partially results in the modality feature of the middle construction in which capability and probability are often involved. (ⅱ) There is no slot at the syntactic level for the agent in that it is suppressed in this construction. However, an agent with arbitrary reference is always implied and it tends to exert some influence on the non-agent. That is why the middle construction tends to describe generic or non-eventive things and is only compatible with the present tense in most cases. (ⅲ) The composite verbs tend to be transitive before they enter the middle construction. In most cases, they are activity verbs that are incongruent with the progressive aspect. These above three features can be taken as the criteria to determine the prototype of the middle construction, but deviations from the prototype are unavoidable.

First, as we have discussed earlier, some intransitive verbs also enter into the middle construction, as in (34). Run and fish are intransitive verbs before they enter the middle construction. Therefore, the two examples are non-prototypes in the category of middles.

(34) a. It's his fountain pen; when the ink doesn't run, he shakes it…(COCA)

b. The top quality rods from Montegue, H&I, South Bend etc. are good rods, fish well and look good.

(Davidse and Heyvaert 2007: 39)

Second, the subject may not be the patient or the theme of the clause, as shown in (35). *This colt* in (35)a is an objective experiencer rather than patient or theme. For (35)b, *a hotel* functions as the location that is responsible for accommodation. *The bag* in (35)c can be construed as a location or an instrument whereas in (35)d, *the machine* is instrumental to a large extent.

(35) a. This colt frightens easily.

(Hale and Keyser 2002: 38)

b. A hotel accommodates 500 guests.

c. The bag holds seven pounds.

(Quirk et al. 1985: 747)

d. The machine prints well.

Third, the implied agent may occur with the *for* prepositional phrase as in (36). In (36)a, *Bill* is the agent who initiates the translating event, and in (36)b, *Tom* is responsible for the action.

(36) a. No Latin text translates easily for Bill.

(Stroik 1992: 131)

b. The bread slices easily for Tom.

Fourth, the middle construction can be used marginally to refer to some specific issue without a generic indication and is compatible with other tenses and aspect as shown in (37).

(37) a. The dried mud scraped off effortlessly.

(Langacker 1991a: 334)

b. With the rebate, these cars are selling quickly.

(Langacker 1991a: 334)

1.1.2   In Terms of Construal

After discussing the role archetype, the composite verb, the degree of prototypicality and their related features, now let us turn to look at how construal works in the middle voice at the clausal level. Before we get to the point, let us first borrow some symbols used by Langacker (2008).

As illustrated in Figure 45, (>) means facilitation in contrast to hindrance (<). The small triangle (Δ) refers to the agent is non-salient or left unspecified. Figure 45 depicts a prototypical middle sentence: *The door opens easily.*

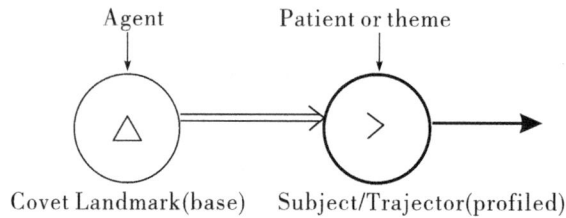

Figure 45   The Construal of the Prototypical Middle Constructions

As can be seen, in the framework of cognitive grammar, it is suggested that the active participant, the agent, is suppressed or demoted into a lower position than that in a passive construction since there is even no slot even available for the agent at the syntactic level. On the other hand, the passive participant is elevated to a large extent and put in a salient position and it can even be partially responsible for the event. Just as Figure 45 shows, the theme or patient is more prominent and therefore serves as the trajector that is profiled in the sentence. On the contrary, the agent is left unstated, and functions as the landmark in the base. In addition, the adverbial element is supposed to facilitate the effect of the subject rather than the implied agent, which greatly weakens the capability of the agent and makes it unable to exert much influence on the non-agent. These factors contribute to the non-eventive feature of middle construction and make it preferable to describe the generic state rather than a specific event.

1.2   Continuous Features

With regard to continuous features, our discussion falls into two aspects. For one, it is evident that middle voice at the clausal level doesn't show a completely unified form at the clausal level. In terms of different components, the role archetypes of subject and composite verbs show continuous features. As we analyzed earlier, the patient or the theme ranks the highest in the hierarchy, but sometimes they will choose the experiencers, instrument, or location as a subject that diverges from the prototype. We will provide further evidence for the continuous features within the category of middle voice. In addition, though most verbs are transitive before they enter the middle voice, some intransitive verbs also show up. And that the implied agent can occur with a prepositional *for-phrase* is another piece of evidence to eliminate absolute discreteness of the middle construction.

For another, at the boundary of the subcategories within the category of grammatical voice, a lot of overlap occurs. It is widely accepted that the middle voice displays properties of both the active and the passive voice. At the syntactic level, the middle voice takes the form of an active voice which can be regarded as one of the marginal members of the active. Semantically speaking, though there are many differences between them, the middle voice tends to be construed as inherently passive in that they both elevate the non-agent and demote the agent. The verbs in both the passive and middle are said to experience a process of detransitivation in contrast to the active. That is why both are regarded as the marked case in the grammatical voice category. The creation of a "mediopassive" voice or "nonactive" voice by some researchers lends further support to the close connection between them. In addition, the middle voice seems to have a close relationship with the anticausative voice that is often shown as the ergative construction in the discourse. Some scholars even think that middle voice can be included in the anticausative in that both two types of voice have no slot for the agent at the syntactic level.

The above features within the category and at the boundary of the categories shed some light on the continuous and fuzzy feature of the grammatical voice in English. It leads us to believe that middle voice is an important part in the continuum of grammatical voices, for it bridges the gap between the active and passive.

1.3   The Schema and Proposed Sketch of the Middle Cognitive Model

In accordance with the above examination and characterization, let us sketch the schema of the middle voice first. Then the cognitive model will be generated.

As illustrated in Figure 46, only one nominal participant, (N/P2)—the non-agent, shows up at the syntactic level, which is profiled in the interaction and becomes partially responsible for the action, whereas (N/P1)—the agent is demoted to a much lower position which has no slot available in the clause. The composite verbs are always congruent with present tense, and take activity process verbs as top priority. These verbs tend to be transitive before they enter the middle construction. The whole clause is generic in meaning and indicates the modality of capability and probability.

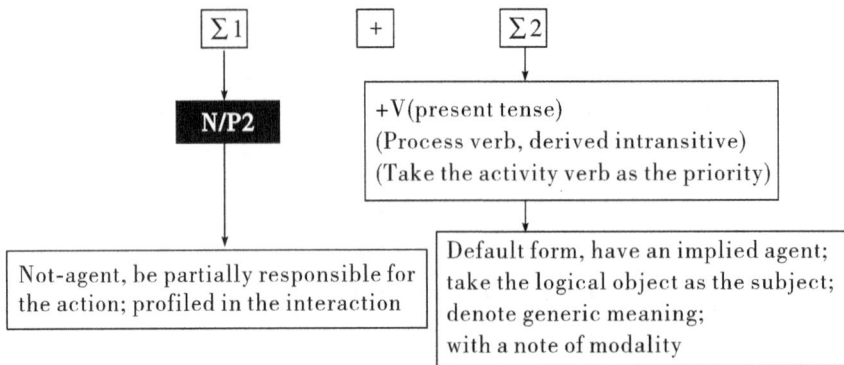

Figure 46   The Schema of the Middle Constructions

Figure 47 demonstrates the rough cognitive model of middle voice at the causal level. It suggests that middle voice, as one of the subcategories of English grammatical voice, shows discrete idiosyncrasies as well as continuous properties. Within the category of the middle, the subject is coded as the patient or theme for the prototype, but it may select an experiencer, instrument, or location as the subject in non-prototypes. In most cases, the agent is implied and covert for the prototype but it also shows up sometimes with the preposition for-phrase. In terms of the verb, activity, process verbs are regarded as prototype, but we cannot eliminate some other non-process or intransitive verbs in the non-prototypes. In the same vein, the generic features sometimes change into specific references in some non-prototypical cases. In addition, the middle voice not only shares similarities with the anticausative, but also denotes commonalities with the two leading voice types: active and passive. This model is supposed to be a reference for correct understanding the status of the middle voice, and it also provides further support for the fuzzy feature of voice in English.

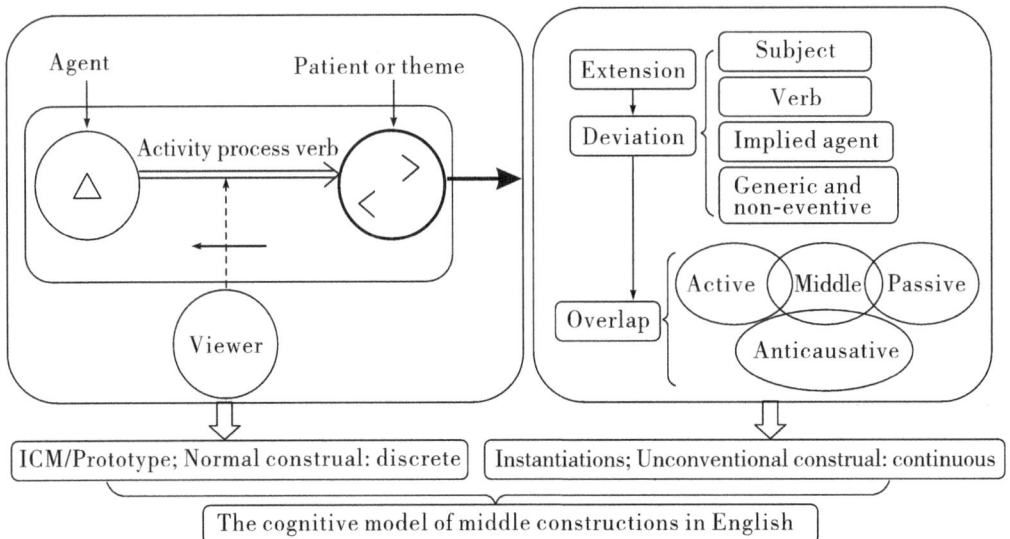

Figure 47   The Cognitive Model of the Middle Constructions in English

2   Causative Constructions

The last seven decades have witness an intensive scrutiny of grammar of causation in that every human language has their own ways to express this notion.

According to Haspelmath et al. (2001: 886), a causative is a verb or verbal construction meaning cause to V_o, make V_o, where V_o stands for the embedded base verb[①]. In Dixon's (2005) view, three types of causatives can be found in English. (i) Simple causatives refer to those lexical causatives, in particular, those ambitransitive verbs, such as *open, break, drop, coil,* etc., whose transitive use can be roughly paraphrased as cause to *V-intransitive*. Consider the sentences in (38), in which the transitive *broke* in (38)a means *cause to become broken,* whereas the intransitive *broke* in (38)b means *become broken.* (ii) Morphological causatives refer to morphemes within words that express causation. They can be considered an additional type of lexical causative, as in (39), where the morphemes *-ify* and *en-* make the verbs *purify* and *enable* have causative meanings. (iii) Periphrastic causatives are also called syntactic causatives in which the causative morpheme is a free form. Typically, it is a construction that consists of the verb such a *cause, force, get, have, etc.* and a complement clause as in (40). (40)a indicates that some difficulties were encountered, where *John* serves as the causer to make *the dog* walk. (40)b shows that the event does not happen naturally.

(38) a. Antonia broke the vase.

b. The vase broke.

(39) a. One tablet will purify a liter of water.

b. The new test enables doctors to detect the disease early.

(40) a. John made the dog walk in the park.

(Dixon 2005: 312)

b. Faulty design caused a bridge to collapse.

(Joshi 2014: 1)

In English pedagogical grammar, few grammarians take the causative as a type of voice. However, the causative is conceived as a discrete type of grammatical voice in a lot of grammatical descriptions. In Mel'ĉuk (1993) and Shibatani's (2000) view, it is reasonable to classify the causative as a separate voice. For one, it changes the lexical meaning of the base verb. For another, it can be combined with several voices. It is generally accepted that causative constructions in English fall into active causative and passive causative at clausal

---

① For a more detailed introduction, see Nedjalkov and Sil'nickij (1969, 1973); Kastovsky (1973).

level. Here, special attention is put on the periphrastic causative. That is, the constructions consist of a causative verb and a non-finite complement clause. By combining the two parts together, the construction usually denotes a causer exerts some influence on the causee to beget some effects, as illustrated in (41). (41)a is an active causative construction and (41)b is a passive causative construction. According to Joshi (2014), five causative verbs—*have*, *get*, *let*, *make*, and *help* are of the most common in causative constructions. But according to survey date, for passive causative constructions, only the first three verbs—*have*, *get*, and *let*—are preferable. Therefore, these verbs will be our focus of discussion in the following section.

(41) a. Tom (Causer) made Joan (Causee) laugh (effect).

b. Bill (Causer) had his house(Causee) painted (effect).

In order to catch the difference of two types of causative constructions, let us discuss the discrete and continuous features of the causative active and causative passive in turn.

2.1 Discrete Features of Causative Active

The combination of causative with active surely denotes the idiosyncrasy in that it is different form the active voice in some ways, and has shared properties in others. Let us address them respectively. To capture the very nature of the causative active, let us first look at the general components of the active causative construction by resorting to some examples as follows:

(42) a. I will have the barber cut my hair.

b. Sophie got her sister to sew her a dress.

c. You should let the school call the student's parents.

d. Emma had made her husband run for a mile.

e. The charity helps people to help themselves.

As illustrated in Figure 48, the general structure of the active causative can be generated below.

As can be seen, the subjects only function as the external causer. In most cases, it is a human realized in pronoun or noun phrases (*I*, *you*, *Sophia*, *Emma*). Sometimes, the subject can be an entity such as *the charity* in (42)e. A close observation reveals that the inflection of tense and aspect only goes to the causative verb (*have*, *get*, *let*, *make*, and *help*) whereas the base verbs (*cut*, *sew*, *call*, *run*, and *help*) maintain the default form. The base verbs are supposed to be preceded by an infinitive particle *to* if the causative verb *get* and *help* are used in the matrix clause, as in (42)b and (42)e. However, *to* is omitted when the causative verb *have*, *let*, and *make* occur in the matrix clause, as in (42)a, (42)c, and (42)d. Moreover, the selection of base word can alternate from transitive, as in (42)a, (42)b, (42)c, (42)e to intransitive, as in (42)d. When a transitive verb is present, it is always followed by an object.

Subject+Causative verb+Agent+(to)+Base verb+(Object)

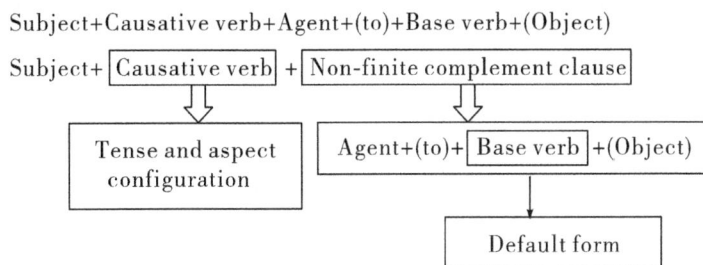

Figure 48   The General Structure of the Active Causative

In contrast to the prototypical active voice, the active causative construction is more complicated in that it always consists of a matrix clause and a subordinate clause. In addition, there are three participants in the construction. Besides the two N/Ps (N/P1 and N/P2) in the complement, another N/P (defined as N/P3 from now on) is added in the matrix clause and serves as the subject. The agent (N/P1) in the subordinate clause is supposed to transfer an action to the patient (N/P2), but it is under the control of (N/P3) which functions as the causer.

As illustrated in Figure 49, there are two interactions and two force transmission phases in active causative constructions. First, there is an interaction between participant 3 in the matrix clause and participant 2 in the complement. Second, the interaction which occurs between the participant 2 and participant 1 in the subordinate clause is construed as the normal active. Both the N/P2 and N/P1 are affected to some extent, but they receive the force from different sources.

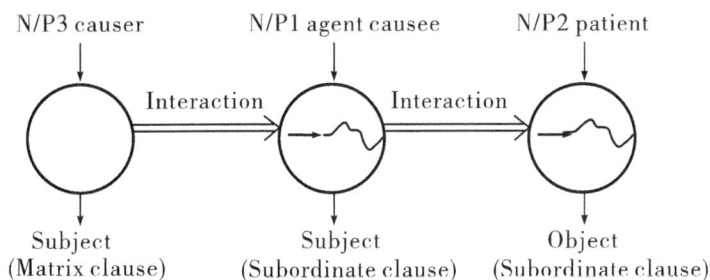

Figure 49   Force Dynamics of the Active Causative Construction

2.2 Discrete Features of Causative Passive

Having discussed the discrete features of the active causative, let us turn to the passive causative to see what the differences between active causative and passive causative, and the differences between the passive causative and a prototypical passive. Observe the following examples first.

(43) a. The student had his application delivered to the head of the university.

    b. The student had someone deliver his application to the head of the university.

(44) a. The bride-to-be got her dress altered by the designer before the wedding.

    b. The bride-to-be got the designer to alter her dress before the wedding.

(45) a. The director will let his deputy be interviewed by the BBC.

    b. The director will let the BBC interview his deputy.

As shown in the above sentences, (43)a-(45)a are typical examples of the passive causative. One difference among them is that they take three different causative verbs, *have* in (43)a, *get* in (44)a, and *let* in (45)a. In contrast to the prototypical passive, the sentences with *have* and *get* cannot take a *be* auxiliary though they have a verbal past participle. For the causative verb *let*, the *be* auxiliary can be attached to the verb participle. What is different between the prototype passive and the passive causative is that the latter falls into two parts: one is a matrix clause consisting of the subject and causative verb; the other is the complement or the subordinate clause consisting of the object of the base verb, the base verb in a past participle form, and the optional by plus agent NP.

As exemplified in (44)a and (45)a, the *by+agent NP* is clearly realized. In contrast to the active causative counterpart, as demonstrated in the corresponding (b) sentences, the subjects of the complement clause—*someone* in (43)b, *the designer* in (44)b and *BBC* in (45)b—are demoted in active causative rather than the NP in the matrix clause. The promotion of the non-agent NP, namely *his application*, and *her dress* and *his deputy* in (43)b, (44)b and (45)b, respectively, seem to be promoted, but the position is not in the matrix subject slot. The tense and aspect inflections of the passive causative go to be matrix causative verbs just like those in the active causative, but the base verbs are realized by the verbal past participle. To sum up, the general structure of the passive causative is as follows in Figure 50.

Subject+Causative verb+Object+(be)+Base verb (pp)+(By+Agent)

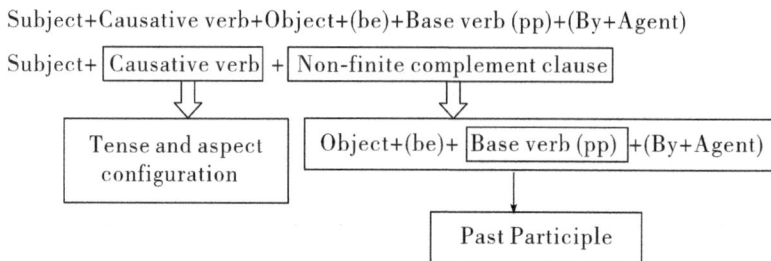

Figure 50   The General Structure of the Passive Causative

It is evident that the passive causative construction is complex in contrast to the prototypical passive voice. This is due to the fact that the passive causative is always made up of the matrix clause and subordinate clause. Moreover, three participants are involved in the construction. In addition to the two N/Ps (N/P1 and N/P2) in the complement, another N/P3 (just like the one in active causative) is added in the matrix clause. The patient (N/P2) in the subordinate is promoted whereas the agent (N/P1) is demoted to the object of the preposition by. Both the subject in the matrix clause and agent in the subordinate clause are supposed to exert some influence on the patient (N/P2).

As illustrates in Figure 51, two interactions and two force transmission phases are incorporated in the passive causative construction. Different from the unidirectional transmission of force in the active causative, the one in the passive construction shows the bidirectional transmission and interaction in that both the subject of matrix clause and the agent in the subordinate clause affect the subject of the subordinate clause that functions as the patient in the complement.

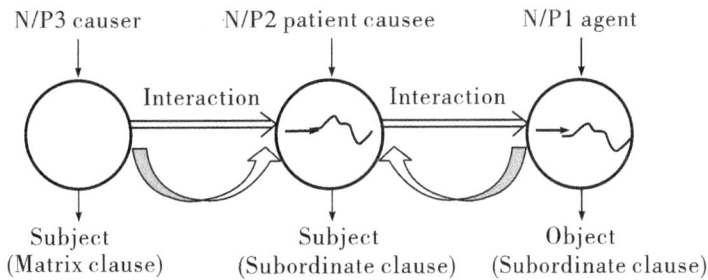

Figure 51   Force Dynamics of the Passive Causative Construction

2.3   The Continuous Features of Active and Passive Causative

Having discussed the discrete features of active and passive causative, we now turn to look into how the continuous feature is shown within the category of the causative and beyond the category of the causative.

First, within the category of the causative, although the causative falls into two types—active and passive, it is only assessed by looking at the complement rather than the sentences as a whole. It is very significant to remember that no matter what causative type the sentence belongs to, the complete causative sentence is active in nature. This is one of the pieces of supporting evidence for continuous features of the causative construction. To facilitate our understanding, consider the following examples.

(46) a. Mary got her transcript delivered by courier to the school.

(Active sentence with a passive causative)

b. Mary was asked to have her transcript delivered by courier to the school.

(Passive sentence with a passive causative)

(47) a. Mary had her brother bring his transcript.

(Active sentence with an active causative)

b. Mary was asked to have her brother bring his transcript.

(Passive sentence with an active causative)

Sentence (46)a and (47)a exemplify two typical causative constructions,the passive causative and active causative. It is clear the two sentences are active. Although we use the passive action verb in (46)a, the complete sentence is still active because we have a subject with an active verb, and the subject is causing something to happen. If we want to make a passive sentence, we need to make the main verb, the causative verb, passive. But as we cannot use *got* or *had* in the passive, it is necessary to resort to other causative verbs. As can be seen, both (46)b and (47)b employ the passive form of the causative verb ask to make the sentence as a whole passive.

Second, looking beyond the category of causatives, it is obvious that the causative voice has many shared properties with the active and passive voices. To some extent, it is suggested that the active and passive voice are embedded in the causative constructions. Because of the double configuration of causative voice, it is feasible to put it in the category of the medial voice in the voice continuum where it plays a bridging role between the active and passive.

2.4 The Schema and Proposed Sketch of the Causative Cognitive Model

Having analyzed the unique features of the causative voice, now let us first generalize all the features of causative constructions in a sketched schema.Then we will address the cognitive model of causatives.

The Schema of Causative Constructions.

Figure 52 illustrates the general schema of the causative construction. As can be seen, the schema is complicated because it needs to be realized by five units of the phonological and semantic pair (Σ). Plus, this structure has to show active and passive variants. They are is N/P3+V1+N/P1+(to)+V2+N/P2 for the active causative and *N/P3+V1+N/P2+(Be)+V2PP+(By+N/P1)* for the passive causative. For variant one, participant *3* in the matrix subject position has interaction with participant1 and participant1 transfers the force to participant *2*. For variant two, participant *2* receives the force both from participant *3* and participant *1* bidirectionally. The complete causative construction is active in form despite the variations of voice in the embedded clauses. In both the active and passive, an external causer is put in the salient position and exerts control over the causee. For the *V1*, five candidates (*have, get, let, make*, and *help*) are of most frequent use for the active, and three candidates (*have, get*, and *let*)

Σ1	+	Σ2	+	Σ3	+	Σ4	+	Σ5

N/P3	(V1) Causative verb	N/P1 in active N/P2 in passive	(V2) Base verb	N/P2 in active By+N/P1 in passive
Subject of Matrix clause	Have, get, let, (make, help)	N/P1 human or entity N/P2 entity(subject of subordinate clause)	(To)+Default form in active; (Be)+past participle in passive	N/P2 object of base verb N/P1 object of by, omitted in most cases

Interaction 1/——→ Force transmission

Interaction 2/ ——→ Force transmission ←——

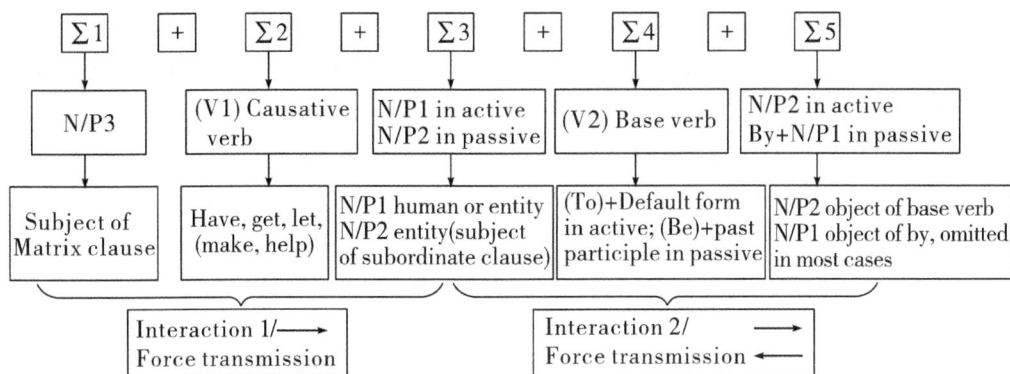

Figure 52   The Schema of Causative Constructions

are preferable for the passive. Given the above properties, it is natural to assume that the causative construction is a marginal member of the active or it serves as an intermediary between the active voice and the passive voice. Meanwhile, it is one of the typical members of the medial voice, which proves the fuzzy feature of English grammatical voice category.

The Cognitive Model of the Causative Constructions.

As we examined earlier, the causative construction itself is active in nature. So we take the active construction as the prototype of the causative construction, and the passive causative construction as the one of the deviations. As shown in Figure 53, for the active causative, the interaction is unidirectional and the force is transmitted in a linear action chain. At the same time, the viewer observes the event from the perspective of the causer in the matrix clause. And the event is observed from an angle of agent in the subordinate sentence. Both observations are

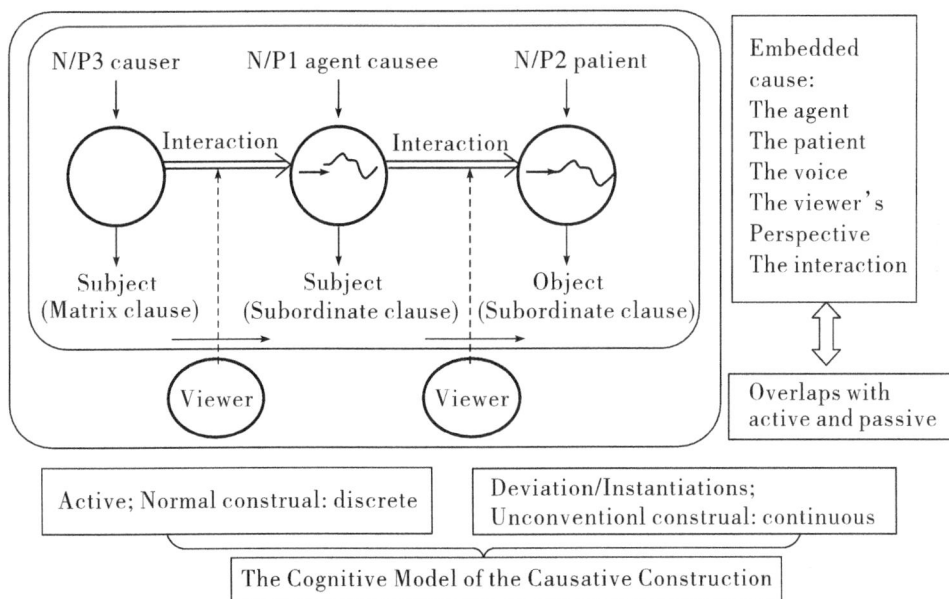

N/P3 causer   N/P1 agent causee   N/P2 patient

Interaction   Interaction

Subject (Matrix clause)   Subject (Subordinate clause)   Object (Subordinate clause)

Viewer   Viewer

Embedded cause:
The agent
The patient
The voice
The viewer's Perspective
The interaction

Overlaps with active and passive

Active; Normal construal: discrete

Deviation/Instantiations; Unconventionl construal: continuous

The Cognitive Model of the Causative Construction

Figure 53   The Cognitive Model of the Causative Constructions

of normal construal. For the passive, the viewer observes the event from the perspective of the patient in the subordinate clause, which is the opposite of the perspective in the matrix clause. In addition, it is evident that the causative construction is more complicated than the active and passive. However, the shared features form a voice continuum where causative is bridging the active and passive to some extent.

3   Anticausative Constructions

Having looked at the discrete and continuous features of causative constructions in the previous section, we now turn our attention to the anticausative voice. As a starting point for our discussion, let us discuss the relationship between causative and anticausative first. It has been generally claimed by some grammarians (Nedjalkov and Sil'nickij 1973; Haspelmath (1993); Zúñiga and Kittilä 2019) that anticaustives amount to the opposite counterpart of causatives.

At first glance, this claim indisputably fits the prototypes of both constructions because the former eliminates an agent from the verbal semantics whereas the latter installs an external causer to denote events (Zúñiga and Kittilä 2019: 41). In spite of this, we need to be aware that the two constructions are definitely not in a symmetrical opposition to each other. For one thing, the causative is a well-established concept whereas the concept of an anticausative has not been universally accepted yet although the term was coined in 1969 by Nedjalkov and Sil'nickij and it frequently occurs in current descriptive and theoretical work. For another, the application of the anticausative is extremely restrained in contrast to the causative, even though it has less variation in form and function. A review of the literature reveals that the anticausative is comparable to the ergative, inchoative, and unaccusative, but in fact, they are not mutual inclusive. To get a thorough understanding of the very nature of the anticausative, let us address its discrete and continuous features in turn.

3.1   Discrete Features

To look into the discrete features of the anticausative, it is necessary to get the general features of the construction first and then discuss the felicity of its components and the relationship between the components. Consider the following example:

(48) a. Martin broke the cup.

     b. The cup broke.

The sentence (48)b represents the most typical anticausative construction and one that is constantly cited in academic works. As can be seen, (48)a and (48)b exemplify a pair of verbs that describe almost the same situation that *the cup* has undergone a change of state. However, (48a) is different from (48b) in that the verb *break* acts as the causative verb whose meaning involves an agent participant who induces the situation. Then, what specific features does the anticaustive have? Let us deal with it by analyzing its role archetype and composite verbs.

3.1.1   In Terms of Role Archetype and Composite Verb

As a starting point for the current discussion, let us go back to sentence (48b), and make a comparison and contrast between the anticausative and its corresponding causative, passive, and middle construction in (48)a, (49)a and (49)b respectively.

As can be observed, (48)b is simple at the syntactic level for it only consists of one nominal participant that functions as the object or patient in the corresponding causative, which is active in nature, as in (48)a. In contrast to the passive construction in (49)a and middle construction in (49)b, (48)b is similar in having a patient-like subject. Just like the verb in (49)a and (49)b, the verb in (48)b shows the property of detransitivation. The difference between (48)b and (49)a is that the latter has the agent exert some influence on the patient the cup which results in the broken condition. The difference between (49)a and (48)b is that the former has an additional adverbial element that serves as an obligatory part directing at the implied agent. But for the verb in (48)b, it seems to exemplify itself by eliminating a causing agent and laying out a situation as occurring spontaneously. In other words, the intransitive verb broke in (48)b shows an action affecting its subject without indicating a causer.

(49) a. The cup was broken by Martin.

b. The cup breaks easily.

Reasoning along these lines, Zúñiga and Kittilä (2019: 41) suggests that the general property of anticausative voice can be defined as follows: (ⅰ) Its semantic and syntactic valency is one less than that of the base. (ⅱ) The agent is removed from argument structure, both semantically and syntactically. (ⅲ) Its subject corresponds to the patient of the non-anticausative voice. (ⅳ) Anticausativization is formally coded on the predicate complex.

Based on these characterizations, it seems necessary for us to determine suitable candidates to fill the slot of the verb in the anticausative. As noted by Zúñiga and Kittilä (2019), causativization usually applies to most verbs in natural languages, while anticausativization is usually available for only those bivalent verbs that allow agents to be omitted altogether. However, this interpretation seems to be far from being satisfactory.

To get the clear idea of the bivalent verbs, let us classify verbs according to its transitivity, and put our focus on the intransitive verbs to see how they can be reclassified in a more thorough way. Observe the following sentences first.

(50) a. Tom opened the door.

     b. The door opened.

(51) a. The cup fell.

     b.*fell the cup.

(52) a. The boy laughed.

     b. laughed the boy.

As illustrated in the above sentences, the verb open in (50)b is a typical anticausative verb that has as its counterpart a causative verb in (50)a. The two verbs form an alternating pair called alternating accusative verbs that belong to the category of unaccusative verbs. The verb *fall* in (51)a is also an intransitive verb which belongs to unaccusative verbs. Unlike the verb *open*, *fall* is a pure unaccusative verb which does not have an alternating feature. According to Haspelmath (2016: 35), unaccusative verbs refer to intransitive verbs with non-agentive meanings implying changes of state, typically of inanimate participants. Moreover, unaccusative verbs fall into two groups: alternating unaccusative verbs and pure accusative verbs, as illustrated in Figure 54.

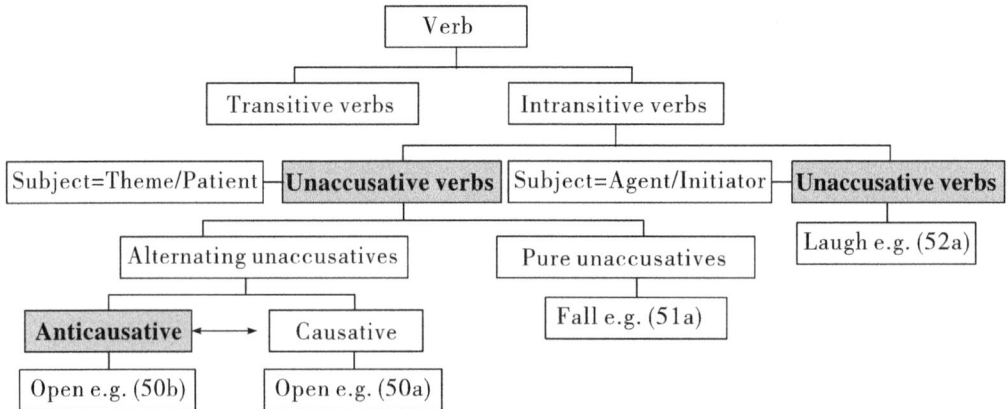

Figure 54   The Transitivity of the Verbs

It is said that unaccusative verbs are often in contrast with unergative verbs that refer to an agentive intransitive that denotes human actions that are not directed specifically at another participant and that have no inherent limit (Haspelmath 2016: 35). Just as the sentence (52a) shows, *laugh* is a typical unergative verb. Given the above analysis, we can divide intransitive verbs into two major groups, one is unergative verbs, and the other is unaccusative verbs, as demonstrated in Figure 54. Therefore, the verbs in the anticausative construction are the alternating unaccusative verbs.

In addition to this, Haspelmath (2016) presents a more expedient classification of the unaccustive. Since the anticausative always involves a spontaneity of action, the classification of automatic and costly unaccusatives seems more persuasive. The former may include verbs such as *melt, freeze, dry, sink*, etc. The latter may consist of verbs such as *break, split, open, change, close*, etc.

3.1.2   In Terms of Construal

After discussing the general property and the components of anticausative construction, we now turn to look at how construal works in the anticausative voice.

As Figure 55 shows, the anticausative voice denotes an anti-causer and spontaneous action that exerts on the patient but without indicating the cause. This automatic force seems to be bidirectional. On the one hand, it is conducive to the patient or theme that is affected. On the other hand, the agent in the corresponding causative is completely kicked out of the sight. Instead, they tend to take the action process as the landmark or base in which the patient or the theme serves as the subject that is profiled as trajector. The pragmatic use of the anticausative is to prevent the agent from taking any responsibilities. In addition, the viewer still observes the event from the patient or theme's perspective.

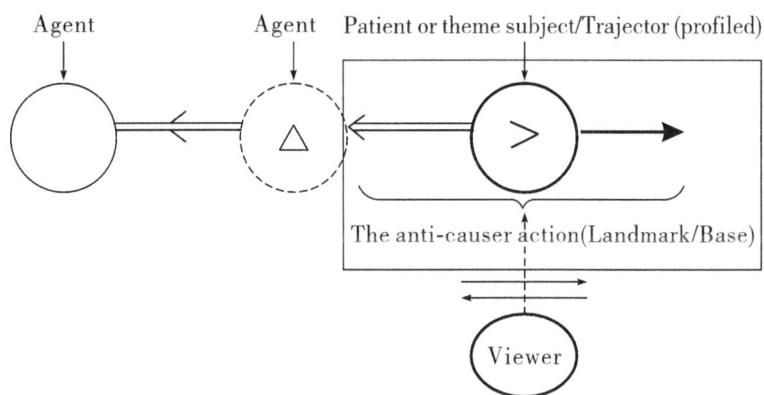

Figure 55   The Construal of the Anticausative Constructions

3.2   Continuous Features

Along the lines of the above reasoning, it is evident to see that the anticausative has many overlaps with the other voice types. Syntactically speaking, it is more similar to the middle construction and active construction in form. Semantically speaking, the middle, the passive and the anticausative all view the event from the perspective of the patient or theme. The three types of construction all put the patient or theme in the subject position and all three involve the demotion of the agent. Pragmatically speaking, the passive, the middle, and the anticausative tend to weaken or completely get rid of the agent's responsibility and make the interlocutor's tone become more objective.

In addition, as put by Zúñiga and Kittilä (2019), the anticausative seems to look more like the agentless resultative construction, one of the marginal members of the passive category. The examples in (53) show that there is a decrease of syntactic valency of the predicate in the agentless resultatives. Like the anticausative, the agentless resultative construction shows a changing of state, though the former is a dynamic process while the latter is more stative.

(53) a. The door is closed.

b. The vase is split.

3.3 The Schema and Proposed Sketch of the Anticausative Cognitive Model

After discussing the discrete and continuous features of anticausative voice, let us generalize its schema first. Then the cognitive model of anticausative constructions will be sketched.

As illustrated in Figure 56, the anticaustive construction is made up of the combination of two Σ. One is the nominal participant 2, which acts as the subject of the sentence and is usually coded as a non-agent and affected by the action. The other is a predicate that is made up of only a verb. The verbs that fill in the slot are supposed to be alternating unaccusative verbs that are intransitive in nature. Though it is compatible with several tenses, it is definitely aspectless. Moreover, the verb denotes an automatic and spontaneous action without an implied agent for the agent is suppressed or coerced in this structure. In addition, the subject is the logical object of the verb in this construction.

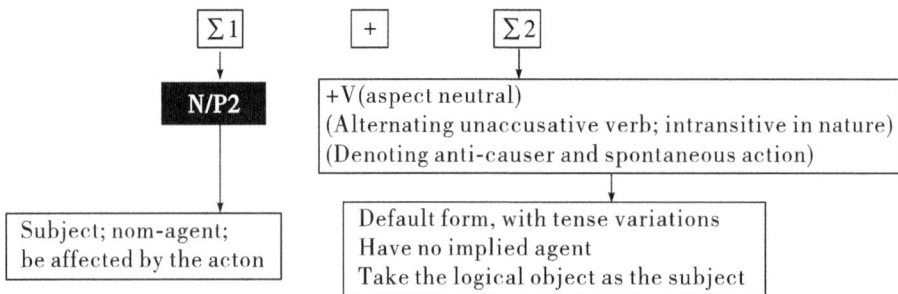

Figure 56　The Schema of the Anticausative Constructions

In terms of the cognitive model, as illustrated in Figure 57, the anticausative, though simple in form, possesses both its own discrete features and shared features with other voice types at the syntactic, semantic, and pragmatic level, three-dimensionally. Within the category of the anticausative, the subject is coded as the patient or theme and is invariably represented by an inanimate entity. The agent is totally suppressed in these constructions. It neither has a slot at the syntactic level nor can one be implied. In terms of the verb, the unaccusative alternating verb is the only candidate. Due to type variations of the alternating verb, it is suggested that the costly alternating accusative is more prototypical than the automatic accusative in that the former has a higher degree of motivation against the causer. In terms of continuous features, causative and anticausative are at the opposite ends of the scale where the former is closer to the active. The latter is more closely associated with the middle, and secondarily with the passive, but it also has some shared features with the active voice. One thing needs to be noted: this model will provide some references for a correct understanding the status of the anticausative voice, and offers further support for the fuzzy features of voice in English.

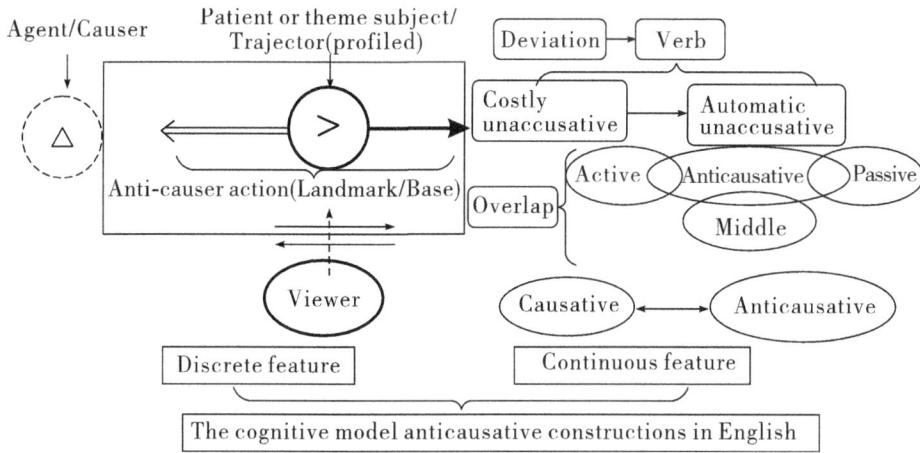

Figure 57   The Cognitive Model of the Anticausative Constructions

4   Antipassive Constructions

Being akin to the causative and anticausative voice alternation, the antipassive is commonly reckoned as a voice on par with the passive. The term antipassive was first coined by Michael Silverstein in 1972 and has received a great deal of attention ever since. To elucidate the concept of the antipassive, a great number of scholars (Foley and Van Valin 1984; Givón 1994; Cooreman 1994; Blight 2004; Spreng 2006, 2010; Guerrero 2011; Malchukov and Comrie 2015; Heaton 2017a, 2017b, 2020; and Polinsky 2017) involve themselves in the identification and generalization of the major properties of the antipassive by resorting to different languages. Originally the antipassive was considered to be restricted to ergative-absolutive languages (Dixon 1994: 146; Palmer 1994: 197; Dixon and Aikhenvald 2000: 7) while the passive is more frequently discussed in nominative–accusative languages. However, a number of scholars (Givón 1984, 1993, 2001; Foley and Van Valin 1985; Lazard 1993) have maintained that antipassives do exist in nominative-accusative languages.

Though there have long been voices claiming that antipassives do indeed exist in nonergative languages (Heath 1976; Postal 1977; Givón 1984; Foley and Van Valin 1985;

Lazard 1993), by and large the examples they discuss are not prototypical antipassives. In the recent decades, with more researchers delving into this notion with access to a wide-scaled corpus, there formed a broad consensus in newly published literature that antipassives are not confined to ergative languages. Heaton (2017a, 2017b) pinpoint 41 nominative-accusative languages that manifest the marked antipassives properties. In terms of English, Heath (1976), Givón (1984, 1993, 2001), Blight (2004), and Heaton (2017a) point out that English, as a nominative–accusative language, does have an antipassive voice or construction though it deviates a bit from the prototypical antipassive.

In this section, we argue for the existence of an antipassive construction in English. Following this basic rationale, we begin with a general definition of the antipassive in prototypical language and aim to gauge the English antipassive by distinguishing its discrete features in terms of role archetypes and composite verbs. And then we turn to addressing the continuous features of the antipassive by examining how it relates to other voices. Finally, we generalize the schema and sketch the cognitive model based on the analysis.

4.1 Discrete Features

To facilitate our understanding, we now turn to how the antipassive is defined in term of the prototypical ergative languages. An observation of the literature reveals that though the definitions of the antipassive vary, there is a general consensus that antipassives are both valency-reducing and detransitivizing constructions. In terms of the function, it is widely believed that antipassives reduce the transitivity of the predicate and make the patient less affected, indefinite, nonspecific, and even omitted completely (Hopper and Thompson 1980; Dixon 1994; Givón 1984, 1994; Cooreman 1994). Resorting to the antipassives in ergative languages, Dixon (1994: 146) sums up four criteria to assess the typical antipassive constructions: (i) Applies to an underlying transitive clause and forms a derived intransitive; (ii) The underlying A NP becomes S of the antipassive; (iii) the underlying O NP goes into a peripheral function, being marked by non-core case, preposition, etc.; this NP can be omitted, although there is always the option of including it; (iv) there is some explicit formal marking of an antipassive construction.[①]

Taking these four criteria as the yardstick, let us investigate what kind of sentences in English can satisfy these requirements. In Givón (1993), and Blight's (2004) view, English antipassives are not confined to one single construction; instead, several constructions instantiate the antipassive by different means. But two researchers' viewpoints differ in recognition of the number and scale of constructions that fit the antipassive. The constructions

---

① A stands for the transitive subject function. O stands for the transitive object function. S refers to the intransitive subject function. For more information, see Dixon (1994: 143-187).

they identify show the degree of hierarchy with regard to their similarity to the prototypical features generalized by Dixon (1994). To get a general view, we intend to analyze their classifications and unify their viewpoints by eliminating any additional overlaps and keeping the different types.

4.1.1   The Variations of Antipassive Constructions

Blight (2004) maintains that only three constructions can be considered as antipassive in English, (1) the unspecified object alternation, (2) the conative alternation, and (3) the preposition drop alternation. To facilitate our understanding, consider the following examples with their active counterparts.

(54) a. Martin ate the fish. (active)

   b. Martin ate. (antipassive)

(55) a. Sophia hummed the tune. (active)

   b. Sophia hummed. (antipassive)

The sentences in (54)b and (55)b are typical examples of the unspecified object for antipassive in English. This type is recognized by Givón (1993, 2001) as the object deletion. Here we follow Givón's naming and define it as type one, with the typical features shown in Table 5. As can be seen, in contrast to (54)a and (55)a, where the verbs are transitive and the patients or theme are definite, specified entities such as *the fish and the tune*, the verbs in (54)b and (55)b become intransitive when the object is deleted. The patient then denotes an indefinite or unspecified interpretation. The object of *ate* in (54)b can be anything than can be eaten, and the object of *hum* in (55)b can be anything that can be hummed. The agent NP in the subject slot in the active remains its position in the antipassive. Comparatively, there is no explicit formal marking *for type one*, so the three criteria can be satisfied.

Table 5   Antipassive Type One and Its Features

Type 1	(i)	(ii)	(iii)	(iv)
Object deletion	√	√	√	?

(56) a. John shot the rat.

   b. John shot at the rat.

(Blight 2004: 113)

(57) a. She kicked the mule.

   b. She kicked at the mule.

(Givón 2001: 171)

Examples (56)b and (57)b demonstrate a conative construction in English in which the patient functions as the object of the preposition *at*, highlighting that the action that was not definitely transferred to the patient. In this way, they differ from the patients in (56)a and (57)a, which present as the object of the transitive verb. We can infer from (56)a and (57)a that the results of the events have been completed or achieved, but for the corresponding (b) sentences, we are not sure. *John* may have shot at *the rat* somehow and missed the target. *She* may try to attack *the mule* by kicking it, but the action may fail. No overt morphological changes occur to the verbs (*shot, kicked*), but the verbs change from transitive in the (a) sentences to the intransitive subjects in the (b) sentences, and the transitive subjects in the (a) sentences turn into intransitive subjects.

As illustrated in Table 6, we define the conative construction as *type two*. In fact, *type one* and *type two* are equal in the category of passives in that they both have three shared features according to the criteria. Detransitivization in the two constructions enables the verbs to alter focus from the object to the action or the subject.

Table 6 Antipassive Type Two and Its Features

Type 2	(i)	(ii)	(iii)	(iv)
Conative construction /Preposition drop	√	√	√	?

(58) a. John climbed the mountain.

b. John climbed up the mountain.

(Blight 2004: 114)

(58)b is considered as the typical example of preposition drop for Blight (2004). As we can see, syntactically, it is identical to the conative construction we discussed in the previous section. But Blight (2004) claims that, semantically, the preposition drop is different from the conative construction in that the verbs which participate in the former tend to be verbs of motion or directed motion. Levin (1993) also has the same viewpoint. In (58)a, the transitive verb is adopted, indicating the goal, to climb the mountain, has been achieved. But for (58)b, we are not sure about the result. Here we do not classify this type as independent; instead, we prefer to categorize it into type two. Then let us discuss the Givón's (1993, 2001) other classification, one that Blight hadn't touched on.

(59) a. The children mow the lawn.

b. The children went lawn-mowing.

(60) a. She sold the books.

b. She is a book-seller.

(Givón 1993: 79)

(59)b and (60)b exemplify the antipassive construction that is defined as object incorporation by Givón. It is clear that the patient-objects *the lawn* and *the books* of the transitive clause in (59)a and (60)a are integrated into nominalized verb phases in the antipassive constructions and render the (b) clauses objectless and the verbs intransitive. The transitive subjects—*the children* and *she* in the (a) sentences become intransitive subjects in the (b) sentences. In this way, the patient is successfully suppressed and non-topical in antipassive constructions. *The lawn*, which has a specific reference as in the active refers to *the lawn* in general in the antipassive. In the same vein, *the books* refer to *the books* in general in the antipassive rather than a specific reference in the active. Given these features, we define object incorporation as the third type of the antipassive construction in English, and, as Table 7 shows, it has equal status with the previous two types.

Table 7   Antipassive Type Three and Its Features

Type 3	(i)	(ii)	(iii)	(iv)
Object incorporation	√	√	√	?

In addition to the above syntactic representations of the antipassive, Givón (1993) points out that there are also some antipassive-like constructions which are only indicated semantically. It is a general rule that a transitive event must have a salient patient and should be cast in the realis modality (Givón 1993: 80), but these two features tend to be subject to the interference from the antipassive-like constructions. Observe the following examples:

(61) a. Kelley likes this dog. (active)

　　b. Kelley likes dogs. (antipassive)

(62) a. The students prefer to buy the pencil case. (active)

　　b. The students prefer to buy a pencil case/any pencil case. (antipassive)

It is conspicuous in (61) and (62) that no transitive and intransitive alternations occur to the verbs between the (a) sentences and (b) sentences. The subjects in the corresponding sentences are identical. The objects of the verbs in (61) change from a singular object (*this dog*) with specific reference in (a) to the plural object (*dogs*) with un-individuated and generic reference, whereas the objects of the verbs in (62) shift from the object with a definite article to the object with an indefinite or non-assertive partitive determiner *any*, indicating non-referring patients. Traditionally, it is widely acknowledged that (61)b and (62)b are active sentences, but to some extent, they are regarded as antipassive-like sentences in that the patient is demoted to some degree and rendered non-topical. Here we define it as *type 4*, as Table 8 shows. It only satisfies two of the features of the prototype.

Table 8   Antipassive Type Four and Its Features

Type 4	(i)	(ii)	(iii)	(iv)
Plural, indefinite or non-referring objects	?	√	√	?

As we mentioned earlier, the prototypical transitive event is always in the realis modality, while the use of non-fact modalities such as habitual, negative, or irrealis often indicate in antipassive clauses. Therefore, sentences in (63)b-(63)d violate the prototypical transitive event and deviate to antipassive to some extent. These are defined as *types five*, as shown in Table 9.

Table 9   Antipassive Type Five and Its Features

Type 5	(i)	(ii)	(iii)	(iv)
Non-fact modalities (habitual, negative, irrealis)	?	√	√	?

(63) a. He took a fantastic photo. (active)

b. He always takes photos. (antipassive)

c. He has never taken a photo. (antipassive)

d. He would rather take a photo. (antipassive)

4.1.2   In Terms of Construal

Having considered the general features of the role archetype, the composite verbs, and five types of antipassive constructions, now let us address how construal works in the antipassive voice at the clausal level.

Figure 58 demonstrates the construal of the antipassive voice at the clausal level. It suggests that the agent that coded as the subject of the clause is put in the salient position and functions as the profiled trajector against the object as the base or landmark, which is always demoted to a large degree and coded as the patient or theme in the clause. The demotion of the objects varies in five ways: (i) It can be deleted; (ii) It can be put in the oblique position; (iii) It can be incorporated in nominal verbal phrases; (iv) It can be rendered non-referring; or (v) It can be rendered to a non-real situation. The patient or theme is less affected: they are not topical, no matter what types do they belong to. The viewer observes the event from the agent perspective and the agent has significant control over the action. The interaction between the agent and patient or theme may succeed or fail.

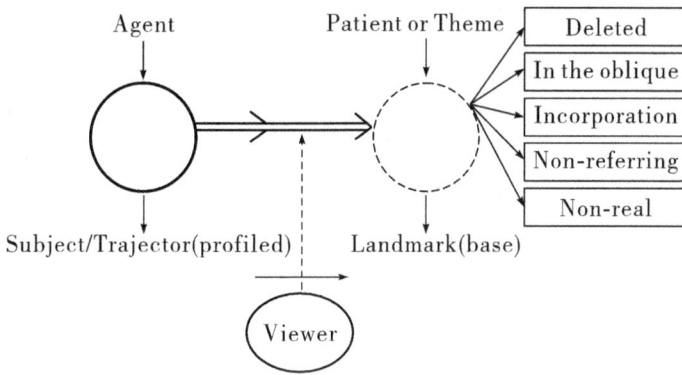

Figure 58   The Construal of the Antipassive Constructions

4.2   Continuous Features

Thus far, we have discussed the discrete features of the antipassive voice in English, but viewing the sample sentences we cited above, there is no denying that the antipassive in English is very similar to the active. In traditional grammar, with looser criteria, these examples will naturally fall into the active category. In terms of the prototypicality of the construction, *type 4* and *type 5* may either be taken as non-typical antipassives or they are seen as overlapping with the active in that they do not show any syntactic configurations but only indicate semantically. *Type 1*, *type 2* and *type 3* are more typical as antipassives for they involve a shift of transitivity. It is generally claimed that the active is the opposite counterpart of the passive. After our investigation, it is better to adjust our view and take a close look at the variations of voice in the discourse. In the active, the agent and patient always play equal roles though the agent is always the initiator of the action. But in the antipassive, the patient is demoted to a large extent just like the agent is demoted in the passive. Therefore, it is reasonable to say that both the active and antipassive are counterparts of their passive. We can thus reach a conclusion that antipassive is an indispensable member of the grammatical voice category in English.

4.3   The Schema and Proposed Sketch of the Antipassive Cognitive Model

So far, we have examined and characterized the discrete and continuous features of antipassive. To see what consists of the antipassive and how the different components interact in antipassive constructions, it is instructive to return to the general features of the antipassive and sketch them in the schema as follows:

As Figure 59 displays, we can generalize that the antipassive construction is a symbolic assembly that includes three complex symbolic units Σ1, Σ2, and Σ3, respectively, designating the complex of semantic structure and the phonological structure. As in the active and passive schema, there are two nominal participants: N/P1 and N/P2. Unlike the passive schema, the position of N/P1 and N/P2 is reversed and N/P2 can be suppressed by deleting it, putting it in the oblique, integrating it into a nominal verbal phrase, getting rid of any specific reference to it, or even transferring it into a non-real situation. Whatever means they take, the use of the antipassive is to make the patient become less affected, indefinite, nonspecific and even omitted so as to emphasize the role of N/P1. In the prototype, the composite verb is always intransitive. But when the antipassive is only indicated semantically, the verb may remain transitive. There seems to be an interaction between the agent and patient, but whether the result is accomplished or not, we may do not know.

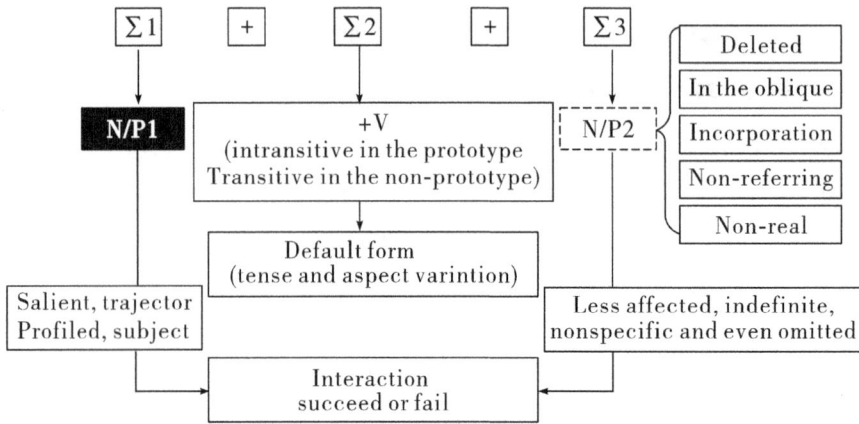

Figure 59   The Schema of the Antipassive Constructions

The induction of the schema helps us organize our knowledge of antipassive in a systematic way, but to get further forward with our study, we first need to generate the cognitive model of the antipassive to make it as vivid as possible.

Figure 60 presents the cognitive model of the antipassive construction in English. As we can see, the five types of this construction fall into two groups: the first three types are considered to be the prototypes of equal status in the category whereas *type 4* and *type 5* are non-prototypes for they do not have obvious syntactic differences in contrast to the active. Thus, it is natural to assume that there are many overlaps between the active and antipassive and antipassive is another opposing alternation for the passive. The prototype typifies the most general features of the antipassive, such as viewing the event from the perspective of an agent, suppressing the patient and making it less prominent, less affected, non-topical, etc. In addition, the intransitive feature of the verb can never be neglected. The deviation, the overlaps and alternation provide further evidence for the continuous feature within the category and beyond the category. All the features presented here render the antipassive as an essential member of grammatical voice in English.

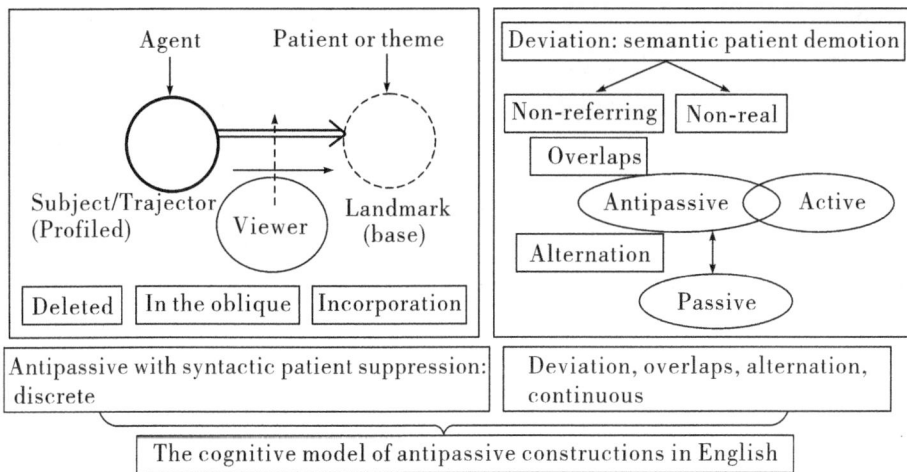

Figure 60   The Cognitive Model of the Antipassive Constructions

5   Reciprocal Constructions

In the last section, we have argued that the antipassive voice at the clausal level in English is closely related to or analogous with the active voice in one way or another. In what follows, we attempt to address the reciprocal voice, one that is frequently considered active in the traditional literature. Despite this, a number of researchers (Klaiman 1991; Givón 1993b; Nedjalkov et al. 2007; Li 2009; Evans et al. 2011) contend that the reciprocal is one subcategory of grammatical voice or that reciprocal constructions are different from active constructions and should be addressed separately. A key assumption made in this dissertation is that reciprocals ought to be treated independently as a voice subcategory. Given this, we begin this section by dealing with discrete and continuous features of reciprocal constructions. Then, resorting to the underlying features, we intend to sketch the schema and cognitive model of reciprocals.

5.1   Discrete Features

To get to know the discrete features, it is necessary to perceive what the reciprocal voice is, what essential components it has, and how it is realized at the clausal level. Let us answer these questions in turn.

5.1.1   In Terms of Role Archetype and Composite Verb

It is generally claimed that voice describes the relationship between the verb and the participants of a clause. As put by Li (2009: 58), in the reciprocal voice, each participant of a clause is both agent and a patient in relation to each other.

Semantically speaking, Nedjalkov (2007: 6-7) maintains that prototypical reciprocals describe situations with at least two participants, called reciprocants. (i) The two participants are in the identical reverse relation to each other, as in (64)a, *Mary* and *Lee* have the same semantic content. It can be construed that *Mary* is *Lee's* friend and vice versa. (ii) The two participants perform two identical roles just as in (64)b, where *Mike* and *Tom* are not only agents but also patients at the same time. Syntactically speaking, the two events are coded as a single reciprocal clause with a conjoined (or plural) subject (Givón 1993b: 82). The object of clause instantiates as *each other* or (*one another*).

> (64) a. Mary and Lee are friends.
>
>   b. Mike and Tom hit each other (one another).

There are always deviations to the prototype, and so non-prototypal reciprocals are not always symmetric or mutual. The extensions mainly fall into two groups:

(1) Deviations in participant numbers.

  In contrast to (64)a, the participants in the sentences of (65) may have three or more participants. In (65)a, the subject is a plural noun with an uncertain number of participants. In (65)b the subject is formed by three singular noun phases indicating three participants whereas the singular collective noun functions as the subject in (65)c. In (65), it is implausible to assume that each participant can perform double roles (agent and patient) and exert the same influence on each other. Their roles are asymmetrical in contrast to the symmetrical roles in the prototype.

> (65) a. The boys hit each other.
>
>   b. John, Bill and Tom killed each other.
>
>   c. People hit one another.

(Nedjalkov et al. 2007: 8)

 (2) Deviations of the base verb meaning in the context.

As exemplified in (66), the verb, *wake up* and *follow* often indicate two participants getting involved in the event. But in the real context, only one of the unspecified participants can transfer the action to the other, not vice versa.

> (66) a. We decided to wake each other up in the morning.
>
>   b. Charles and Bill followed each other.

(Nedjalkov et al. 2007: 9)

In addition, Nedjalkov (2007) suggests that there are mainly two types of reciprocals.

One type is the lexical reciprocals. These are often labeled as explicit and inherent reciprocals and instantiated by words without a reciprocal marker such as *to meet, to argue, to kiss, to quarrel, etc.*, as in (67). The concept of a lexical reciprocal in English is identical with the light reciprocal defined by Givón (1993) and the single event symmetry reciprocal defined by Maslova (2008).

(67) a. John and Mary kissed.

b. The player and the referee argue all the time.

The other type is the grammatical reciprocals, which has three subcategories: syntactic reciprocals, morphological reciprocals, and clitic reciprocals. English is said to only have syntactic reciprocals; that is, reciprocals with syntactic marking such as *each other* and *one another*. The concept of grammatical reciprocals in English is identical with the concept of the heavy reciprocal defined by Givón (1993) and the binary conjunctive reciprocals presented by Maslova (2008).

(68) a. John and Mary kissed each other.

b. The player and the referee argue with each other all the time.

In this dissertation, we mainly focus on the grammatical reciprocals. Having discussed the participant role of the reciprocal construction, we know they often occur in the subject position in English grammatical reciprocal. How about the composite verb and related pronoun? Consider the following examples. It is clear that the verb in the reciprocal can be transitive as in (69)a, intransitive as in (69)b and ditransitive, as in (69)c. The pronoun each other can function as the direct object as in (69)a and indirect object as in (68b) and (69c).

(69) a. The boy and the girl saw each other.

b. The student and the teacher talked to each other.

c. The lad and the girl give gifts to each other.

Moreover, there are also some constraints for grammatical reciprocals in English. (i) Objectless intransitive verbs cannot occur in the reciprocal construction, as in (70)a. (ii) Subjects and objects of the different semantic types are incompatible given the semantic specificity imposed by the verb, as in (70).

(70) a. *Charlie and Johnson went one another.

b.* Lewis and the table call each other.

In addition, as the grammatical marker, *each other* and *one another* may be used in different conditions, but they do not have any apparent effect on the valency of the verb. According to Hurst and Nordlinger (2011:76), *each other* is number one choice (variant one) for a reciprocal pronoun in an NP slot in primary English reciprocals in that it can be used with the full range of non-subject grammatical functions. *One another* (variant two) appears to be a secondary variant used in less common conditions. Ostensibly, the two pronouns seem to be interchangeable in most cases. However, some researchers have pointed out their differences in various contexts. It is said that variant one puts emphasis on the agents whereas variant two on the shared action (Krusinga and Erade 1953). Variant one is more colloquial whereas variant two is more stylistic (Kjellmer 1982). Variant one is more commonly employed in chained situations while variant two is used more in symmetric reciprocal situations (Stuurman 1987).

5.1.2   In Terms of Construal

After examining the components, the classification, and restrictions of the reciprocal construction in English at the syntactic and semantic level, now let us see how these constructions connect with the way we view the world by means of construal.

Figure 61 illustrates how construal works for the reciprocals in English. As it is suggested, neither the agent and nor the patient are put in the salient position. Instead, the participants are of equal status and both play double roles in the prototypical reciprocals. They are agents and patients at the same time in most cases. Both can initiate an action and receive an action. Both can exert some influence on the other and be affected by the other. The action chain is complete but it is bidirectional rather than unidirectional as in the prototypical active. Moreover, the viewer can observe the event from two perspectives rather than one, which is a unique feature of reciprocals. In addition, both the participants under most circumstances are coded as subject while the objects are realized by the pronoun *each other* or *one another* for the grammatical

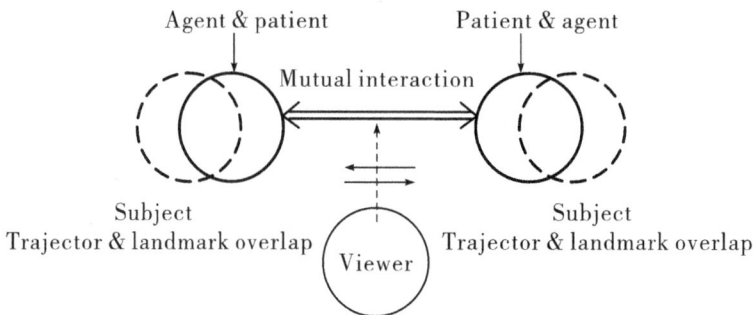

Figure 61   The Construal of the Reciprocal Constructions

reciprocal in English. It is evident that the agent and patient are promoted and demoted if we view the events from different perspectives, but the demotion and promotion offset each other in the interaction process. These features may provide some evidence that reciprocals though similar to the actives, are not identical with the active in one way or another.

5.2   Continuous Features

The discrete properties discussed above may help us understand the idiosyncrasies of the reciprocals in English. However, we also argue that as a subcategory of grammatical voice, the reciprocals are related to active and passive in one way or another. Traditional grammarians tend to believe that reciprocals are actives in that they have shared formal properties. We agree with them partially but not completely. Regarding the continuous feature, we have discussed the lexical reciprocal in Chapter V where we treat the words *resemble*, and *intersect* with inherent reciprocal meaning as one of the peripheral member of the active. Here, we see the reason why they are marginal. They overlap with reciprocals at the boundary of the categories.

Here we also maintain that reciprocals are closely associated with the passive and reflexive in one way or another. The reason why we mention the passive here is concerning the double roles of the both participants. Syntactically, reciprocals don't seem to have the same verb configuration as passives, but semantically there are some similarities. If one volitionally affects the other, the other tends to be affected. In terms of the relationship with the reflexive, we intend to give an explanation in the reflexive section (cf. 6.2).

5.3   The Schema and Proposed Sketch of the Reciprocal Cognitive Model

The discrete and continuous features discussed above present us with a guideline about how the schema and the cognitive model of the reciprocal constructions should be. Based on the relationships between the components of the reciprocal constructions, we assume that the schema of the reciprocal construction in English can be illustrated in Figure 62.

As Figure 62 shows, the reciprocal constructions in English in most cases consist of three complex symbolic units $\Sigma1$, $\Sigma2$, and $\Sigma3$, each representing the complex of semantic structure and the phonological structure. Like the active and passive schema, two nominal participants: N/P1 and N/P2 take part in the event most of time. Unlike the active and passive schema, the N/P1 and N/P2 are often considered to be in one chunk and perform as the subject of the clause together. They are often instantiated by plural noun phrases or conjuncted singular noun phrases. At the same time, the reciprocal pronoun takes the object position and acts as an anaphora that is coreferential with the subject that functions as the antecedent. The composite verb is realized in the default form with tense and aspect variations. It can be both transitive and intransitive, but intransitive verbs without an object are ineligible the reciprocal

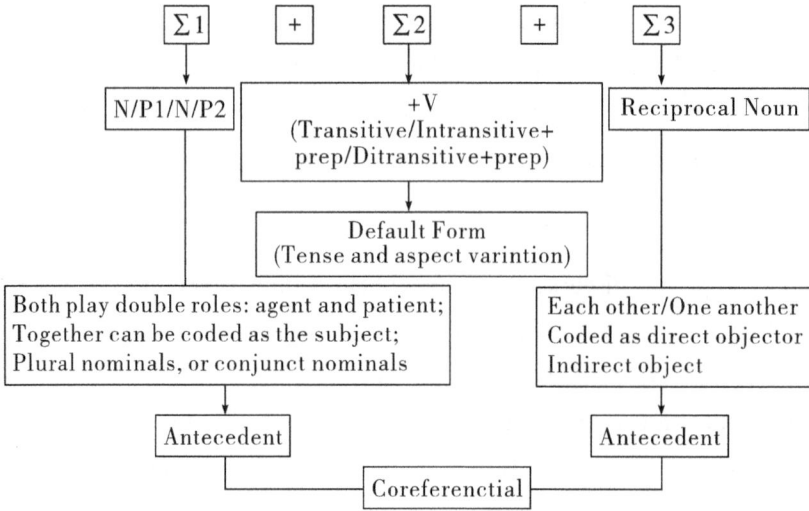

Figure 62 The Schema of the Reciprocal Constructions

constructions.

The generalization of the schema presents a general picture of the most typical reciprocal constructions. The cognitive model of the reciprocal constructions illustrated in Figure 63 may help us to see how the deviation occurs and evolves as the extensions of non-canonical and asymmetric reciprocals and merges with other categories at their boundary of the categories. As we can observe, grammatical reciprocals with syntactic marking are the typical reciprocal in English, but we take the one with two participants and unrestrained base verb as the prototype. Deviation may occur in two aspects within syntactic reciprocals. One is the participants' number; the other is the meaning of base verb. In addition, those lexical reciprocals with no

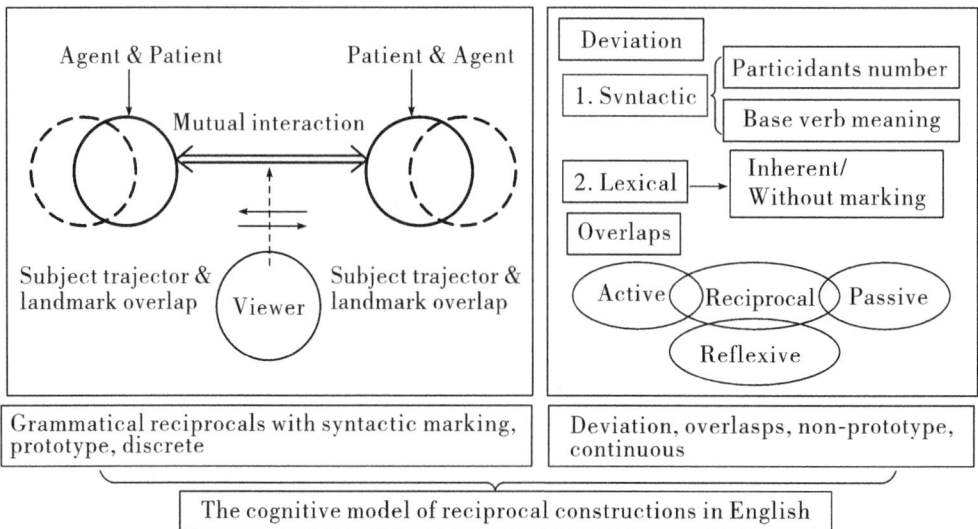

Figure 63 The Cognitive Model of the Reciprocal Constructions

marking or inherent reciprocal meanings are also seen as deviations of the prototype. At the boundary of the reciprocals, it overlaps with the active, passive, and reflexive in one way or another. The combinations of discrete and continuous features that reside in the reciprocals provide further support for the fuzzy feature of the grammatical voice category.

6   Reflexive Constructions

As put by Katkova (2008), while the meaning and ways of its expression show disconformity in the category of voice, other voices other than active and passive need to be recognized. Among them, the reflexive voice in English, though being disputable, is readily seen in lots of academic research (Kruisinga 1925, Barber1975, Alexeyeva 2007, Van Pelt 2010, etc.). In most cases, it is widely accepted that the reflexive voice resides in reflexive constructions (Givón 1993, Stephens 2006, Dixon 2012, Kulikov, 2011). As discussed earlier, this dissertation assumes that reflexive is an independent voice type having its idiosyncrasy as well as commonalities with other voices types. As a consequence, both the discrete features and continuous features will be dealt with in turn and based on which the schema and cognitive model are deduced and sketched.

6.1   Discrete Features

A review of literature reveals that reflexive constructions are not restricted to one type. Given this, it is instructive to sort out the most typical reflexive form, figure out its general properties and take them as the benchmark to evaluate other types of reflexives. To understand the typical reflexive, it is wise to know (1) How is the reflexive defined in the literature? (2) What constitutes the reflexive? and (3) How do the reflexive constructions vary in the discourse? These issues will be addressed consecutively.

6.1.1   In Terms of Role Archetype and Composite Verb

A lot of research contributes to the expounding of the reflexive voice and reflexive constructions in English. Let us see some cases in point. Van Pelt (2010: 76) points out that, with the reflexive voice, the subject of the verb performs and receives the verbal action. In Alexeyeva's (2007) view, in the case of the reflexive voice, the doer of an action and the object of the action coincide; that is, the doer experiences his own actions.

In terms of reflexive construction, it falls into several types rather being confined to one construction. Despite the variations in construction, generally, as put by Givón (1993), reflexive constructions can be defined in terms of two properties: (i) The same referent is mentioned twice in the nature of clause. (ii) The same referent participates in the clause in two different roles. In the same vein, Faltz (1977: 3) holds that a typical reflexive context is made up of a simple clause conveying a two-participant predication in which one participant is the agent or the experiencer and the other is the patient. The most conspicuous feature is that the two participants refer to the same entity. To smooth the way for our understanding, observe the following examples:

(71) a. The Prophets of Baal mocked themselves.

(Van Pelt 2010: 77)

    b. She poured herself a cup of tea.

(Geniušiene 1987: 189)

As indicated in (71)a, the reflexive pronoun *themselves*, the patient, functions as a direct object referring to the same thing: the subject of the verb, the *prophets of Baal*, which is the agent of the action. Unlike (71)a, the pronoun *herself* in (71)b serves as the indirect object instantiating the recipient or beneficiary role. Though *she* and *herself* have different roles, they indicate the same thing in the clause.

When it comes to the classification of the reflexive construction, the grammarians' generalization oscillates. Three representatives' classifications are drawn out to clarify our thought. That is Geniušiene's (1987) classification, Givón's (1993b) classification, and Kemmer's (1993) classification. One thing needs to be noted, Kemmer (1993) lays emphasis on the connection of the reflexive with middle voice. Givón (1993b) attaches great importance to its functional analysis, whereas Geniušiene (1987) mainly focuses on the reflexive verbs. In what follows, the three grammrians' generalization will be integrated by eliminating the overlaps and making them an organic whole.

Kemmer (1993: 43) highlights two basic reflexive types. One is a direct reflexive that is taken as the prototypical reflexive. The other is anindirect reflexive. To see the differences, observe the following examples:

(72) a. Joshua saw himself.

    b. The woman stabbed herself.

Sentences in (72) typify the direct reflexive construction. Three properties can be taken into consideration concerning the direct reflexive. First and foremost, the referential feature, which refers to the coreferences involved in the construction. The discussion of coreference is closely related to the reflexive marker which refers to the grammatical device that is used obligatorily to mark direct reflexive contexts in at least the third person (Kemmer 1993: 47). In English, the marking of the reflexive varies according to person and number, as shown in Table

10. As indicated in (72)a, the object *himself*, functioning as the reflexive marker and patient is coreferentical with the subject *Joshua*, the experiencer. In (72)b, the object *herself*, acting as the reflexive marker and a patient is coreferentical with the agent, the woman, the subject of the clause.

Table 10   The Variation of Reflective Pronoun with Number and Person

Person	Singular	Plural
1st	myself	ourselves
2ed	yourself	yourselves
3rd	himself/herself	themselves

Next, in terms of the scope of the basic reflexive, both Kemmer (1993) and Faltz (1977) claim that the direct reflexive construction is supposed to consist of a simple main clause, as shown in (72) and those muticlausal constructions should be eliminated, as in (73). Or semantically, it involves only a single event frame, therefore, the sentences in (74) should be excluded in that (74a) indicates a nominalized clause that involves two event frames and (74)b demonstrates a comparison relation that involves two two-participant events.

(73) a. John asked Bill to turn himself in.

    b. The girl who shot herself survived.

(Kemmer 1993: 44)

(74) a. John's killing himself sent her over the edge.

    b. Peter defends Max better than himself.

The third feature concerning the direct reflexive pertains to the thematic roles specified within it. As we mentioned earlier, the subject is instantiated by the agent or experiencer. However, the object in (72)a, in Kemmer's view, should be coded as stimulus in correspondence with the experiencer, in that the verb see always indicates mental events.

With reference to the indirect reflexive construction, as put by Kemmer (1993), it often consists of three participants, an agent, a patient and a recipient or beneficiary, as shown in (75). In (75)a, the agent *Minna* is coreferential with the beneficiary *herself* that acts as the indirect object of the verb buy. In (75)b, the agent *the boy* corefers with the recipient *himself* that serves as the indirect object of the verb give.

(75) a. Minna bought herself a new coat.

    b. The boy gave himself a gift.

Unlike Kemmer's (1993) view, Givón (1993b) argues that there are three types of reflexive constructions: (i) the simple reflexive; (ii) the emphatic reflexive, and (iii) the possessive reflexive. The simple reflexive in Givón (1993b) is equivalent to a combination of the direct reflexive and indirect reflexive in Kemmer (1993). The additional contribution made by Givón (1993b) is that he designates a restriction on composite verbs in the simple reflexive. Just like the reciprocals, it can appear with a transitive verb as direct object, as in (72), and a ditransitive indirect object, as in (75). In addition to the above two, it can also occur with an intransitive verb serving as the indirect object, as in (76)a, and in a ditransitive verb acting as the indirect object, as in (76)b.

(76) a. The lady spoke to herself.

    b. The fire-fighters told the student about themselves.

Next, the emphatic reflexive and possessive reflexive will be addressed. To see the difference, compare the sentences in (77) and (78). The former stands for the emphatic reflexive whereas the latter typifies the possessive reflexive. The emphatic reflexive is often used to lay emphasis or make contrast. It can occur in subjects with the pronoun being coreferential with the subject as in (77)a or in the object with the pronoun being coreferential with the object as in (77)b. As indicated in (78), the possessive reflexives often have *own* combined with an anaphoric possessive pronoun. To be concrete, the subject is the possessor of the object (Givón 1993b: 98).

(77) a. I myself refused to vote for Joe.

(Givón 1993b: 95)

    b. I gave it to the president himself.

(Givón 1993b: 96)

(78) a. Mary killed her own mother

(Givón 1993b: 98)

    b. The president carried his bags to the plane.

(Givón 1993b: 98)

According to Geniušiene (1987), there are two major types of reflexives in English: (i) reversible reflexives and (ii) non-reversible reflexives. The former falls into two major groups: formal class I and formal class II. In terms of formal class I, reflexive verbs are usually derived from transitive non-reflexive verbs by means of the pronoun marker alone. Both syntactic classification and semantic classification are taken into account. Generally speaking, these reflexives show three variations. The sentences in (79)a-(81)a are simple reflexives as claimed by Givón (1993b) and typify subjective reflexives, objective reflexives, and dative reflexives, respectively. Compare (79)a and (79)b, the verb *blame* is a subjective reflexive verb taking the human as the subject. The pronoun marker *himself* is used to replace a direct object Rose in the non-reflexive construction. The verb *manifest* in (80) is an objective reflexive verb. Unlike (79)a, (80)a takes an inanimate entity, *his impatience*, as the surface subject that acts as the object of in the non-reflexive construction. There is a promotion of object from the non-reflexive construction to the reflexive construction. The verb *bake* in (81)a represents a dative reflexive verb with the pronoun marker *himself* replacing the indirect object in the non-reflexive construction as in (81)b.

(79) a. Wade blames himself.
     b. Wade blames Rose.

(80) a. His impatience manifested itself.
     b. He manifested his impatience.

(Geniušiene 1987: 188)

(81) a. Vito baked himself a piece of the bread.
     b. Vito baked the child a piece of the bread.

In terms of formal class II, the reflexive verbs are often derived from intransitive non-reflexive verbs by adding a pronoun marker. It falls into two types. One is reflexives with the postpositive particle out, as shown in (82), and the other is reflexives with a prepositional noun phrase, or an adjective in the resultative clause, as in (83).

(82) a. The wind blew itself out.
     b. The storm raved itself out.

(Geniušiene 1987: 213)

(83) a. The child cried himself to sleep.
     b. The child cried himself hoarse.

(Geniušiene 1987: 187)

Moreover, non-reversible reflexives are also worth our attention. The notion of non-reversibility refers to the way derivative words enjoy an independent semantic and formal development unrelated to the development of the base words (Nedjalkov 1971: 14).

As indicated in (84), the verb *pride* is compatible with the reflexive pronoun *herself* rather than the normal noun phrase *their son*. In contrast, the verb *pique* takes a direct object in the non-reflexive construction in (85)b whereas in the reflexive construction, it takes a pronoun marker as well as a prepositional object, as in (85)a.

(84) a. Mary had always prided herself on her achievement.

b.* The parents always pride their son.

(85) a. John piqued himself on being punctual.

b. John (John's attitude) piqued me.

All of the above facts suggest that reflexives in English are expressed in diverse ways. Taking all the classifications into consideration, we claim that direct reflexive construction with a reversible subjective reflexive verb is to be regarded as the prototype of the reflexive form in English. The rest are non-prototypes. For how these deviations evolve, further discussion will be made while we address the cognitive model of the reflexive constructions.

6.1.2 In Terms of Construal

Having dealt with the general features, the components, and the classification of the reflexive construction in English at the syntactic and semantic level, let us investigate how the interactions between the participants work in terms of construal.

As illustrated by Figure 64, in the direct reflexive construction, it seems that there are two participant roles, agent/experiencer versus patient/stimulus, but, in actuality, the two participants are coreferential, referring to the same entity. There are interactions, but the interactions and force transmission reside in one entity. Whatever action the agent initiates, it may exert some influence on itself. The action chain is complete and unidirectional and similar to the prototypical active. Moreover, the viewer observes the event from the agent's perspective. In addition, the agent/experiencer is coded as the subject acting as the profiled trajector, the patient/stimulus serving as the landmark is instantiated as the reflexive pronoun marker and coded as the direct object. Moreover, there is an additional participant in the indirect reflexive; that is, a recipient or beneficiary, as shown in the latter part of Figure 64, as an additional element, where the agent/experiencer is the initiator of an action. By exerting some influence on the patient or stimulus, it affects the third participant while it remains the same as the initiator and some interaction happens between A and B.

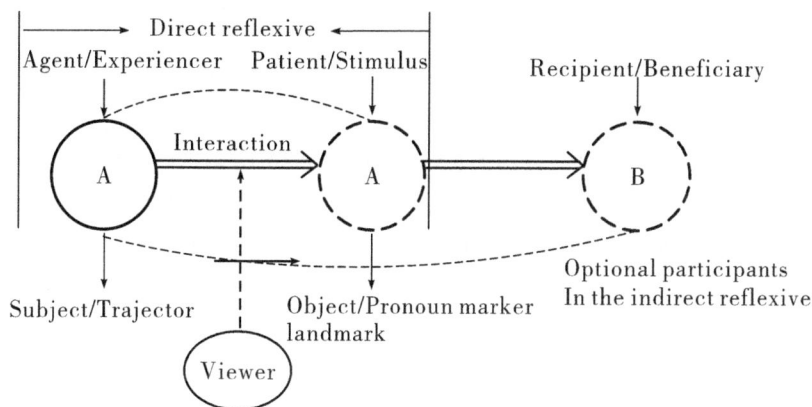

Figure 64   The Construal of the Reflexive Constructions

6.2   Continuous Features

As we mentioned earlier, the reflexive voice is one of the most disputable voice categories. Many researchers believe it is active in nature since the sentences in reflexive do not have very conspicuous features, nor do they form a paradigm in contrast to the active construction except in the use of pronoun marker *oneself*. Just as shown in the reversible reflexive, the reflexive and non-reflexive are very similar to each other. In addition, the transitive verb without a pronoun may also have reflexive meaning such as *Tom dressed* or *Mary combed*. This provides evidence for the fuzzy boundary between the active and reflexive.

Some researchers also present continuous features of the reflexives. For example, Van Pelt (2010) argues that the reflexive voice is a combination of the active and passive voices in that the action moves away from the subject in the active voice whereas the action moves toward the subject in the passive voice. However, the action of the verb moves both away from and back toward the verbal subject in the reflexive. Steinbach (2002) argues that the anticausative construction and middle construction do not contain a reflexive pronoun, but verbs of grooming and verbs indicating the change in body posture also permit a reflexive explanation without a reflexive pronoun, as in (86). In the same vein, it is suggested by Kemmer (1993) that a number of middle types are closely related to the reflexive.

(86) a. The children are washing themselves.

　　b. Tom is shaving.

6.3   The Schema and Proposed Sketch of the Reflexive Cognitive Model

The discussion of the discrete and continuous features facilitates our understanding of reflexive constructions. However, some abstractions and generalizations of the reflexive constructions still need to be dealt with by the schema and cognitive model. In what follows, the reflexive schema will be sketched first, and then the cognitive model will be drawn out based on this analysis.

As Figure 65 illustrates, the reflexive construction in English is generally comprised of three complex symbolic units $\Sigma 1$, $\Sigma 2$, and $\Sigma 3$, each of which represents the complex of semantic structures and the phonological structures. It designates a two-participant event where N/P1 is the agent/experiencer and is coded as the subject. N/P2 is the patient or stimulus that instantiated by reflexive pronoun suffix varying with person and number and is coded as direct or indirect object. Moreover, N/P1 serves as an antecedent that is coreferiential with the N/P2, which acts as the anaphora. The most important point is that N/P1 and N/P2 refer to the same entity. The composite verb is realized in the default form with tense and aspect variation and falls into three groups: the subjective reflexive verb, the objective reflexive verb, and the dative reflexive verb, as we discussed earlier. In addition, the composite verbs can be both transitive and intransitive, an intransitive verb plus a preposition and an object or ditransitive verb with a preposition plus an object.

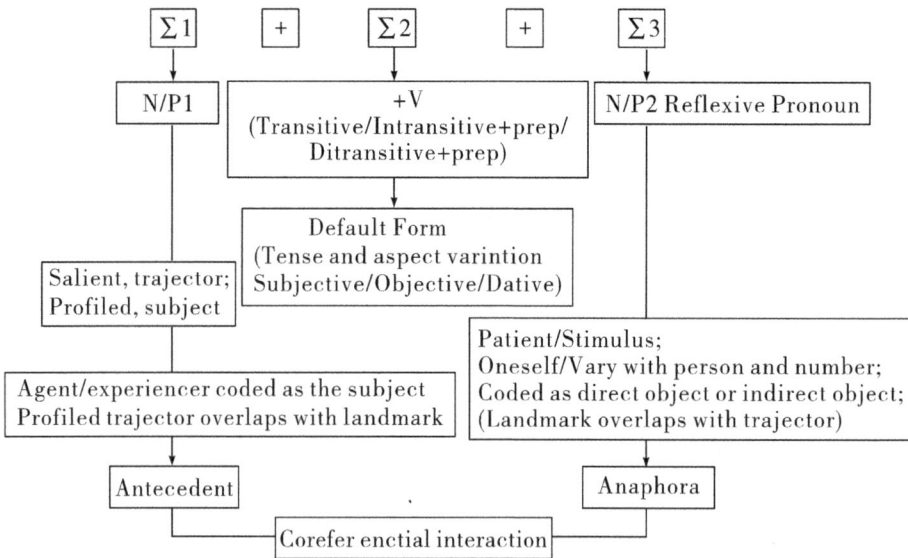

Figure 65　The Schema of the Reflexive Constructions

The induction of the schema helps us abstract the main properties of the reflexive construction based on its discrete and continuous features. The generalization of the cognitive model of the reflexive construction will pave the way for the comprehensive understanding of the reflexive.

By combining the prototype and its deviations, the cognitive model of reflexive construction in English can be sketched in Figure 66. As we can see, the direct reflexive with a subjective reflexive verb in simple clause is the prototype of the reflexive. The deviation falls into two groups. The first is the internal deviation which is mainly concerning the composite verb. The verb diverges from the subjective transitive reflexive verb in the prototype to the objective or dative reflexive verb on the one hand, and intransitive verb plus preposition or ditransitive verb plus preposition, on the other hand. The second is the classification deviation. It ranges from the direct reflexive in the prototype to the indirect reflexive, the emphatic reflexive and the possessive reflexive in the non-prototypes. Moreover, it shares similar features with the active, passive, reciprocal, and middle voices at the boundary of the subcategories. All in all, the integration of discrete and continuous features and the combination of prototypes and non-prototypes reside in the reflexives shown in the cognitive model may not only shed further light on the fuzzy feature of the grammatical voice category but also present us with a holistic picture of the reflexive voice in English.

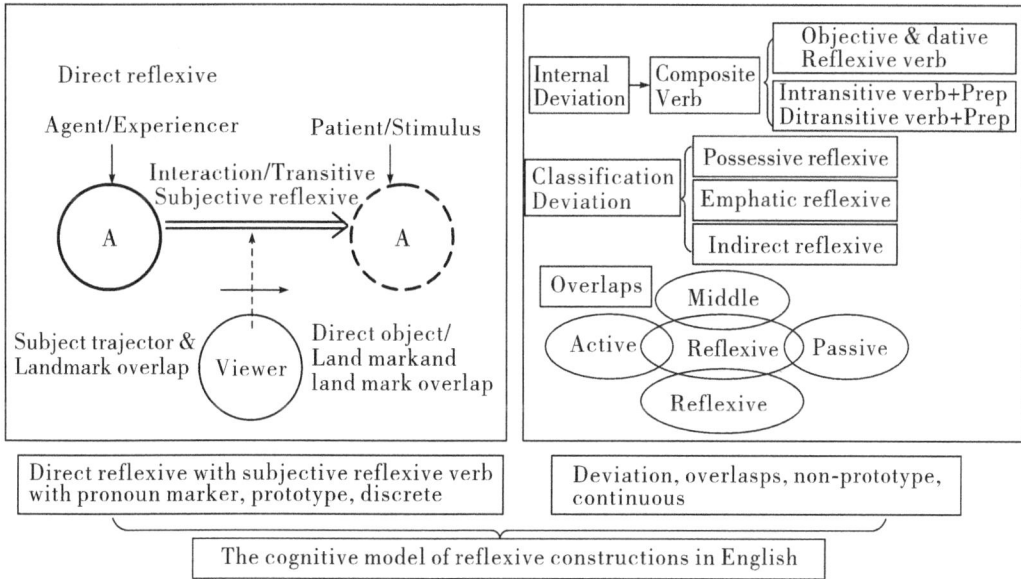

Figure 66   The Cognitive Model of the Reflexive Constructions

7   Applicative Constructions

The applicative voice is a concept that is frequently mentioned in the literature. It refers to a grammatical voice that involves promoting an oblique argument of a verb to the (core) object argument. Prototypically, the applicatives goes with intransitive verbs. The peripheral object can be elevated to the centre serving as a direct object (Dixon and Alexandra 1999). It can also be applied to transitive verbs and results in ditransitive verbs. The applicative voice is clearly designated in Bantu languages and Austronesian languages (Kikusawa 2012; Jerro 2016), where morphological affixes are clearly seen in the applicative. It is generally said that English does not have a particular type of prefix or suffix to indicate the applicative, but some similar constructions can achieve applicative effects.

7.1 Discrete Features

Though the applicative in English is only recognized as a peripheral member in contrast to the applicative construction in agglutinative languages, three types of similar constructions are regarded as applicative in English in the literature.

First, prepositions can be compounded with verbs for an applicative effect. As indicated in (87)-(89), the verbs, *run, live*, and *grow* are intransitive in the (a) sentences, but they change into transitive verbs in (b) sentences. At the same time, the peripheral objects, *the giant, his wife and his shoes*, are promoted in the (a) sentences and brought to the centre as the direct objects in the (b) sentences.

(87) a. Jack ran faster than the giant.

    b. Jack outran the giant.

(88) a. The man lived longer than his wife.

    b. The man outlived his wife.

(89) a. The boy grew out of his shoes again.

    b. The boy outgrew his shoes.

Another type can be designated by pairs of intransitive/transitive verbs with rather similar (although not identical) meanings. As put by Dixion (2012b), in these constructions, an optional peripheral argument for the intransitive verb corresponds to the obligatory object argument for the transitive, as in (90)-(92), where *the problem, their children*, and *the murder* in the (a) sentences serve as peripheral arguments, but they all change into direct objects in the (b) sentences. Though the composite verbs changes, the intransitive verbs in (a) have similar meaning to the transitive verb in (b).

(90) a. John thought about the problem.

    b. John considered the problem.

(Dixon 2012b: 330)

(91) a. Most parents give birth to their children in late twenties.

    b. Most parents bear their children in late twenties.

(92) a. She confessed to the murder.

   b. She admitted the murder.

In addition, though Dixon (2012b: 338) claims that the alternative structure shown by the verb give in English does not qualify as an applicative because there is no marking on the verb. Both Marantz (1993) and Tallerman (2005) argue that dative shifting or dative movement construction in English, as in (93)-(95), is actually an applicative construction with a non-overt applicative marker.

(93) a. Jessica gave a gift to Michael.

   b. Jessica gave Michael a gift.

(94) a. I read a letter to Mary.

   b. I read Mary a letter.

(Marantz 1993)

(95) a. My brother sold his bike to Sue.

   b. My brother sold Sue his bike.

(Tallerman 2005: 201)

As can be seen, dative shifting occurs with three-argument verbs such as give, read, and sell, as illustrated in (93)-(95), respectively. In the (a) sentences these verbs take direct object NPs such as *a gift*, *a letter* and *his bike* followed by oblique preposition phrases. However, in the (b) sentences, the objects of the preposition, *Michael*, *Mary* and *Sue*, have been promoted to the position immediately after the verb while the original objects are demoted into the secondary position. This alternation seems to align with the notion of applicative construction. In terms of the role archetype, these constructions seem to be very similar to the active construction. The subject can be the agent, while the object can be the patient or the beneficiary in the applicative construction. The resultative forms of the applicative constructions are transitive in nature.

In terms of construal, it seems that the applicative is similar to the active in form, but it has to indicate the changing role of the oblique object to the direct object. Therefore, it is rather abrupt to take the (b) sentences in (87)-(95) as the applicative without referring to the corresponding (a) sentences.

As illustrated in Figure 67, the applicative construction shows the interaction between two or three participants. The subject is coded as the agent and put in the profiled trajectory position while the object is coded as the patient put in the landmark position. One thing that needs to be noted is that the object demonstrates certain variations. One is consistent with the object of preposition in the oblique position in intransitive clause before it is promoted to the direct object position in the transitive clause. The other shows in the dative construction where the recipient /beneficiary is promoted to the direct object position by deleting the preposition and demoting the original direct object into a secondary position. The viewer observes the event from the agent perspective. The agent stays stable, but the patient is in a dynamic state varying from non-dative construction to dative construction.

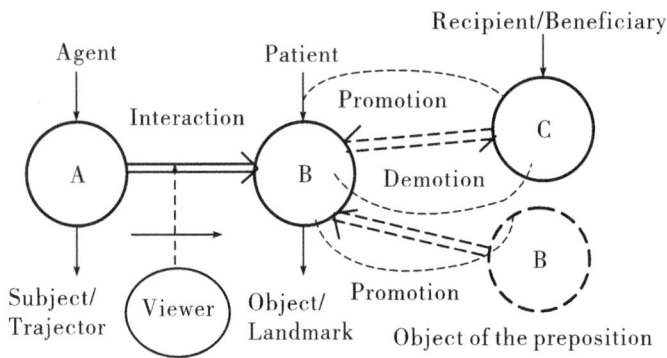

Figure 67   The Construal of the Applicative Constructions

7.2   Continuous Features

Applicative constructions in English resemble the active to a great extent. Observing the (b) sentences in (87)-(95), we can change them into the passive voice easily. In addition, it seems that there are no formal differences between the applicative and active if we only look at the resultative (b) sentences without referring to (a) sentences. However, there are differences if we dig deeper to find the very nature of each construction. The formation of the applicative takes the non-applicative as a reference point. It provides further evidence to the fuzzy feature at the boundary of the voice category. Moreover, applicative construction does not confine to one structure, its variations show the transitive continuum where the transitivity of the verb varies from the intransitive verb with one argument to transitive verbs with two arguments and then to ditransitive verbs with three arguments.

7.3   The Schema and Proposed Sketch of the Applicative Cognitive Model

Different from other voice types, the applicative voice in English seems not to have unique feature superficially. But its difference resides in the dynamic changing from intransitive sentence with the preposition oblique to the transitive sentences taking the direct object on the one hand, or the changing role of the object in a dative movement. Based on above analysis, let us sketch its schema and cognitive model in turn.

As we can see, in Figure 68, the applicative constructions fall into three types and have two variations in components in English. It may consist of three complex symbolic units $\Sigma 1$, $\Sigma 2$, and $\Sigma 3$ or four complex symbolic units $\Sigma 1$, $\Sigma 2$, $\Sigma 3$, and $\Sigma 4$. Each represents the complex of the semantic structure and the phonological structure. It specifies a two-participant event or a three-participant event. In the former case, the N/P1 is the agent and is coded as the subject. The N/P2 is the patient and is coded as a direct object. In the latter case, the N/P1 remains the same: it is still the agent and is coded as the subject, but the N/P2 moves to the secondary object position and the slot is replaced by the N/P3 that is the beneficiary and recipient in the original sentences. In the *type one* and *type two* as we discussed above, there is an interaction between N/P1 and N/P2. In the *type three*, the interaction happens among three participants, N/P1, N/P2 and N/P3. Both the N/P2 and N/P3 can serve as the primary landmark and secondary landmark, but there are type variations. The composite verbs have to undergo the process from the intransitive form to the transitive form or from the transitive form to the ditransitive form. Syntactically, it presents in the default verb form with tense and aspect variations.

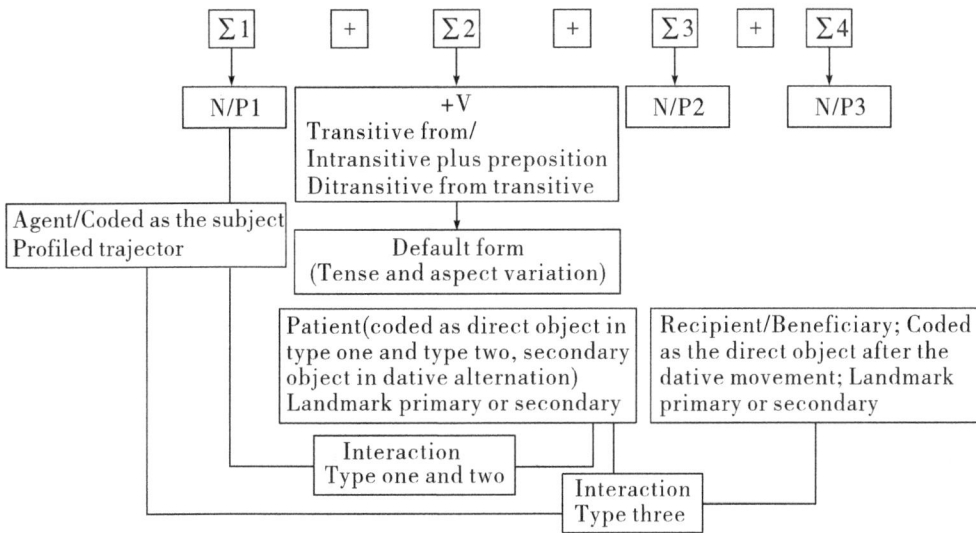

Figure 68   The Schema of the Applicative Constructions

The sketch of the schema presents us with the essential components of applicative construction and how these constitutes interact with each other. Next, it is still necessary to generalize the cognitive model of applicative construction to make our understanding of applicative construction connected and instantiated in a comprehensive way.

Given the above analysis, we sketch the cognitive model of the applicative construction in English in Figure 69. Taking every type of applicative construction into account, we assume that type one and type two are more typical in that type three is evolved from type one and type two to some extent. It is suggested that the applicative prototype resides in the dynamic process from the intransitive clause to the transitive clause, where there is a valency increasing for the final clause. There are two participants (A and B) involved in the event. The agent is in the salient position and acts as the profiled trajector while the patient appears only after the object of the preposition, which is promoted when the applicative voice is exerted. In addition, we assume the dative alternation as being non-prototype. Its deviation manifests itself in having one more participant (C) which will be elevated to the direct object position and make the original object downgraded to the secondary position.

Furthermore, there are overlaps between the active and the applicative since it seems that there is no syntactic difference. However, for applicative constructions, it is better to assume them to be the combination of two sentences, the original one and the resultative one, since there is no overt marker for applicative in English in contrast to the applicative in some other languages.

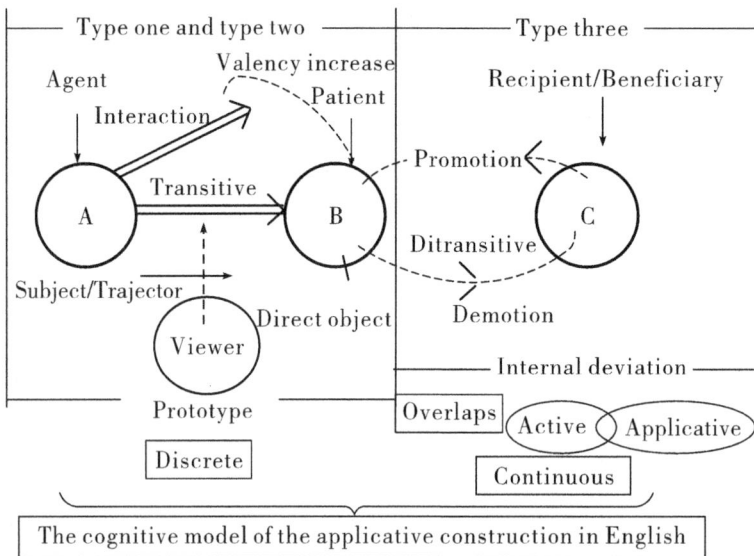

Figure 69 The Cognitive Model of the Applicative Constructions

8 Summary

This chapter has primarily been concerned with the fuzzy features shown in the medial voice constructions and their cognitive models. Our examination and characterization of medial voice falls into seven sections. In each section, we discuss the discrete features of each subcategory by investigating their classifications, components (the role archetype and the composite verb), and interaction between the components, on the one hand. On the other hand, the continuous features of each subcategory are addressed by designating how the members of the subcategories of medial voice deviate within the category and how they overlap with other voice types. Moreover, we sketch the schema for each voice subcategory and generalize the cognitive model of each voice types by taking all the factors into account.

Section one has been dedicated to the middle voice at the clause level. It is argued that the idiosyncrasies of middle construction lie in three aspects: (ⅰ) It has an implied agent with arbitrary reference and often denotes a generic meaning. (ⅱ) A non-agent is partially responsible for the occurrence of the action and it echoes to the modality of capability or probability. (ⅲ) In most cases, the composite verbs tend to be transitive before they enter into the middle construction, but some intransitive verbs can also be qualified candidates. Moreover, not all the members can satisfy all the three features above, and deviations are unavoidable. The continuous features not only show within the category of middle voice but also at the boundary among the active, passive and the anticausative.

Section two has dealt with the causative constructions in English. It is argued that causatives in English are made up of two major subtypes, the causative active, and the causative passive. Each has discrete features. However, the similarity is that there is a causative verb added in both the causative active and passive in the matrix clause, and the voice of the whole sentence is active even though the complement sentences tend to vary in voice, which makes them closely related to both the active and passive voice by continuous features to some extent.

Section three has elaborated the anticausative constructions which are regarded as the opposite counterpart of the causative construction. It is suggested that there is only one participant available. It is coded as the subject of the clause and shows affectedness by the action in the anticausative construction. The verbs tend to be alternating unaccusative verbs that are intransitive in nature. In addition, it has overlaps with the active, passive and middle voices in one way or another.

Section four has examined the very nature of antipassive constructions in English. It is claimed that there are five variations in antipassive constructions; that is, the object deletion, the conative construction/preposition drop, object incorporation, plural, indefinite or non-referring objects, and non-fact modalities. The agent plays a very important part in the antipassive while the patient is less affected, indefinite, non-specific and sometimes even omitted. In terms of continuous features, it is often regarded as another opposite counterpart for the passive in that it is very similar to the active construction to some extent.

Section five has characterized the discrete features and continuous features of the reciprocal constructions. We maintain that the unique feature of reciprocal constructions lie in the fact that each participant plays the role of both agent and patient in relation to each other. In addition, the subject serving as the antecedent is coreferential with the object which realizes itself as the anaphora. Moreover, there are deviations showing at the syntactic level and lexical level. Overlaps also occur between the active, passive and reflexive.

Section six has addressed the unique features and continuous feature of reflexive constructions in English. We claim that reflexive constructions fall into four categories, namely, the direct reflexive, the indirect reflexive, the emphatic reflexive, and the possessive reflexive. The direct reflexive is construed as the prototype, and the other three types are non-prototypes. The most conspicuous feature of the reflexive is that that N/P1 and N/P2 refer to the same entity. In addition, it overlaps with active, passive, reciprocal and middle in one way or another.

Finally, our effort has been devoted to the applicative constructions in English. It is claimed that there are three types of constructions for applicative in English though there is no clear morphological marker in English for the applicative. Among the three types, type one and type two involve converting the intransitive verb with a prepositional phrase from the original clause to the transitive clause with the object of the preposition promoted to direct object. For type three, it evolves from the type one and type two and can be regarded as non-prototypes in that it converts a transitive sentence with two arguments into a ditransitive one with three arguments.

VIII

Conclusion

It has been widely accepted that grammatical voice is an absolutely vital part of the English grammar teaching syllabus for ESL/EFL learners. However, those ESL/EFL learners who make great effort to acquire the grammatical rules of the dichotomy voice system often are confused and frustrated because there are always so many cases in natural language that are not compatible with the rules taught in class. Given this, efforts have been made to account for categorization in the grammatical voice system in English on the basis of prototype theory, force dynamic theory, construal theory, and schema theory from the perspective of cognitive grammar. The major findings can be encapsulated as follows:

First, it is suggested that the grammatical voice in English is a symbolic assembly residing in the symbolic relationship between a semantic unit and phonological unit. As a grammatical category, it is formulated by schematizing and sorting out the actual cases of language use rather than some abstract generative or transformational rules.

Second, contrary to the active-passive dichotomy presented in most grammar books and research works, it has been argued that English grammatical voice consists of three major subcategories: active, passive and medial, where the active voice is the unmarked, entrenched representative for other voices to take as a reference point. The medial voice and passive voice are marked and different from the active voice in some aspects, but the shared features enable both of them to be incorporated into the category of grammatical voice, though their statuses vary. Moreover, the medial voice is not an independent voice type, but falls into seven subcategories, that is, middle voice, causative voice, anticausative voice, antipassive voice, reciprocal voice, reflexive voice and applicative voice. These seven voice types not only bear their unique features but also possess some shared features with other voice types which certify them as one of the eligible members of the category of grammatical voice.

Third, in accordance with the above classification, the schema and cognitive model of each voice subcategory are deduced and sketched based on the discrete features of the prototype, continuous features of non-prototypes, different construal models, and overlaps with other categories. It has been claimed that these discreteness-continuity schematic models will provide a reference for grammar teaching and learning for sure.

Forth, the active voice, at the clausal level, is far more complicated and diversified than most grammar books have presented. For the prototype of the active construction, we argue that it profiles an action chain which takes the agent as the head of energy that is fully responsible for the action and the patient as the tail of energy that is affected by the influence of the agent. Syntactically, the agent is coded as the subject and the patient is coded as the object of the clause. The composite verb is supposed to be a concrete verb that denotes a resultative state so as to validate that the patient is actually affected by the agent's volitional action. However, in the discourse, the language data deviate greatly. The verbs that enter into the active construction may be perfective or imperfective or concrete or abstract. The agent may not be a prototypical human; the patient may not be prototypical inanimate entity. They deviate in one way or another from the prototype. As far as the sentence types are concerned, the simple, affirmative, declarative clause is assumed to be the prototype, while more complex non-prototypes such as negatives, interrogative, and complex sentences, are omnipresent. The discussion and investigation of active construction lends support to the assumption that the active voice is a voice category that has various members, and the prototype is the typical exemplar of the category that has the discrete features. The other instantiations or members share some commonality with the prototype but they do not have equal status and display the continuous features within the active category. The examination of the active voice category reveals that the active voice is fuzzy rather than clear-cut.

Next, in contrast to the active voice category, we contend that the passive voice category is marked in that it not only possesses syntactic configurations but also manifests itself in various types. In this dissertation, it has been maintained that passive category comprises prototype and non-prototype members. By evaluating the formal features and acceptance scale in the literature, the agentful true passive in the Be+V-en construction is selected as the prototype. Semantically, it profiles an action chain in which the patient is construed as the trajector though it acts as the terminus of the energy transmission whereas the agent is often left implicit and construed as the landmark that is backgrounded. Since the viewer is observing the event from the perspective of patient, the patient is coded as the subject of the clause while the agent is the object of the oblique phrase. The morpheme Be_2 combining with $PERF_3$ is the clause head of the prototype passive. However, deviations from the prototype occur in various ways. First, there are internal divergences concerning the role archetypes and composite verbs in the prototypical passive sentences. Second, the category of Be+V-en construction consists of not only the prototype, but also the semi-passive, pseudo-passive, and statal passive. Next, syntactic deviations of passive manifest themselves in the Get+V-en construction and prepositional passive in which the Get+V-en construction has many variations that show a hierarchy of membership within the category itself. Finally, the marginal members of the passive voice are also taken into consideration. Special focus is put on the unaccusasative progressive construction, Be+V-able construction and [V1+V2-ing] construction. Taking all the factors into account, we have concluded that the category passive voice is not clear-cut but fuzzy and there is gradience among the six types of passive constructions. The degree of passivization is diminishing progressively from the prototype to non-prototypes.

Moreover, after addressing the seven types of medial voice, it has been argued that it is very necessary to look into the voice categories in a fine-graded way in that some clauses that have specific features are not eligible for being members of the active or passive voice. On the other hand, the existence of the medial voice can further validate the continuous features within the category of grammatical voice. In terms of role archetypes, the middle voice at clausal level exemplifies itself by showing one participant of the event, that is, the patient or the theme is coded as the subject that is profiled. Causative voice often involves three participants in the event, and though it falls into the causative active and causative passive, its matrix clause is active in nature. The subject of the matrix clause is often coded as causer and the subject of the subordinate clause is often coded as the causee. The anticausative voice has only one participant shown at the syntactic level, that is, the patient or theme. Different from the middle voice which may have an implied agent, the anticausative lays emphasis on the affectedness of the theme or patient and ignores the responsibility of the agent completely. In case of the antipassive, it is the patient or theme that is demoted or is rendered into a less affected, indefinite, nonspecific entity or even omitted whereas the agent is more salient and profiled than that of agent in the active. With regard to the reciprocals, the two participants, the agent and patient are often construed to be in one chuck and coded as the subject together while the pronoun in the object position is coreferential with the subject. For the reflexive, we argue that it involves a two-participant event, one is the agent or experiencer, and the other is the patient or stimulus. The key point is that the two participants refer to the same entity. In the applicative, it often involves two participants or three participants. The most important feature is that there is a promotion of oblique object to the central position as the patient.

As far as the composite verb is concerned, the middle construction is more compatible with the activity verb that confines itself to the derived intransitive verb. The causative construction has two verbs in its constructions, for the V1, *have*, *get*, *let*, *make* and *help* are top five choice for causative active, *have*, *get* and *let* are more preferable for the passive. For the V2, in most cases, it is transitive in nature. Next, the composite verb in anticausative construction is intransitive in nature. To be concrete, the verb slot is suitable for an alternating unaccusative verb. Moreover, in the antipasssive construction, the composite verb in the prototypical case is intransitive, but for the non-prototypes, transitive verbs are also accepted.

For both the reciprocal construction and reflexive construction, the composite verbs show three variations: transitive verb, intransitive verb plus preposition, or ditransitive verbs plus preposition. Moreover, applicative construction does not confine itself to one structure, and its composite verbs vary from the intransitive verb with one argument to the transitive verb with two arguments and then to the ditransitive verb with three arguments.

Finally, we maintain that the fuzzy feature of grammatical voice is not only shown in the subcategory but also at the boundary of the subcategories since there is always no precise conformity between the meaning and the syntactic expressions. Therefore, it is necessary to regard grammatical voice as a continuum rather than a rigid binary dichotomy. In addition, it is reasonable and instructive to think of the category of voice as covering all the verbs rather than only the transitive ones when treating the category of voice, since transitivity is also a fuzzy concept. Furthermore, the archetype roles in each slot are appropriate for different candidates rather than a stable one under different circumstances.

There is no denying that addressing the discrete and continuous features of the members of the grammatical category and sketching the schemas and cognitive models for each subcategory is a dauntless and tentative effort. Few attempts to do so have been found in the literature. The study may, to some extent, bridge the gap between theoretical research and teaching and learning practice in that its detailed analysis is certain to provide some reference and revelations for the tricky questions met in the grammar study. Despite this, limitations are unavoidable.

Grammatical voice, though it may seem like an easy topic, it is actually pertinent to all the most challenging and most wide-scaled aspects of modern linguistics, and it seems to be interest of semantics, syntax, pragmatics, etc. Hard as we may try, there is still so much confusion concerning voice and limitations reside.

First, since nine subcategories of the voice have been examined in this dissertation, some constructions may not have been fully investigated and characterized due to the limitation of the space and time.

Second, the cognitive grammar approach to grammatical voice is comparatively new and persuasive in some aspects, but there are still some limitations for the theory itself. In addition, in some areas, the combination of theory with language facts may not be well-organized and well-interpreted, or it might look a bit far-fetched.

Third, the deduction of the schema and cognitive model will offer a powerful tool to ESL and EFL learners in that they are vivid, and the main points of the grammatical voice will be easy to catch sight of. However, our discussions are tentative and preliminary, and practical evidence needs to be provided from teaching practice and reading practice to learn how they can be well applied.

Despite the above deficiencies, a cognitive grammar approach to grammatical voice still provides us with a more satisfactory and powerful tool in that it tends to look into grammatical voice by connecting it with human cognition and conceptualization.

In the future, special focus needs to be put on the complex sentences or discourse to see how grammatical voice exemplifies itself in the context. Moreover, we will further investigate how the cognitive model and schema of grammatical voice can be operable in grammar teaching and be of real help in our learning and teaching practices.

Finally, some cross-lingual research could be done concerning grammatical voice in the native languages of EFL and ESL learners to see how the native language can exert some influence on the grasping of grammatical voice in English.

All in all, it must be pointed out that this study is only a small step along the long journey of voice exploration. We still have a lot to do in this field.

References

[1]   AARTS B, DENISON D, KEIZER E, et al. Fuzzy grammar: a reader [M]. Oxford: Oxford University Press, 2004.

[2]   AARTS B, CHALKER S, WEINER E. The Oxford dictionary of English grammar [M]. 2nd ed. Oxford: Oxford University Press, 2014.

[3]   AARTS B. Syntactic gradience [M]. Oxford: Oxford University Press, 2007.

[4]   ABNEY S. The English noun phrase in its sentential aspect [D]. Massachusetts: MIT, 1987.

[5]   ACKEMA P, SCHOORLEMMER M. The middle construction and the syntax-semantics interface [J]. Lingura, 1994, 93: 59-90.

[6]   ACKEMA P, SCHOORLEMMER M. Middles and nonmovement [J]. Linguistic Inquiry, 1995, 26: 173-197.

[7]   ALEXEYEVA I. Theoretical grammar course of modern English [M]. Vinnysya: Nova Knyha, 2007.

[8]   ALEXIADOU A, DORON E. The construction of two non-active voices: passive and middle [J]. Journal of Linguistics, 2012, 48: 1-34.

[9]   ALSINA A. Passive types and the theory of object asymmetries [J]. Natural Language and Linguistic Theory, 1996, 14 (4): 673-723.

[10]   ALSINA A. The prepositional passive as structure-sharing [C]// Miriam B and King T. Proceedings of the LFG09 conference. Stanford, CA: CSLI Publications, 2009: 44-64.

[11]   ARMSTRONG S, GLEITMAN L, GLEITMAN H. What some concepts might not be [J]. Cognition, 1983, 13: 263-308.

[12]   AUTHIER G, HAUDE K. Ergativeity, valency and voice: empirical approaches to language typology [M]. Berlin: De Gruyter, 2012.

[13]   BAKER M. Incorporation: A theory of grammatical function changing [M]. Chicago: Chicago University Press, 1988.

[14]   BARBER E. Voice: beyond the passive [C]//Annual meeting of the Berkeley Linguistics Society, 1975, 1: 16-24.

[15]   BARLOW M, KEMMER S. A schema-based approach to grammatical description [J]. The Reality of linguistic rules, 1993, 19: 19-42.

[16]   BARRY A. English grammar: language as human behavior [M]. 2nd ed. London: Pearson education, Inc, 2002.

[17]   BARTLETT F. Remembering: a study in experimental and social psychology [M].

Cambridge: Cambridge University Press, 1932.

[18] BIBER D, JOHANSSON S, LEECH G, et al. Longman grammar of spoken and written English [M]. London: Longman, 1999.

[19] BLACK C A. A step-by-step introduction to the government and binding theory of syntax [J]. SIL-Mexico branch and university of north Dakota, 1998,4(3): 11-76.

[20] BLEVINS J. Passives and impersonals [J]. Journal of linguistics, 2003, 39(3): 473-520.

[21] BLIGHT R. Head movement, passive, and antipassive in English [D]. Austin: The University of Texas at Austin, 2004.

[22] BOLINGER D. Generality, gradience, and the all-or-none [M]. The Hague: Mouton, 1961.

[23] BOLINGER D. Form and meaning [M]. London: Longman, 1977.

[24] CARTER R., MCCARTHY M. The English get-passive in spoken discourse: description and implications for an interpersonal grammar [J]. English language & linguistics, 1999, 3(1): 41-58.

[25] Chandler D. Semiotics: the basics [M]. Routledge, 2002.

[26] CHAPPELL H. Is the get-passive adversative? [J]. Research on language & social interaction, 1980, 13(3): 411-452.

[27] CHOMSKY N. Syntactic structure [M].The Hague: Mouton, 1957.

[28] CHOMSKY N. Aspects of the theory of syntax [M]. Cambridge: The MIT Press, 1965.

[29] CHOMSKY N. Remarks on nominalization [M]//KRATZER A, HEIM I. Studies on semantics in generative grammar. The Hague: Mouton, 1970: 11-61.

[30] CHOMSKY N, LASNIK H. Filters and control [M]//Essays on restrictiveness and learnability. Dordrecht: Springer, 1990: 42-124.

[31] CHOMSKY N. Lectures on government and binding: the pisa lectures [M]. Dordrecht: Foris, 1981.

[32] CHOMSKY N. Some concepts and consequences of the theory of government and binding [M]. Cambridge, MA: The MIT Press, 1982.

[33] CHOMSKY N. Barriers [M]. Cambridge, MA: MIT Press, 1986.

[34] COHEN H, LEFEBVRE C. Handbook of categorization in cognitive science [M]. NJ: Elsevier, 2005.

[35] COLLINS P C. Get-passives in English [J]. World Englishes, 1996, 15(1): 43-56.

[36] COMRIE B. Language universals and linguistic typology: syntax and morphology [M]. Oxford: Blackwell, 1981.

[37] COMRIE B. Language universals and linguistic typology: syntax and morphology [M]. 2nd ed . Chicago: University of Chicago press, 1989.

[38] CONDORAVDI C. The middle: where semantics and morphology meet [J]. MIT

working papers in linguistics, 1989, 11: 18-30.

[39]   COOREMAN A. Topicality, ergativity, and transitivity in narrative discourse: evidence from Chamorro [J]. Studies in Language, 1982, 6(3): 343-374.

[40]   COOREMAN A, FOX B, GIVÓN T. The discourse definition of ergativity [J]. Studies in Language, 1984, 8(1): 1-34.

[41]   COOREMAN A. Transitivity and discourse continuity in chamorro narratives [D]. Eugene: University of Oregon, 1985.

[42]   COOREMAN A. Transitivity and discourse continuity in chamorro narratives [M]. Berlin: Mouton de Gruyter, 1987.

[43]   COOREMAN A. The antipassive in Chamorro: variations on the theme of transitivity [M]//SHIBATANI M. Passive and voice. Amsterdam: Benjamins. 1988: 561-593.

[44]   COOREMAN A. A functional typology of antipassives [J]. Voice: Form and Function, 1994: 49-88.

[45]   CORRIGAN R. The internal structure of English transitive sentences [J]. Memory & Cognition, 1986, 14(5): 420-431.

[46]   CORRIGAN R. Sentences as categories: is there a basic-level sentence? [J] Cognitive Linguistics, 1991, 2(4): 339-356.

[47]   COUPER K E. The prepositional passive in English: a semantic-syntactic analysis, with a lexicon of prepositional verbs [M]. Tubingen: Max Niemeyer Verlag, 1979.

[48]   COWAN R. The teacher's grammar of English [M]. Cambridge: Cambridge University Press, 2008.

[49]   CROFT W. Typology and universals [M]. Cambridge: Cambridge University Press, 1990a.

[50]   CROFT W. Possible verbs and the structure of events [M]//TSONATZIDIS S. Meanings and prototypes. London: Routledge, 1990b: 58-83.

[51]   CROFT W. Syntactic categories and grammatical relations: the cognitive organization of information [M]. Chicago: University of Chicago Press, 1991.

[52]   CROFT W. Case marking and the semantics of mental verbs [M]//PUSTEJOVSKY J. Semantics and the lexicon. Dordrecht: Kluwer, 1993: 55-72.

[53]   CROFT W. Voice: beyond control and affectedness [M]//FOX B, HOPPER P. Voice: form and function. Amsterdam: John Benjamins, 1994, 27: 89-117.

[54]   CROFT W. Linguistic evidence and mental representations [J]. Cognitive Linguistics, 1998, 9: 151-73.

[55]   CROFT W. Radical construction grammar: syntactic theory in typological perspective [M]. Oxford: Oxford University Press, 2001.

[56]   CROFT W, CRUSE D. Cognitive linguistics [M]. Cambridge: Cambridge University

Press, 2004.

[57] CROFT W. Verbs: aspect and causal structure [M]. Oxford: Oxford University Press, 2012.

[58] CRYSTAL D. A dictionary of linguistics and phonetics [M].Oxford: Blackwell, 1985.

[59] CRYSTAL D. A dictionary of linguistics and phonetics [M]. 3rd ed. Oxford: Blackwell, 1991.

[60] CURME G. A grammar of the English language [M]. Boston: D. C. Heath, 1931.

[61] DAVIDSE K, HEYVAERT E. On the middle voice: an interpersonal analysis of the English middle [J]. Linguistics, 2007, 45: 37-83.

[62] DAVIDSON W, ALOCK J. English grammar and analysis [M]. London: Allman, 1876.

[63] DIK S. Basic principles of functional grammar [M]//DIK S. Advances in functional grammar. Dordrecht: Foris Publications, 1983: 3-28.

[64] DIK S. The theory of functional grammar: the structure of the clause [M]. Dordrecht: Foris Publications, 1997.

[65] DIXON R. Ergativity [M]. Cambridge: Cambridge University Press, 1994.

[66] DIXON R, ALEXANDRA W, AIKHENVALD Y. The Amazonian languages [M]. Cambridge: Cambridge University Press, 1999.

[67] DIXON R, AIKHENVALD A. Introduction [M]//DIXON R, AIKHENVALD A. Changing valency: case studies in transitivity. Cambridge: Cambridge University Press, 2000: 1-29.

[68] DIXON R. A semantic approach to English grammar [M]. Oxford: Oxford University Press, 2005.

[69] DIXON R. Basic linguistic theory: Vol 3, further grammatical topics [M]. Oxford: Oxford University Press, 2012.

[70] DIXON R. Applicatives [M]//Dixon R M. Basic linguistic theory: Vol 3. Oxford: Oxford University Press, 2012: 294-342.

[71] DOWNING A. The semantics of get-passives [M]//Ruqaiya H, Carmel C, David B. Functional descriptions: theory in practice. Amsterdam: Benjamins, 1996: 179-205.

[72] ECKERSLEY C. A concise English grammar for foreign students [M]. London: Longman, 1958.

[73] EVANS N, LEVINSON S, GABY A, et al. Reciprocals and semantic typology [M]. Amsterdam: John Benjamins, 2011.

[74] EVANS V, GREEN M. Cognitive linguistics: an introduction [M]. Edinburgh: Edinburgh University Press, 2006.

[75] EVANS V. Language and cognition: the view from cognitive linguistics. [M]//COOK V, BASSETTI B. Language and bilingual cognition. New York: Psychology Press, 2011:

69-107.

[76] FAGAN S. The English middle [J]. Linguistic inquiry, 1988, 19: 181-203.

[77] FAGAN S. The syntax and semantics of middle constructions [M]. Cambridge: Cambridge University Press, 1992.

[78] FALTZ L. Reflexivization: a study in universal syntax [D]. San Francisco: University of California Berkeley, 1977.

[79] FALTZ L. Reflexivization: a study in universal syntax [M]. New York: Garland, 1985.

[80] FELLBAUM C. On the middle constructions in English [M]. Bloomington: Indiana University Linguistic Club, 1986.

[81] FINDLAY J. The prepositional passive: a lexical functional account [D]. Oxford: University of Oxford, 2014.

[82] FINDLAY J. The prepositional passive in lexical functional grammar [J]. 2016,12(4): 255–275.

[83] FLECK D. Antipassive in Matses [J]. Studylanguage, 2006, 30(3): 551-573.

[84] FODOR J, LEPORE E. The red herring and the pet fish: why concepts still can't be prototypes [J]. Cognition, 1996, 58(2): 253-270.

[85] FOLEY W, VAN VALIN V. Functional syntax and universal grammar [M]. Cambridge: Cambridge University Press, 1984.

[86] FOLEY W, VAN VALIN V. Information packaging in the clause [M]//Shopen T. Language typology and syntactic description: Vol I, Clause structure. Cambridge: Cambridge University Press, 1985: 282-364.

[87] FOWLER R. An introduction to transformational syntax [M]. London: Routledge and Kegan Paul Ltd, 2017.

[88] GEERAERTS D, GRONDELAERS S, BAKEMA P. The structure of lexical variation: meaning, naming, and context [M]. Berlin: Mouton de Gruyter, 1994.

[89] GENIUŠIENE E. The typology of reflexives [M]. Berlin: Mouton de Gruyter, 1987.

[90] GIVÓN T. On understanding grammar [M]. New York: Academic Press, 1979.

[91] GIVÓN T. Typology and functional domains [J]. Studies in Language. 1981, 5(2): 163-193.

[92] GIVÓN T. English grammar: a function-based introduction: Vol I [M]. Amsterdam: John Benjamins, 1993a.

[93] GIVÓN T. English grammar: a function-based introduction: Vol II [M]. Amsterdam: John Benjamins, 1993b.

[94] GIVÓN T. Voice and Inversion [M]. Amsterdam: John Benjamins, 1994.

[95] GIVÓN T, BOMMELYN L. The evolution of de-transitive voice in Tolowa Athabaskan [J]. Studies in Language, 2000, 24(1): 41-76.

[96]   GIVÓN T. Syntax: an introduction: Vol I [M]. Amsterdam: John Benjamins, 2001a.

[97]   GIVÓN T. Syntax: an introduction: Vol II [M]. Amsterdam: John Benjamins, 2001b.

[98]   GIVÓN T. Ute Reference grammar [M]. Amsterdam: John Benjamins, 2011.

[99]   GOLDSTEIN B. Cognitive psychology: connecting mind, research and everyday experience [M]. 3rd ed. Wadsworth: Cengage Learning, 2011.

[100]   GOLDBERG A E, ACKERMAN E. The pragmatics of obligatory adjuncts [J]. Language, 2001: 798-814.

[101]   GRANGER S. The be+past participle construction in spoken English with special emphasis on the passive [M]. Amsterdam: North-Holland, 1983.

[102]   GREENBAUM S. The Oxford English grammar [M]. Oxford: Oxford University Press, 1996.

[103]   GRONEMEYER C. On deriving complex polysemy: the grammaticalization of get [J]. English Language & Linguistics, 1999, 3(1): 1-39.

[104]   GUERRERO M P. An antipassive interpretation of the English "conative alternation": semantic and discourse-pragmatic dimensions[M]//MEDINA P. Morphosyntactic alternations in English: functional and cognitive perspectives. Sheffield: Equinox, 2011:182-206.

[105]   HAEGEMAN L. The get-passive and Burzio's generalization [J]. Lingua, 1985, 66(1): 53-77.

[106]   HALE K, KEYSER S. A view from the middle lexicon [M]. Cambridge: MIT Press, 1987.

[107]   HALE K, KEYSER S. Prolegomenon to a theory of argument structure [M]. Cambridge: MIT Press, 2002.

[108]   HALLIDAY M A K. An introduction to functional grammar [M]. London: Edward Arnold Limited, 1985.

[109]   HALLIDAY M A K. An introduction to functional grammar [M]. 3rd ed. London: Arnold, 2004.

[110]   HALLIDAY M A K. Studies in English language [M]. London: Continuum Language, 2005.

[111]   HASPELMATH M. The grammaticization of passive morphology [J]. Studies in Language, 1990, 14(1): 25-72.

[112]   HASPELMATH M. More on the typology of inchoative/causative verb alternations [M]//COMRIE B, POLINSKY M. Causatives and transitivity. Amsterdam: John Benjamins, 1993: 87-120.

[113]   HASPELMATH M, KÖNIG E, OESTERREICHER, W, et al. Typology and language universals [M]. Berlin: Walter de Gruyter, 2001.

[114] HASPELMATH M. Further remarks on reciprocal constructions [M]//VLADIMIR P. Reciprocal constructions. Amsterdam: Benjamins, 2007: 2087-2115.

[115] HASPELMATH M. Universals of causative and anticausative verb formation and the spontaneity scale [J]. Lingua Posnaniensis, 2016, 58(2): 33-63.

[116] HATCHER A G. To get/be invited [J]. Modern Language Notes, 1949, 64(7): 433-446.

[117] HE W Z. Middle constructions in Chinese and West-Germanic language: toward a unified cognitive account [M]. Beijing: Science Press, 2007.

[118] HEATH J. Antipassivization: a functional typology [C]//Annual Meeting of the Berkeley Linguistics Society. 1976, 2: 202-211.

[119] HEATON R. A typology of antipassives, with special reference to mayan. [D]. Mānoa: University of Hawaii, 2017a.

[120] HEATON R. A featural Description of Antipassive-type Structures [C]// Paper presented at the 12th conference of the association for linguistic typology (ALT), Canberra, 2017b: 10-15.

[121] HEATON R. Antipassives in crosslinguistic perspective [J]. Annual review of linguistics, 2020, 6: 131-153.

[122] HERRING P. Complete English grammar rules [M]. Dublin: Farlex International, 2016.

[123] HINKEL E. Why English passive is difficult to teach (and learn) [M]//HINKEL E, FOTOS S. New perspectives on grammar teaching. Mahwah, NJ: Lawrence Erlbaum Associates, 2002: 223-260.

[124] HINKEL E. Tense, aspect and the passive voice in L1 and L2 academic texts [J]. Language teaching research, 2004, 8(1): 5-29.

[125] HIRTLE W. Lessons on the English verb: no expression without representation [M]. Montreal and Kingston: McGill-Queen's University Press, 2007.

[126] HOEKSTRA T, ROBERTS I. Middle constructions in Dutch and English. [M]// REULAND E, ABRAHAM W. Knowledge & language: volume 2, Lexical and conceptual structure. Dordrecht: Kluwer, 1993: 183-220.

[127] HOPPER P, THOMPSON S. Transitivity in grammar and discourse [J]. Language, 1980: 251-299.

[128] HUDDLESTON R. Introduction to the grammar of English [M]. Cambridge: Cambridge University Press, 1984.

[129] HUDDLESTON R, PULLUM G. The Cambridge grammar of the English Language [M]. Cambridge: Cambridge University Press, 2002.

[130] HURST P, NORDLINGER R. Reciprocal constructions in English: each other and beyond [M]//EVANS N, GABY A, LEVINSON S, et al. Reciprocals and semantic

typology. Amsterdam: John Benjamins, 2011: 75-90.

[131] JACKENDOFF R. Multiple subcategorization and the theta-criterion: The case of climb [J]. Natural language & linguistic theory, 1985, 3(3): 271-295.

[132] JACKENDOFF R. Semantic structure [M]. Cambridge, MA: The MIT Press, 1990.

[133] JACKENDOFF R. Conceptual semantics and cognitive Linguistics [J]. Cognitive linguistics, 1996 (7): 93-129.

[134] JACOBS R, ROSENBAUM P. Readings in English transformational grammar [M]. Waltham, MA: Ginn, 1970.

[135] JERRO K. The syntax and semantics of applicative morphology in Bantu [D]. University of Texas at Austin, 2016.

[136] JESPERSEN O. The philosophy of grammar [M]. London: George Allen and Unwin, 1924.

[137] JESPERSEN O. A modern English grammar [M]. Heidelberg: Carl Winter, 1927.

[138] JESPERSEN O. Essentials of English grammar [M]. London: George Allen and Unwin, 1933.

[139] JOHNSON M. The body in the mind: the bodily basis of meaning, imagination, and reason [M]. Chicago: University of Chicago Press, 1987.

[140] JOOS M. Description of language design [J]. The journal of the acoustical society of America, 1950, 22(6): 701-707.

[141] JOSHI M. English causative sentences: active and passive causatives [M]. Bloomington: Booktango, 2014.

[142] KASTOVSKY D. Causatives [J]. Foundations of Language, 1973, 10(2): 255-315.

[143] KATKOVA N. The problem of modern English verbs and interchangeability of active and passive constructions [M]//POLENOVA T and BONDARETS O. Collected articles of the 2nd international linguistics conference. Cambridge: Cambridge Scholar Publishing, 2008: 191-194.

[144] KEMMER S. The middle voice [M]. Amsterdam: John Benjamins, 1993.

[145] KEENAN E, DRYER M. Passive in the world's languages [M]//SHOPEN T. Language typology and syntactic description: Vol 1. Cambridge: Cambridge University Press, 2007: 325-361.

[146] KEYSER S, ROEPER T. On the middle and ergative constructions in English [J]. Linguistic inquiry, 1984, 15(3): 381-416.

[147] KIKUSAWA R. On the development of applicative constructions in Austronesian Languages [J]. Bulletin of the national museum of ethnology, 2012, 36(4): 413-455.

[148] KITAZUME S. Middles in English [J]. Word, 1996, 47(2): 161-183.

[149] KITTILÄ S. Trasnstivity: towards a comprehensive typology [M]. Turku/Abo: Abo

Akademis Tryckeri, 2002.

[150] KLAIMAN M. Affectedness and control: a typology of voice systems [M]// SHIBATANI M. Passive and voice. Amsterdam: John Benjamins, 1988: 25-83.

[151] KLAIMAN M H. Grammatical voice [M]. Cambridge: Cambridge University Press, 1991.

[152] KLAMMER T, SCHULZ M. Analyzing English grammar [M]. Boston: Allyn and Bacon, 1992.

[153] KJELLMER G. Each other and one another: on the use of the English reciprocal pronouns [J]. English Studies, 1982, 63(3): 231-254.

[154] KRIFKA M, PELLETIER F, CARLSON G, MEULEN A, et al. Genericity: An introduction [M]//CARLSON G, PELLETIER F. The deneric book. Chicago: University of Chicago Press, 1995: 1-124.

[155] KRUISINGA E. Retained accusatives in passive sentences[J]. English Studies, 1927, 9: 38-40.

[156] KRUISINGA E. A handbook of present-day English: part II, English accidence and syntax I [M]. 5th ed. Groningen: P. Noordhoff, 1931.

[157] KRUSINGA E, ERADES P. An English grammar [M]. Groningen: Noordhoff, 1953.

[158] KULIKOV L. Voice typology [M]//SONG J. The Oxford handbook of linguistic typology. Oxford: Oxford University Press, 2011: 368-398.

[159] LABOV W. Language in the inner city [M]. Philadelphia: University of Pennsylvania Press, 1973.

[160] LAKOFF G. Women, fire, and dangerous things: what categories reveal about the mind [M]. Chicago: University of Chicago Press, 1987.

[161] LANGACKER R. The integration of grammar and grammatical change [J]. Indian Linguistics Poona, 1981, 42(4): 82-135.

[162] LANGACKER R. Space grammar, analysability, and the English passive [J]. Language, 1982, 58(1): 22-80.

[163] LANGACKER R. Foundations of cognitive grammar I: theoretical prerequisites [M]. Stanford: Stanford University Press, 1987a.

[164] LANGACKER R. Nouns and verbs [J]. Language, 1987b, 63: 53-94.

[165] LANGACKER, R. An overview of cognitive grammar [M]//RUDZKA-OSTYN B. Topics in cognitive linguistics. Amsterdam: John Benjamins, 1988: 3-48.

[166] LANGACKER R. Foundations of cognitive grammar II [M]. Stanford: Stanford University Press, 1991a.

[167] LANGACKER R. Concept, image and symbol: the cognitive basis of grammar [M].

Berlin: Mouton de Gruyter, 1991b.

[168]   LANGACKER R. Reference-point constructions [J]. Cognitive Linguistics, 1993, 4(1): 1-38.

[169]   LANGACKER R. Conceptualization, symbolization, and grammar [M]//TOMASELL M. The new psychology of language. Hillsdale, NJ: Erlbaum. 1998: 1-39.

[170]   LANGACKER R. Grammar and conceptualization [M]. Berlin: Mouton de Gruyter, 2000.

[171]   LANGACKER R. Dynamicity in grammar [J]. Axiomathes, 2001, 12(1): 7-33.

[172]   LANGACKER R. Concept, image, and symbol: the cognitive basis of grammar [M]. 2nd ed. Berlin: Mouton de Gruyter, 2002.

[173]   LANGACKER R. Foundations of cognitive grammar: Vol II. [M]. Beijing: Beijing University Press, 2004a.

[174]   LANGACKER R. Metonymy in grammar [J]. Journal of Foreign Languages, 2004b, 6: 2-24.

[175]   LANGACKER R. On the continuous debate about discreteness [J]. Cognitive Linguistics, 2006, 17(1): 107-151.

[176]   LANGACKER R. Sequential and summary scanning: a reply [J]. Cognitive Linguistics, 2008a, 19: 571-584.

[177]   LANGACKER R. Cognitive grammar: a basic in troduction [M]. Oxford: Oxford University Press, 2008b.

[178]   LANGACKER R. Investigations in cognitive grammar [M]. Berlin: Mouton de Gruyter, 2009.

[179]   LANGACKER R. Essentials of cognitive grammar [M]. Oxford: Oxford University Press, 2013.

[180]   LARSEN-FREENMAN D, MARIANNE C M. The grammar book: form, meaning, and use for English language teachers [M]. 3rd ed. Boston: Heinle Cengage Learning, 2016.

[181]   LAURENCE S, MARGOLIS E. Concepts and cognitive science [M]//MARGOLIS E, LAURENCE S. Concepts: core readings. Cambridge, MA: MIT Press, 1999: 3-81.

[182]   LAZARD G. Transitivity revisited as an example of a more strict approach in typological research [J]. Folia Linguist 1993, 36: 41-90.

[183]   LEECH G, COATES J. Semantic indeterminacy and modals studies [M]//GREENBAUM S, LEECH G, SVARTVIK J. English linguistics. London: Longman,1980: 79-90.

[184]   LEES R B. A multiply ambiguous adjectival construction in English [J]. Language, 1960, 36(2): 207-221.

[185] LEES R B. The grammar of English nominalizations [M]. The Hague: Mouton, 1963.

[186] LEGENHAUSEN L. Mediopassives: fuzziness and speaker evaluation [M]// WOLFGANG K. Language as structure as process: in honor of Gerhard Nickel on the occasion of his 70th birthday. Trier: Wissenschaftlicher Verlag, 1998: 47-62.

[187] LEHMANN C. Predicate classes and participation [M]//SEILER H, PREMPER W. Partizipation: das sprachliche erfassen von sachverhalten. Tubingen: Narr, 1991: 183-239.

[188] LEKAKOU M. In the middle, somewhat elevated: the semantics of middles and its cross linguistic realization [D]. London: University of London, 2005.

[189] LEKAKOU M. A comparative view of the requirements for adverbial modification in middles [M]//LYNGFELT B, SOLSTAD T. Demoting the agent: passive, middle, and other vice phenomena. Amsterdam: John Benjamins, 2006: 167-196.

[190] LEVIN B. English verb classes and alternations: a preliminary investigation [M]. Chicago: University of Chicago Press, 1993.

[191] LI T. The verbal system of the aramaic of daniel: an explanation in the context of grammarticalization [M]. Leiden: Brill Hotei Publishing, 2009.

[192] MA L. Clarification on linguistic applications of fuzzy set theory to natural language analysis [C]//Eighth international conference on fuzzy systems and knowledge discovery (FSKD), Shanghai, 2011: 811-815.

[193] MALCHUKOV A, COMRIE B. Valency classes in the world's languages [M]. Berlin: Mouton de Gruyter, 2015.

[194] MALDONADO R. Grammatical voice in cognitive grammar [M]//GEERARERTS D, CUYCKENS H. The Oxford handbook of cognitive linguistics. Oxford: Oxford University Press, 2007: 829-868.

[195] MANNINEN S. Generative grammar [M]//CHAPELLE C. The encyclopedia of applied linguistics. Malden, MA: Blackwell Publishing Ltd, 2013: 1-8.

[196] MARANTZ A. Implications of asymmetries in double object constructions [M]// MCHOMBO S. Theoretical aspects of bantu grammar. Stanford: CSLI Publications, 1993: 113-150.

[197] MASLOVA E, KÖNIG E, GAST V. Reflexive encoding of reciprocity: cross-linguistic and language internal variation [M]//DIMITRIADIS A, König E, Gast V. Reciprocals and reflexives: theoretical and typological explorations. Berlin: Mouton de Gruyter, 2008, 225-258.

[198] MASSAM D. Null objects and non-thematic subjects [J]. Journal of Linguistics, 1992, 28(1): 115-137.

[199] MATTHIESSEN C, TERUYA K, LAM M. Key terms in systemic functional linguistics [M]. London: Continuum, 2010.

[200] MEINTS K. Prototypes and the acquisition of the English passive [J]. Perspectives on cognitive science, 1999, 4: 67-77.

[201] MEL'ČUK I. The inflectional category of voice: towards a more rigorous definition [M]//COMIE B, POLINSKY M. Causatives and transitivity. Amsterdam: Benjamins, 1993:1-46.

[202] MELNARK L. Caddo verb morphology [D]. Chicago: The University of Chicago, 1998.

[203] MICHAEL I. English grammatical categories and the tradition to 1800 [M]. Cambridge: Cambridge University Press, 1970.

[204] MITHUN M. Voice without subjects, objects, or obliques [M]//SHIBATANI M, TSUNODA T, Kageyama T. Voice and grammatical relations: in honor of Masayoshi Shibatani. Amsterdam: John Benjamins, 2006: 195-216.

[205] MÖHLIG-FALKE R. The early English impersonal construction: an analysis of verbal and constructional meaning [M]. Oxford: Oxford University Press, 2012.

[206] MOLCZANOW A. Quantification: transcending beyond frege's boundaries: a case study in transcendental-metaphysical logic [M]. Leiden: Brill Academic Publishers, 2012.

[207] MOLTMANN F. Parts and wholes in semantics [M]. Oxford: Oxford University Press, 1997.

[208] NAN C. On raising of the theme object: a minimalist perspective [D]. Changsha: Zhong Nan University, 2012.

[209] NESS A. Prototypical transitivity [M]. Amsterdam: John Benjamins. 2007.

[210] NEDJALKOV V, SILNITSKY G. The typology of morphological and lexical causatives [M]//KIEFER F. Trends in soviet theoretical linguistics. Dordrecht, Boston: Reidel, 1973: 1-32.

[211] NEDJALKOV V, GENIUSIENE E, GUENTCHÉVA Z. Reciprocal constructions. Amsterdam: John Benjamins, 2007.

[212] NEWMEYER F. Grammatical theory: its limits and its possibilities [M]. Chicago: University of Chicago Press, 1983.

[213] NEWMEYER F. Language form and language function [M]. Cambridge, MA: MIT, 1998.

[214] O'GRADY W. The derived intransitive construction [J]. Lingua, 1980, 52: 57-72.

[215] PALMER F. The English verb [M]. London: Longman, 1987.

[216] PALMER F. Grammatical roles and relations [M]. Cambridge: Cambridge University Press, 1994.

[217] PARROTT M. Grammar for English language teachers [M]. Cambridge: Cambridge University Press, 2000.

[218] PESETSKY J. Zero syntax: experiences and cascades [M]. Cambridge, MA: MIT Press, 1995.

[219] PETERSON D. Applicative constructions [M]. Oxford: Oxford University Press, 2007.

[220] POLINSKY M. Antipassive [M]//COON D, MASSAM L, TRAVIS J. The Oxford handbook of ergativity. Oxford: Oxford University Press, 2017:308-331.

[221] POUTSMA H. A grammar of late modern English. [M].Groningen: Noordhoff, 1926.

[222] POSTAL P. Antipassive in French [J]. Lingvisticae investigationes, 1977, 1(2): 333-374.

[223] PUCKICA J. Passive constructions in present-day English. [J]. GAGL: Groninger Arbeiten zur germanistischen Linguistik, 2009 (49): 215-235.

[224] PYLKKÄNEN L. What applicative heads apply to [J]. University of Pennsylvania Working Papers in Linguistics, 2000, 7(1): 197-210.

[225] QUIRK R, GREENBAUM S, LEECH G, SVARTVIK J. A comprehensive grammar of the English language [M]. London: Longman, 1985.

[226] RADFORD A. An introduction to English sentences [M]. Cambridge: Cambridge University Press, 2009.

[227] RAPER J. Multidimensional geographic information science [M]. London: Taylor and Francis, 2000.

[228] RAPOPORT T. The English middle and agentivity [J]. Linguistics inquiry, 1999, (30)1: 147-155.

[229] RICE S. Towards a transitive prototype: evidence from some atypical English passives [C]//Annual Meeting of the Berkeley Linguistics Society. 1987a, 13: 422-434.

[230] RICE S. Towards a cognitive model of transitivity [D]. San Diego: University of California, 1987b.

[231] RIVANDI M, RAZALI S, HUSIN N, et al. The correct use of passive voice in report writing by Somali SPACE students in UTM [J]. Social and behavioral science, 2012 (56): 284-291.

[232] ROBERTS I. The representation of implicit and dethematized subjects [M]. Dordrecht: Foris Publications, 1987.

[233] RONA B. Turkish in three months [M]. London: Hugo' s Language Books, 1998.

[234] ROSCH E. Categories [J]. Cognitive psychology, 1975, 4 (3): 328-350.

[235] ROSCH E. Cognitive representations of semantic categories [J]. Journal of experimental psychology, 1975, 104: 192-233.

[236] ROSCH E, MERVIS C. Family resemblances[J]. Psychology, 1975, 7: 573-605.

[237] ROSCH E. Principles of categorization [M]//ROSCH E, LLOYD B. Cognition and categorization. Hillsdale, NJ: Lawrence Erlbaum Associates, 1978: 27-48.

[238] ROSS H. Islands and syntactic prototypes [J]. Chicago linguistic society papers, 1987, 23: 309-320.

[239] RUBIN E. Visuell wahrgenommene figuren [M]. Copenhagen: Glydendalkse Boghandel, 1921.

[240] RUBIN M. The passive in 3- and 4-year-olds [J]. Journal of psycholinguist research, 2009, 38: 435-446.

[241] RUMELHART D. Schemata: The building blocks of cognition [M]//SPIRO R, BRUCE B, BREWER W F. Theoretical issues in reading comprehension. Hillsdale, NJ: Lawrence Erlbaum, 1980: 33-58.

[242] RUMELHART D, NORMAN D. Representation of knowledge [M]//AITKENHEAD A, SLACK J. Issues in cognitive modelling. Hillsdale, N J: Lawrence Erlbaum, 1985: 15-62.

[243] RUMELHART D, ORTONY A. The representation of knowledge in memory [M]// ANDERSON R, SPIRO J, MONTAGUE N. Schooling and the acquisition of knowledge. Hillsdale, N J: Erlbaum, 1976: 99-135.

[244] RYDER M. Mixers, mufflers and mousers: the extending of the -er suffix as a case of prototype reanalysis [J]. Proceedings of the Berkeley linguistics society, 1991, 17: 299-311.

[245] SCHEURWEGHS G. Present-day English syntax [M]. London: Longman, 1959.

[246] SCHLEPPEGRELL M. The language of schooling: a functional linguistics perspective [M]. Mahwah, NJ: Lawrence Erlbaum, 2004.

[247] SHIBATANI M. Passives and related constructions: a prototype analysis [J]. Language, 1985, 61: 821-848.

[248] SHIBATANI M. Introduction [M]//SHIBATANNI M. Passive and voice. Amsterdam: John Benjamins, 1988: 1-8.

[249] SHIBATANI M. Issues in transitivity and voice: Japanese perspective [J]. Bull. Faculty of Letters, University of Kobe, 2000, 27: 523-586.

[250] SHIBATANI M. On the conceptual framework for voice phenomena [J]. Linguistics, 2006, 44: 217-269.

[251] SIEWIERSKA A. The passive: A comparative linguistic analysis [M]. London: Croom Helm, 1984.

[252] SILVERSTEIN M. Chinook jargon: Language contact and the problem of multi-level generative systems [J]. Language, 1972, 48(2): 378-406.

[253] SLEEMAN P. Verbal and adjectival participles: position and internal [J]. Lingua, 2011, 121: 1569-1587.

[254] SLOBIN D, BEVER T. Children use canonical sentence schemas: a cross-linguistic study of word order and inflections [J]. Cognition, 1983, 12 (3): 229-265.

[255] SPRENG B. Antipassive morphology and case assignment in Inuktitut [M]//JOHNS A, MASSAM D, NDAYIRAGIJE J. Ergativity: emerging issues. Dordrecht, Neth: Springer, 2006: 247-270.

[256] SPENCER A. Morphological theory [M]. Oxford: Blackwell, 1991.

[257] SPRENG B. On the conditions for antipassives [J]. Lang. Linguist. Compass, 2010, 4: 556-575.

[258] STEINBACH M. Middle voice [M]. Amsterdam: John Benjamins, 2002.

[259] STEPHENS N. Agentivity and the virtual reflexive construction [M]//BENJAMIN L, TORGRIM S. Demoting the agent. Amsterdam: John Benjamins, 2006: 275-330.

[260] STRANG B. A history of English [M]. London: Methuen and Co. Ltd, 1970.

[261] STROIK T. Middle construction and movement [J]. Linguistic Inquiry, 1992, 23: 127-137.

[262] STROIK T. On middle formation [J]. Linguistic Inquiry, 1995, 26: 165-171.

[263] STROIK T. Middles and reflexivity [J]. Linguistics Inquiry, 1999, 30: 119-131.

[264] SUNG K M. Case assignment under incorporation [D]. Los Angeles: University of California at Los Angeles, 1994.

[265] STUURMAN F. Each other & one another: there will always prove to be a difference [J]. English Studies, 1987, 68(4): 353-360.

[266] SVARTVIK J. On voice in the English verb [M]. The Hague: Mouton, 1966.

[267] SVARTVIK J, STENSTRÖM A. Words, words, words: the rest is silence? [M]// TEOKSESSA S, BÄCKMAN H, KJELLMER G. Papers on language and literature: presented to Alvar Ellegård and Erik Frykman. Göteborg: ACTA University Gothoburgensis, 1985: 342-353.

[268] SVOROU S. The grammar of space [M]. Amsterdam: John Benjamins, 1994.

[269] SWEET H. A new English grammar, logical and historical, Part I: introduction, phonology, and accidence [M].Oxford: Clarendon Press, 1892.

[270] SWEET H. A new English grammar, Part two: syntax [M]. Oxford: Clarendon Press, 1900.

[271] SWEETSER E. From etymology to pragmatics: metaphorical and cultural, aspects of

semantic structure [M]. Cambridge: Cambridge University Press, 1990.

[272] TALLERMAN M. Understanding syntax [M]. London: Arnold, 2005.

[273] TAMBA K. The argument structure of passive and antipassive in Paloor [J]. International Journal of Linguistics, 2018, 10(6): 263-274.

[274] TALMY L. The relation of grammar to cognition: a synopsis [M]//WALTZ D. Theoretical issues in natural language processing Vol 2. New York: Association for Computing Machinery, 1978: 14-24.

[275] TALMY L. Lexicalization patterns: semantic structure in lexical forms [M]//SHOPEN T. Language typology and syntactic description: Volume Ⅲ, grammatical categories and the lexicon. Cambridge: Cambridge University Press, 1985: 57-149.

[276] TALMY L. Force dynamics in language and cognition [J]. Cognitive science, 1988, 12: 49-100.

[277] TALMY L. Toward a cognitive semantics: Vol 1, concept structuring system. [M]. Cambridge: The MIT Press, 2000a.

[278] TALMY L. Toward a cognitive semantics: Vol 2, typology and process in concept structuring [M].Cambridge: The MIT Press, 2000b.

[279] TALMY L. Concept structuring systems in language [M]//TOMASELLO M. The new psychology of language. Mahwah, NJ: Erlbaum, 2002: 15-46.

[280] TARANTO G. An event structure analysis of causative and passive get: manuscript [M]. San Diego: University of California, 2004.

[281] TAYLOR J. Linguistic categorization: prototypes in linguistic theory [M]. Norwood, NJ: Clarendon Press, 1989.

[282] TAYLOR J. Linguistic categorization: prototypes in linguistic theory [M]. Oxford: Oxford University Press, 1995.

[283] TAYLOR J. Linguistic categorization: prototypes in linguistic theory [M]. Beijing: Beijing Foreign Language Teaching and Research Press, 2001.

[284] TAYLOR J. Cognitive grammar [M]. Oxford: Oxford University Press, 2002.

[285] TAYLOR J. Linguistic categorization [M]. 3rd ed. Oxford: Oxford University Press, 2003.

[286] TOYOTA J. An adversative passive in English: in search of origins [M]//DELBECQUE N, CORNILLIE B. The construction of meaning and the meaning of constructions: data-based approaches to transitivity, motion and causation. Berlin: Mouton de Gruyter, 2007: 143-169.

[287] TOYOTA J. Diachronic in the English passive [M]. Basingstoke: Palgrave Micmillan, 2008.

[288]   TOYOTA J. Fossilization of passive in English: analysis of passive verbs [J]. English Studies, 2009, 90 (41): 476-497.

[289]   TOYOTA J. The grammatical voice in Japanese: a typological perspective [M]. Newcastle upon Tyne: Cambridge Scholars Publishing, 2011.

[290]   TRASK R. A dictionary of grammatical terms in linguistics [M]. London: Routledge, 1993.

[291]   TRUSWELL R. Preposition stranding, passivisation, and extraction from adjuncts in Germanic [J]. Linguistic Variation Yearbook, 2008, 8: 131-178.

[292]   TSUNODA T. Remarks on transitivity [J]. Journal of Linguistics, 1985, 21: 385-396.

[293]   TSUNODA T. Transitivity [M]//ASHER R. Encyclopedia of language and linguistics. Oxford: Pergamon, 1994: 4670-4677.

[294]   TUGGY D. Schematicity [M]//GEERAERTS D., Cuyckens H. The Oxford handbook of cognitive linguistics. Oxford: Oxford University Press, 2007: 82-116.

[295]   UNGERER E, Schmid H. An introduction to cognitive linguistics [M]. London: Longman, 1996.

[296]   UNGERER E, SCHMID H. An introduction to cognitive linguistics [M] 2nd ed. London: Pearson Education Limited, 2006.

[297]   VAN OOSTEN J. Subject and agenthood in English [J]. CLS, 1977, 13: 459-471.

[298]   VAN OOSTEN J. Subject, topic, agent, and passive [D]. San Francisco: University of California, Berkeley, 1984.

[299]   VAN OOSTEN J. The nature of subjects, topics and agents: a cognitive explanation [M]. Bloomington: Indiana University Linguistics Club, 1986.

[300]   VAN PELT M. English grammar to Ace Biblical Hebrew [M]. Grand Rapids, MI: Zondervan, 2010.

[301]   VAN VALIN R. Exploring the syntax-semantics interface [M]. Cambridge: Cambridge University Press, 2005.

[302]   VANRESPAILLE M. A semantic analysis of the English get-passive [J]. Interface, 1991, 5(2): 95-112.

[303]   VENDLER Z. Linguistics in philosophy [M]. Ithaca: Cornell University Press, 1967.

[304]   VISSER F. A historical syntax of the English language [M]. Leiden: E. J. Brill, 1963-1973.

[305]   WANNER A. Deconstructing the English passive [M]. New York: Mouton de Gruyter, 2009.

[306]   WITTGENSTEIN L. Philosophical investigations [M]. Oxford: Blackwell, 1953.

[307]   WOODS C. The grammar of perspective: the sumerian conjugation prefixes as a

system of voice[M]. Leinde: Brill, 2008.

[308]   XIONG X L. An ICM approach to (Chinese) zero subject [J]. Modern Foreign Languages, 2001, 24(1): 34-43.

[309]   ZADEH L. Fuzzy sets: information and control [J]. Information & Control, 1965, 8: 338-353.

[310]   ZRIBI-HERTZ A. On Stroik's analysis of English middle constructions [J]. Linguistic Inquiry, 1993, 24: 583-589.

[311]   ZÚÑIGA F, KITTILÄ S. Grammatical voice [M]. Cambridge: Cambridge University Press, 2019.